Hong Kong

World Cities series

Edited by
Professor R.J. Johnston and Professor P. Knox

Published titles in the series:

Forthcoming titles in the series:

Other titles in preparation

Hong Kong

C.P. Lo

Belhaven Press
London

Co-published in the Americas by Halsted Press,
an imprint of John Wiley & Sons, Inc., New York

First published in Great Britain in 1992 by
Belhaven Press (a division of Pinter Publishers Ltd)
25 Floral Street, London WC2E 9DS

*Co-published in the Americas by Halsted Press, an imprint of
John Wiley & Sons, Inc., 605 Third Avenue, New York,
NY 10158-0012*

British Library Cataloguing in Publication Data
A CIP catalogue record for this book is available from the
British Library

ISBN 1 85293 053 5 (UK)

Library of Congress Cataloging in Publication Data
A CIP catalog record for this book is available from the
Library of Congress

ISBN 0–470–21957–2 (in the Americas only)

Typeset by Mayhew Typesetting, Rhayader, Powys
Printed and bound in Great Britain by Biddles Ltd, Guildford and King's Lynn

To Christine and Kit

Contents

Contents

List of figures

List of figures

List of tables

List of tables

List of plates

List of plates

Preface

Hong Kong is at the threshold of change as its sovereignty will be returned to China by Britain on July 1 1997. A lot of attention has focused on this small piece of land because Hong Kong is the world's third most important banking and financial centre. This thriving world city with an energetic population is also China's window to the West. A central question that has been constantly asked by many people is: what will become of Hong Kong after 1997? Will Hong Kong continue to distinguish itself as an international finance centre or will it become eclipsed by its neighbours? Many people have attempted to answer this question from social, political and economic points of view. In this book, I propose to look at the root of the problem: what are the ingredients that have contributed to Hong Kong's development as a world city, and how will these ingredients be changed in the years to come? I believe that an understanding of the spatial development of Hong Kong and the evolution of its ecological structure will shed light on its future urban form. An efficient urban form is essential to Hong Kong's economic development: the daily rapid movement of people and goods is needed to sustain the large volume of transactions and interactions. Throughout the years Hong Kong has integrated its separate physical components into a unified whole while its uni-centre urban morphology has evolved into a multi-centred one. Typically, this represents a balancing of two major forces of spatial development in Hong Kong: centrifugal and centripetal. The construction of the new airport in Lantau Island, the western extremity of Hong Kong, is an example of the centrifugal growth while the Metroplan embodies the spirit of centripetal development. This art of balancing opposite forces characterizes Hong Kong's history of development.

Preface

This book intends to provide a comprehensive survey of Hong Kong with special emphasis on its urban development. The style of writing reflects my training as a geographer and my roots in Hong Kong. Hong Kong is an amazing city: it is always full of life, it is ever changing and advancing and it is a beautiful city if you look at it from a distance, say, from the Peak or from an airplane. I sincerely hope that its vitality will remain unchanged after 1997. This book would not have been written without the encouragement of Dr. Iain Stevenson, Editorial Director of Belhaven Press. I am grateful to Professor Paul Knox at the Center for Urban and Regional Studies, Virginia Polytechnic Institute and State University for valuable comments on the book outline and for tolerating my tardiness in completing the book. I am eternally grateful to my former classmate and colleague, Professor Chi-Keung Leung, Head of the Department of Geography and Geology, University of Hong Kong, Hong Kong, for giving me the opportunity to rejoin the Department for a short-time and for allowing me to use the excellent technical and secretarial staff in his Department to assist me in completing this book. By writing the book in Hong Kong, I have benefited not only from access to the most current works on Hong Kong, but also from becoming a part of Hong Kong myself and once again feeling its throb of life. In particular, I wish to thank cartographers H.K. Kwan, Martin Chiu, and T.B. Wong, and photographer T.T. Chen for their help with the illustrations in this book. I am also indebted to Mrs Betty Lai, Secretary in the Department, for helping with word processing and the production of the final typescript. Colleagues in the Department of Geography and Geology at the University of Hong Kong gave me a very warm home-coming which I will never forget.

Last but not least, I must thank my wife Christine and my son Kit for being so tolerant of my long absence from home. Without their understanding and support, I could not have completed this task. I hope I can make up for being such a negligent husband and father. This book is dedicated to them with love and gratitude.

C.P. Lo
December, 1991

1
From barren island to world city: the economic transformation of Hong Kong

Hong Kong's most valuable asset is not its land, but its water; between the island and the mainland, only a quarter of a mile away at its narrowest part, lies a magnificent harbour, almost landlocked and an ideal anchorage for shipping. Hong Kong is the product of its harbour. . .

G.B. Endacott, *A History of Hong Kong*, 1964

Hong Kong (Xiang Gang in Chinese pinyin system), or literally the Fragrant Harbour, is a British Crown Colony with a total land area of about 1,070 sq km. This includes the island of Hong Kong, Kowloon Peninsula and the New Territories comprised of a portion of the Chinese mainland and 235 islands (Figure 1.1). Therefore, unlike other world cities, Hong Kong is a city state. Indeed, the history of development of Hong Kong has been one of territorial expansion and consolidation in order to achieve better integration of its various components so that the city state can function more efficiently as a unified whole. The Colony, initially based on the island of Hong Kong, was acquired by the British from China during the rule of the Qing Dynasty on June 26 1843. It was subsequently expanded to include Kowloon Peninsula in October 1860 and a 99-year lease on the New Territories dating from July 1, 1898. On December 19, 1984, an agreement between Britain and China was signed restoring the sovereignty of Hong Kong to China on July 1 1997, the date when the 99-year lease of the New Territories will expire.

Despite its lowly status as a colony, Hong Kong has developed through its 148 years of existence into a city state of great importance which

From barren island to world city

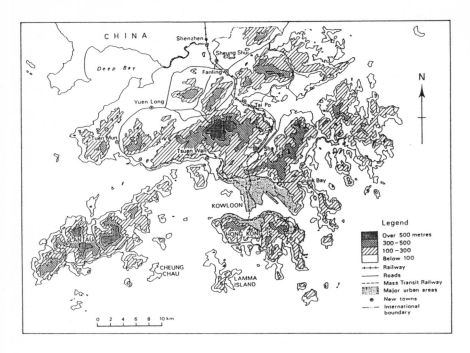

Figure 1.1 The areal extent of Hong Kong, showing the topography, transportation lines, and major place names

supports a population of about 5.8 million. Hong Kong is now one of the world's greatest ports and trade centres with commercial links extending to all the inhabited continents. In terms of goods alone, it is the 13th largest trading entity in the world with total imports and exports amounting to some 180 per cent of its gross domestic product (GDP). If trade in services is included, total trade comes to more than double the GDP (Hong Kong Government, 1987). It is the financial capital of Asia and the world's third most important banking and financial centre, trailing only behind London and New York. Hong Kong's own bank, the Hongkong and Shanghai Banking Corporation, is among the world's top 20 banks and is the biggest based outside the major industrialized countries of Europe, North America and Japan (Hong Kong Government, 1986). All these achievements meet the criteria of world cities which, as originally defined by Hall (1966), should be both national centres of government and trade and great ports where professional talents of all kinds congregate. World cities should contain a significant proportion of the richest members of the community, have great department stores, specialised shops and luxurious restaurants. In

2

the 1970s, as a result of the emergence of a new world-economic order based on the internationalization of capital and the international division of labour, the world-economy is no longer confined to a single core, but has become multipolar, with capitalist production encompassing an increasing number of newly industrializing countries in the semi-periphery (King, 1990). The term 'world cities' is now broadened to designate 'nodal points' which co-ordinate and control this global economic activity (Sassen-Koob, 1984) or cities which constitute 'a worldwide system of control over production and market expansion' (Friedman and Wolff, 1982). In other words, the 'world cities' are a linked set of markets and production units organized and controlled by transnational capital. More appropriately, they should be called 'global cities' (King, 1990). Hong Kong has received a fair share of international finance and capital, and has been cited as a secondary city in semi-peripheral countries in the world city hierarchy identified by Friedmann (1986). What then are the forces that have propelled Hong Kong forward to become a world city?

It is suggested here that historical, geographical, and political factors have *accidentally* created a favourable environment in Hong Kong where the best of Eastern and Western cultural traits meet. In this chapter, the transformation of Hong Kong is traced in the light of the impact of these factors.

The colonial heritage

The founding of the British Crown Colony of Hong Kong in 1843 was the result of clashes in cultural values between the East and the West. This occurred at a time when Britain, by virtue of her commercial and political control in India, was the most powerful European country and leading China in trade. The items of trade were Chinese tea and silk which were in great demand in Britain. China, under the rule of the Qing Dynasty at that time, had always been the superior civilization in Asia and regarded all foreigners as barbarians who demanded favours from her. Great restrictions were therefore imposed on all European merchants and they were only allowed to trade through the city of Guangzhou (Canton) and had to stay in small enclosures called 'factories' erected outside the city. They also had to trade solely with the Co–Hong group of Chinese merchants. In an effort to improve the trading conditions the British government had attempted several times to establish diplomatic relations with China, but all these efforts failed because the Chinese Court would not admit the British claim to equality. The British government therefore had developed a desire to secure an island or islands off the Chinese coast to replace Guangzhou as the centre of trade in order to avoid the difficulties in Guangzhou. Such an island would also be capable of becoming a great emporium of trade along the lines of Bombay and Singapore, could serve as a naval base for strategic reasons and maintain law and order among the British merchants. Such an island obviously could not be acquired from China without the use of force. Hong Kong was suggested by Lord Napier, the British Chief Superintendent of Trade in 1834, as a possible site to be acquired (Endacott, 1964).

The eventual acquisition of Hong Kong was the result of wars between Britain and China between 1840 and 1841, triggered by the problem of opium, and therefore referred to as the Opium Wars. Opium had been used in China as a medicinal drug since the Tang Dynasty (618–907 AD), but when the practice of smoking it was introduced in the 17th century it became a major problem. The supply of opium came mainly from India which was under British control. Hence, the opium trade fell predominantly into British hands and brought them huge profits. The Chinese government had passed edicts against the smoking of opium in the eighteenth century and prohibited its importation in 1800. However, Chinese officials were corrupt and allowed opium to be smuggled into China by the merchants. In 1839, a special Imperial Commissioner by the name of Lin Ze-xu was sent to Guangzhou to stamp out the opium trade. He had a good reputation as a just, humane man and an efficient official. He acted drastically and ordered foreign merchants to surrender all their opium and to sign a bond promising not to import any in future on pain of death. The Western merchants were virtually imprisoned in the factories and sixteen of them were held as hostages until the opium was given up. The British Superintendent of Trade, Captain Charles Elliot, agreed to surrender all the opium in British hands but would not agree to the signing of the bond by the merchants. When the British merchants were freed they withdrew to Macao. The British felt that they had been unfairly treated because not all British merchants were involved in the opium trade. They viewed Commissioner Lin's actions as high-handed and a blow to British prestige. From the Chinese point of view, however, opium was an illegal commodity and they were within their rights to seize it in their own territory. Clearly, clashes between two different cultures were inevitable. Lord Palmerston, the British Foreign Secretary, sent an expedition to China in the' hope of settling the matter with a treaty which would arrange for the cession of a British-ruled island to secure the safety of British merchants. Wars between the two countries ensued. China was defeated and Hong Kong was occupied by a British naval force on January 26 1841. However, its cession as a colony to Britain was not recognized officially by both Britain and China until June 26, 1843 when the Treaty of Nanjing (Nanking) was ratified. But during the intervening period the growth of Hong Kong as a city had already begun.

This brief episode on the acquisition of Hong Kong by the British presages the direction of its future development as a centre of free trade, and indeed Captain Elliot intended it to become a permanent trading station with China. The British rule in the Colony meant that all British subjects and foreigners were to be given full security and protection according to British laws, while native Chinese had free and full permission to come to Hong Kong. All Chinese trade was to be exempted from charge and duty of any kind to the British government and all heads of villages were to be held responsible that the commands of the government were observed. By December 1841 there were over 12,000 Chinese living on the island, mostly workers attracted by the employment prospects. The colonial status of Hong Kong gave it a very important element of stability because British law and order meant freedom from the influences of political upheavals in China. Of course, all these would not have been possible without the co-operation of China. This is still the most essential factor in sustaining the growth of Hong Kong as a world city.

Geographical characteristics

The cession of Hong Kong as a British Colony off the Chinese coast did not impress Lord Palmerston, the Foreign Secretary, who called it 'a barren island with hardly a house on it', and relieved Captain Elliot of his post. He did not feel that Hong Kong was the proper place from which to trade with Guangzhou and China. Indeed, when Captain Elliot occupied Hong Kong on January 26 1841, it was virtually uninhabited. There were a few Chinese villages and hamlets along the coast as well as fishermen living on boats. The most extensive cultivated land was found in the southern coast of the island at a farming village called Hong Kong (pronounced as Heong Kong by the local fishermen) from which the island obtained its name (Figure 1.2). To the Chinese, the name Hong Kong which means 'fragrant harbour' refers to the sweet-smelling incense trees found in this same area. Archaeological evidence indicates that the region around Hong Kong was inhabited by hunters and fishermen since neolithic times, but more permanent settlement of the area seems to have occurred since the Han Dynasty (207 BC–220 AD). In May 1841 the total Chinese population was estimated to be 5,650, which rapidly increased to about 12,250 by October (Tregear and Berry, 1959).

There are certain geographical characteristics of Hong Kong that set it apart from other islands in the area. First, Hong Kong's geographical position is unique. It is located at the entrance of the Zhujiang (Pearl River) which, with Dongjiang, Xijiang and Beijiang, forms one of the

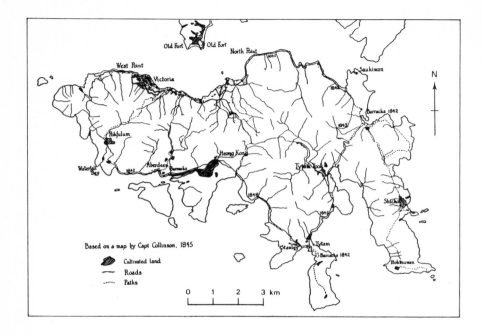

Figure 1.2 Hong Kong Island in 1845
Source: Tregear and Berry, 1959

richest agricultural delta areas of China. Hong Kong is therefore directly open to the South China Sea and the Pacific Ocean. It occupies a central position in South-east Asia and serves as a focal point for major shipping routes from Europe and North America. This makes Hong Kong highly suited as a transhipment point for goods for other parts of Asia. The advent of air transport further enhances the centrality of Hong Kong. This explains why Hong Kong has been very successful with its entrepôt port function (Davis, 1949).

Second, Hong Kong's harbour is unique. Hong Kong is well endowed with a natural deep-water harbour which is relatively free from silting. The eastern half of the harbour and the main central channel allow 12 metres of draught (Chiu, 1973). This makes it superior to Macao where the harbour suffers from silting from sediment plumes swinging south-westwards from Zhujiang. This can be clearly seen in the satellite photograph in Figure 1.3. The tidal range for most days of the year is about 1.5 metres, which has little effect on the navigability of the waters in and around the harbour. The strength and direction of the tidal currents tend to preserve the depth of the harbour. Guangzhou, which

Figure 1.3 A satellite image (0.61–0.68 um) of Hong Kong and the New Territories, acquired by SPOT on January 8, 1988

is about 145 km away from Hong Kong, suffers from heavy silting, and an outport, Huangbu, has to be used.

Third, as a partially submerged, dissected, upland terrain rising to over 500 metres in height, the island of Hong Kong and the Kowloon peninsula together produced a harbour which is 12.9 km long in its east-west extent and 1.6 km by 3.2 km wide. Thus, the harbour is quite well sheltered from wind and the occasional typhoon.

Fourth, because the coastline was formed by submergence, there is not much level land around the harbour for development and the inland area is also very hilly. Fortunately, the near-shore areas are shallow enough to permit reclamation to take place. This is the only way that Hong Kong can obtain new land immediately adjacent to the harbour (So, 1986). But this also means that the land price is high.

Fifth, Hong Kong has no natural resources of its own. Its arable land is limited in areal extent, and mineral resources are scarce. Geologically, Hong Kong is made up of granite and acid volcanic rocks with sedimentary intercalations (Peng, 1986). Because of its location on the margin of the Pacific Basin, marine fish are important primary products. Hong Kong also has sufficient fresh water to support a small population. Apart from these Hong Kong is basically a resource-poor area.

All these geographical characteristics have had a great impact on the economic development of Hong Kong.

Stages of economic transformation

The economic transformation of Hong Kong has not always been smooth. There were times when Hong Kong appeared to be losing ground, but miraculously the resilience of the population and the flexibility of the economic system helped Hong Kong to overcome its worst moment, and put it back on the proper path of development.

1. The founding and consolidating period (1841–61)

When the island of Hong Kong was first occupied by Captain Elliot, it was largely military in nature, and three batteries were immediately established to counter two Chinese forts on the tip of Kowloon peninsula. The hilly topography restricted the development of the settlement on the northern coast of the island near to the West Point (Figure 1.2). This area was named Victoria and became the residential and commercial centre of the settlement. While the most intensive development of the settlement rapidly took place on steeper slopes which had deeper inshore water, urban development generally proceeded along the coast from East Point to West Point. Land reclamation was also involved as the settlement spread outwards. Such early reclamations were piecemeal and unplanned. Bitter arguments between the government and private lot holders invariably occurred. The government's efforts to build a continuous bund or praya along the coast was opposed by private lot holders. It was not until 1873 that a more or less continuous praya running approximately along the present site of Des Voeux Road was built.

Another serious problem in the early period of the colony was the presence of some poor elements in the population, both foreigners and Chinese, who came to the colony looking for profits. Also, there were health hazards, notably fever and dysentery, which killed many residents. Because of the makeshift nature of the houses, fires were rampant in the dry season and typhoons caused considerable damage to property. All this added to the uncertainty of life and possessions in Hong Kong. Also trade did not increase as rapidly in the early years as had been expected, largely because British merchants continued to maintain their offices in Guangzhou and British ships tended to trade directly with other treaty ports. Opium which was an important component of British trade had been discouraged by the British government and many opium ships by-passed Hong Kong. But, despite these miscalculations, trade did increase in Hong Kong albeit slowly. Hong Kong registered more and more ships coming from the China coast, Guangzhou and India although opium continued to be the big export item with merchants using Hong Kong as a transhipment point to transfer cargo into smaller vessels adapted for the coastal trade.

Despite all these difficulties the Colony survived, probably because of its important role as a naval and military centre which provided security for headquarters of important British merchant houses. Hong Kong also served as a very much needed service centre for ships coming from Europe, America or India for repairs and stocking up with supplies. As Hong Kong's population grew, trade increased because of local demands for food and other goods. The Chinese gradually acquired the habit of using European goods and Hong Kong naturally became the centre for the supply of British goods to China. Banks were established as trade continued to grow. In 1857 the Chartered Mercantile Bank of India, London and China opened a branch in Hong Kong, followed by the Chartered Bank of India, Australia and China (now the Chartered Bank) in 1859, and the Hongkong and Shanghai Banking Company (later Corporation) was opened in 1864 by a group of leading Hong Kong merchants to become, from 1866 onwards, the most important bank in China. Another very important development was shipping which had been responsible for the growth of Hong Kong's trade. The local firm, Jardine, Matheson and Company was particularly prominent in this area. Other companies were established including the French Messageries Maritime in 1866 and Butterfield and Swire of the China Navigation Company in 1872. It is not surprising that Hong Kong developed its ship-repairing and shipbuilding industries at a very early stage at the East Point of the island. In 1843 the first ship was launched, and in 1857 the first dry dock was built in Aberdeen. In 1863 some of the existing companies were consolidated into Hong Kong and Whampoa Dock Company.

Thus, during this early founding stage, Hong Kong had gradually strengthened its position as a transhipment centre and a trade centre with China by providing much needed services to the merchants. Its economic base was therefore firmly established.

2. The expanionist period (1861–98)

During this period, the original territory of Hong Kong was considerably expanded. In 1861, the Kowloon peninsula opposite Hong Kong Island was added to Hong Kong as a result of the Second Anglo–Chinese War (1856–8) which forced China to open up more treaty ports with the signing of the treaties of Tianjin (Tientsin) and Beijing (Peking) in 1858 and 1860 respectively. The territory extended from the coast to present-day Boundary Street and included Stonecutters Island (Figure 1.1). This acquisition not only allowed Hong Kong to control the whole harbour from the defensive point of view, but also provided more land for development. At the time of take-over there were about 3,000 people, mainly farmers, living in small villages on the peninsula. Unlike Hong Kong Island the development of Kowloon was planned from the beginning. Areas to be reclaimed were laid out (Figure 1.4). These included the Tsim Sha Tsui bay and the east and west coasts. Military installations were set up on the peninsula. By 1887 three areas had emerged: Tsim Sha Tsui, the development core; Yau Ma Tei, a small town with shipbuilding industries, and Hung Hom, an industrial village based on the dock companies premises.

The population growth of Kowloon was gradual, and no wholesale transfer of population from Hong Kong Island occurred immediately. By 1887 the population had risen to 15,000 (Tregear and Berry, 1959) and by 1897 it had increased to 25,000. Very rapid population increase in Kowloon did not occur until the New Territories were leased from China in 1898. The New Territories are a very large piece of land extending from Boundary Street to the Shenzhen River and including Lantau and other smaller islands. This lease was triggered by Britain's fear of the growth of Russian and French power in the Far East which, after the French acquisition of Tongking following the Sino-French War of 1884–1885, threatened to control China's southern provinces. The acquisition of the New Territories therefore provided a buffer zone to allow the proper defence and protection of Hong Kong. The New Territories were essentially rural in nature with about 423 villages scattered throughout the area. The total population was estimated to be 100,000 at the time of the take-over. There were also some village industries in existence, such as, notably, lime-burning, brickmaking, salt production, shipbuilding, and joss-stick manufacturing. But, most importantly, the New Territories provided the much-needed water supply for the continued development of Hong Kong as its population grew. They also provided an agricultural base (rice and vegetables) for the population.

During this period, trade continued to grow in Hong Kong because of the development of shipping services, banking and insurance. By 1880 Hong Kong handled 21 per cent of the value of China's total export

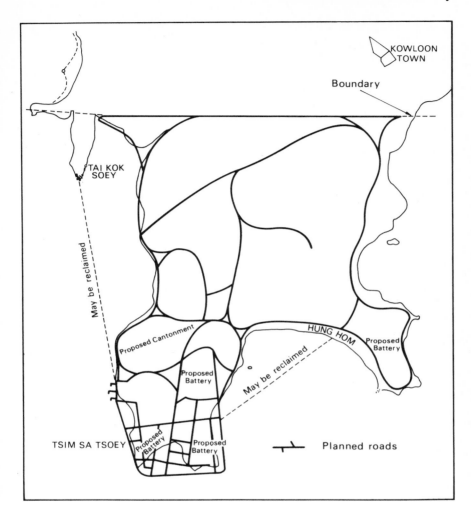

Figure 1.4 A map of Kowloon in 1861

Source: Tregear and Berry, 1959

trade and 37 per cent of its import trade. It was also the centre of the opium trade which constituted about 45 per cent of the total value of China's import trade. The opium trade did not end until 1909 when Britain adopted a policy to stop the use of opium in the UK, although the use of opium was not forbidden in Hong Kong until 1940. Industries other than shipbuilding began to appear by the end of the 19th century including factories for making matches and soap, rattan work, sugar refining and a cement company were established.

3. The First World War and growth (1914–39)

Hong Kong had prospered as a free port following a Victorian *laissez-faire* policy which allowed private enterprise to develop with the minimum interference from the government. During the First World War period (1914–18), Hong Kong suffered a decline in trade but, as soon as the war was over, Hong Kong regained its importance as one of the world's principal ports. However, as Endacott (1964) observed, major changes in the balance of power in the world and in British political ideology had begun to affect Hong Kong's economic development. After the war Japan emerged as the principal rival to Britain in the Far East, while the British share of industrial production and world trade steadily declined as developing countries began to industrialize. In 1931 Britain relinquished the principle of free trade in favour of protectionism. The *laissez-faire* policy was also out of favour. Because of the importance of British commercial ties, Hong Kong experienced increasing difficulties in maintaining its role as a free port. Most important of all was the emergence of a new China after the 1911 Revolution led by Dr. Sun Yat Sen which overthrew the Manchu Empire in favour of a Republic. After the death of Dr. Sun in 1925, civil war broke out between the National government of the Republic of China led by Chiang Kai Shek (belonging to the Kuomintang Party) and the Communists led by Mao Zedong. The Japanese militarists were interested in North East China (Manchuria) and its control. Growing nationalism in China resulted in repealing the unequal treaties and abolition of extraterritoriality, foreign concessions, settlements, and foreign control of Chinese customs. Hong Kong, however, remained under British rule. In view of all these political changes, Hong Kong needed to adapt to a new world order for its survival.

All these changes were reflected by the decline in importance of British shipping using Hong Kong and a sharp fall in exports to China. On the other hand, trade with South-east Asia and the Western Pacific had increased. The political instability in China had driven a lot of Mainland Chinese to Hong Kong in search of a more peaceful environment to make a living. The availability of capital and labour provided the impetus for the development of light industries in Hong Kong. The most notable was textiles which employed 5,867 people, mostly women, by 1939. Other industries, according to the 1934 Hong Kong Chamber of Commerce list, included processed goods such as preserved food products, sugar refining, knitted clothing, rattan furniture, rubber shoes, flashlight torches and batteries, rope, cement, perfumes, soap and firecrackers. However, the population increase did have the bad effect of straining public facilities, such as housing and water supplies. This had worsened by 1939 when the Sino-Japanese hostilities intensified in the build-up to the Second World War.

4. The Second World War (1939–45) and Korean War (1950) impacts

During the period of the Second World War, Hong Kong experienced the greatest setback in the history of its development. The Japanese invaded and occupied Hong Kong for three years and eight months from December 25 1941 to August 30 1945. The population declined dramatically to about one-third of its pre-war (1941) level or about 650,000 by May 1945. The economy stagnated while law and order deteriorated during the period of the Japanese Occupation. The defeat of the Japanese in August 1945 ushered in a period of uncertainty about the restoration of Hong Kong's sovereignty to Nationalist China (the Kuomintang) under the leadership of Generalissimo Chiang Kai Shek. It was only with the United States' influence that the British were able to reassume their authority in Hong Kong and face the immediate problems of rehabilitation. The Chinese population returned to Hong Kong in great numbers as soon as the Japanese occupation ended and the wave of immigration was further accelerated by the political instability caused by the civil war between the Nationalists and the Communists in China. By 1946 the population of Hong Kong had exceeded a million, and by late 1947 it had soared to 1.8 million.

The post-war years were hard for Hong Kong although it continued to maintain its status as an important trade centre. With the decline in British influence in the Pacific region, the American and Russian influence increased. Hong Kong had to further diversify its economy to lessen its dependence on the entrepôt trade. In 1949 the Communists defeated Chiang Kai Shek and drove his Nationalist armies to an island off the South China coast, Taiwan. This triggered an influx of Chinese refugees to Hong Kong. Many of these were experienced industrialists and skilled labourers from Shanghai who also brought capital with them. Conditions were ripe for the further development of industries in Hong Kong. The Korean War between China (for North Korea) and the United States (for South Korea) resulted in a United Nations embargo placed on trade in strategic articles with China in 1951. This further reduced Hong Kong's trade with China and caused tremendous suffering during the war which made Hong Kong see clearly the urgent need to develop industry.

5. Early industrialization and opening up to the world market (1951–61)

The early types of industries developed were unsophisticated and small scale. They focused on the use of cheap labour and were export-oriented by nature. Thus, light industries with an emphasis on textiles (spinning and weaving cotton yarn and grey cloth) were the most important. There were many small factories and workshops housed in residential areas and congested high-rise buildings producing cheap garments, simple plastic goods, rubber footwear, enamelware, cheap electrical and metal products and toys. During all this time, the role of the government was relatively unimportant, and the Hong Kong industrialists had been able to adjust rapidly to the internal and external economic environment. The importance of the Hong Kong government was its ability to provide a secure and stable environment, undisturbed by the political upheavals in China, for the people to fully engage their energies in economically productive pursuits to improve their standard of living. Thus, Hong Kong was among the first of the Newly Industrializing Countries (NIC) which adopted an outward-looking policy of export-oriented industrialism. The success of this policy was revealed by the fact that while in 1951 clothing exports had been only one-twentieth of the value of total exports, they represented over one-third of domestic exports by 1962. The United States and the United Kingdom replaced China as Hong Kong's biggest export markets.

6. Self-sustaining economic growth (1961–71)

This decade was marked by the beginning of the transformation of Hong Kong into a world city. The economic take-off was made possible by the savings generated in the previous decade, which financed capital investment and expansion of exports and trade, thus achieving a state of self-sustaining growth. By 1963 total exports had recovered to exceed the 1951 level, and real wage increases also occurred. People were fully employed. The building regulations were modified to allow the construction of high-rise buildings leading to a building boom. Such modern buildings as the Hong Kong Hilton and Mandarin Hotels were constructed at this time. The decade was not all plain sailing for Hong Kong. The building boom resulted in a banking crisis in 1964–5 because of the over-extension of credit, to be followed by the 'Star Ferry' riots of 1966 (to protest against an increase in the ferry fare) and the disturbances of 1967 (inspired by the Cultural Revolution in China). The latter disturbances indicated the political influence of China on the destiny of Hong Kong. Hong Kong's colonial status embarassed hard-lined Chinese communists, who, guided by the thoughts of Chairman Mao Zedong, vehemently opposed Hong Kong's capitalist pursuits. Hong Kong's ability to survive the disturbances reflected the strong support given by the Hong Kong Chinese residents to the British government whose policy of minimum interference (or *laissez-faire*) was bringing along prosperity. The banking crisis resulted in better legislation by the government to prevent future occurrences. Strong confidence in local banks, effective legislation and popular support of the government were the necessary prerequisites for Hong Kong to develop into a world city.

7. Sophistication and diversification of industries and the growth of financial and business services sector (1971–81)

To maintain its competitiveness in the world market, Hong Kong invested heavily in plant, machinery and equipment in order to increase productivity and to improve the quality and level of sophistication of its products. Hong Kong's investment in this area has increased from 16 per cent of the GDP (Gross Domestic Product) in the mid-1960s to over 33 per cent of the GDP in 1980 and 1981. Hong Kong also attempted some degrees of diversification in its industrial products. A good example is the electronics industry. The stock market provided an important source of capital to local enterprises and began to attract interest from overseas investors. Because of rapid industrial development and the lack of natural resources, Hong Kong also relied heavily on imports of raw materials, fuels, foods, and other consumer goods to satisfy the needs of its population. The success of trade depends on an efficient banking and telecommunication system. Services in shipping, aviation, tourism, and finance have become more and more important. By 1980, for the first time, the contribution of financial services to GDP (26 per cent) surpassed that of manufacturing (25 per cent) (Chen, 1984). This period was not without its problems. The most serious of which was the collapse of the stock market bubble in 1973 followed by the world recession in 1974–5 after the first oil crisis. But by 1976 Hong Kong had fully recovered from all these setbacks due to its high degree of flexibility in adapting to adverse economic conditions and the shrewdness of its industrialists. When Chairman Mao died in September 1976, and Deng Xiaoping, a pragmatist, took over control in China a new open policy was announced and implemented in 1978 so as to attract foreign investment. As a result a strong revival of Hong Kong's entrepôt trade with China occurred in 1979. In other words, Hong Kong once again became important to China as its window onto the West in its pursuit of modernization.

8. A world city in the face of the 1997 uncertainties (1981–91)

The economic growth of Hong Kong during the 1980s was aided by the recovery from the oil crisis and also by China's Open Door Policy. Hong Kong excelled in the production of light consumer goods and was the biggest exporter in the world by value of clothing, toys and electrical

15

hairdressing apparatus, as well as the biggest exporter by volume of watches and radios. But Hong Kong also began to diversify its industries further in the face of stiff competition from its neighbours. Hong Kong attempted to move up-market and to increase the value per unit of output. Some examples were optical goods, metal and chemical products and electronics manufacturing of all types. By 1984 electronics became the largest export item among manufactured goods. Hong Kong has also become well established as an international finance centre by virtue of its excellent air transport and telecommunication facilities and a pool of well educated and highly efficient service personnel and technocrats. Because of China's open policy which makes it rely heavily on Hong Kong to export its products overseas, Hong Kong has regained its former importance as an entrepôt port. Indeed, in 1985 as much as 56.1 per cent of domestic exports and 57.7 per cent of re-exports went to just two markets – the United States and China – while China and Japan supplied almost half of all Hong Kong's imports (Hong Kong Government, 1987). This reliance on China made the negotiation on the future of Hong Kong between China and Britain particularly significant. The negotiation started as early as May 1982 and by December 19, 1984, a Sino–British Joint Declaration on the Future of Hong Kong was signed by Mrs Margaret Thatcher, the Prime Minister of Great Britain, and Mr. Zhao Ziyang, the Prime Minister of the People's Republic of China. Britain agreed to return the sovereignty of Hong Kong to China on July 1 1997 while China promised to maintain a policy of 'one country, two systems' by converting Hong Kong into a Special Administrative Region which will continue to follow a capitalist economic system and hopefully maintain its status as a world city. Initially, this declaration was quite well received by the people of Hong Kong. But very soon doubts as to whether the Chinese government will keep its promise, and whether the prosperity of Hong Kong can be maintained, spurred some Hong Kong residents, mostly the well educated and highly skilled, to think seriously of emigration. Their favourite destination is Canada which has relaxed its immigration policy to attract some of the talented and wealthy residents of Hong Kong. The confidence of the Hong Kong people was further eroded by the Chinese government's brutal crackdown on the pro-democracy demonstration by students in Tiananmen Square on June 4, 1989 and the ensuing downfall of the more open-minded premier Zhao Ziyang, the very person who signed the Sino-British Joint Declaration. In 1990, the Basic Law was completed, but it was drafted under such tight constraints from Beijing that less local autonomy to post-1997 Hong Kong would be allowed. Hong Kong is now experiencing the most severe brain drain. In 1989 about 55,000 people, or about 1,000 per week, emigrated from Hong Kong. This number is anticipated to increase as 1997 draws near. Surprisingly, Hong Kong's prosperity is apparently not affected and continued to maintain a respectable growth rate in GDP. In 1987 it was 14 per cent, although by 1989 it had declined to 2.5 per cent, which probably reflected the world market condition at the time. Such is the vitality and resilience of Hong Kong's economy.

Conclusion: determinants of economic growth

This brief survey indicates a number of important factors that help explain the transformation of Hong Kong from a barren island into a world city within a period of about 140 years.

First, the geographic location of Hong Kong on the rim of the Pacific Basin in relation to North America and Europe has grown in importance since 1841, and has been crucial in assuring its success as a world trade centre.

Second, the government's policy of maintaining Hong Kong as a free port devoted to free trade combined with low taxation and free movement of money attracted capital, skill, and technology to the colony.

Third, the government's *laissez-faire* policy (officially known as 'positive non-interventionism') has been particularly favourable for Adam Smith's theory to fully develop. The wealth of a nation is solely the amount and quality of the labour it possesses and the efficiency with which it sets to work. Hong Kong has a hard-working Chinese labour force whose work ethic follows that of Confucius. As time goes by, this labour force is improved by gaining skills, education and diverse influences from Western cultures.

Fourth, British law and order and the colonial status have brought political stability and security to Hong Kong for its economic transformation. During Hong Kong's existence as a British colony, China has undergone tremendous political upheavals which hampered its economic development. Hong Kong, like the eye of a typhoon, survived the turbulence relatively unscathed.

In the course of Hong Kong's transformation into a world city, distinct characteristics of people, politics and cityscapes emerge, which form the subjects of more detailed discussions in subsequent chapters.

References

Chen, E.K.Y. 1984. The economic setting. In *The business environment in Hong Kong*, D.G. Lethbridge (ed.). Hong Kong: Oxford University Press, pp. 1–51.

Chiu, T.N. 1973. *The port of Hong Kong: a survey of its development*. Hong Kong: Hong Kong University Press.

Davis, S.G. 1949. *Hong Kong in its geographical setting*. London: Collins.

Endacott, G.B. 1964. *A history of Hong Kong*. London: Oxford University Press.

From barren island to world city

Friedmann, J. 1986. The world city hypothesis. *Development and Change.* 17: 69–83.

Friedmann, J. and Wolff, G. 1982. World city formation: an agenda for research and action. *International Journal of Urban and Regional Research.* 6: 309–344.

Hall, P.G. 1966. *The world cities.* London: Weidenfeld and Nicolson.

Hong Kong Government, 1986. *Hong Kong 1986 – a review of 1985.* Hong Kong: Government Printer.

Hong Kong Government, 1987. *Hong Kong 1987 – a review of 1986.* Hong Kong: Government Printer.

King, A.D. 1990. *Global cities: post-imperialism and the internationalization of London.* London and New York: Routledge.

Peng, C.J. 1986. Geology. *A geography of Hong Kong*, T.N. Chiu and C.L. So (eds). Hong Kong: Oxford University Press, pp. 7–33.

Sassen-Koob, S. 1984. Capital mobility and labor migration: the expression in core cities. In *Urbanization in the world system*, M. Timberlake (ed.). New York: Academic Press.

So, C.L. 1986. Landforms. In *A geography of Hong Kong*, T.N. Chiu and C.L. So (eds). Hong Kong: Oxford University Press, pp. 35–68.

Tregear, T.R. and Berry, L. 1959. *The development of Hong Kong and Kowloon as told in maps.* Hong Kong: Hong Kong University Press.

2
Demographic transition and economic development: population growth, composition and distribution

Hong Kong people have been described as having an almost instinctive grasp of economic reality, and as being pragmatic in outlook

Hong Kong Government: *Hong Kong 1986: A Review of 1985*

The economic development of Hong Kong reflects the responses to the challenges posed by its population in various stages of growth. Because of its poor resource-base and unique political status, most of these responses attempted to maximize the benefits of its natural harbour and the resourcefulness of its people. Despite this uniqueness, the growth of population in Hong Kong has exhibited characteristics no different from those experienced by other developing countries of the world during the same period. The most dominant characteristic has been the influx of rural population from the adjoining territories in Mainland China to the urban area which is Hong Kong. In fact, Hong Kong has played and continues to play a distinct role as a magnet to the people in South China ever since its founding day as a British Colony in 1843. It is therefore not surprising that, despite its small size, Hong Kong has undergone a demographic cycle closely associated with its stages of economic growth.

Population before 1841

The present territory of Hong Kong has exhibited archaeological evidence of its cultural associations with the southeastern coastal areas of China. These are characterized by the distinctive cord-marked pottery and chipped stone tools which began to appear in the fourth millennium BC and continued to the mid-third millennium BC when polished stone tools showing better workmanship and proliferation of forms also appeared. This was followed by the appearance of bronze dated at about the middle of the second millennium BC (Chang, 1986). All these artefacts suggest a strong maritime orientation of Hong Kong's ancient inhabitants during neolithic times. The end of the fourth millennium BC marked a dramatic rise in the sea levels with vast tracts of coastal plain being submerged and the modern shoreline being established. Human adaptations to the environmental change must have been tremendous during this period. From Chinese literary records, it was determined that the maritime peoples occupying the southeast coast were known as 'Yue', and there were different types of Yue people. Today, the term 'Yue' is also used to refer specifically to the province of Guangdong, to which Hong Kong belongs geographically and culturally.

During the Qin (221–207 BC) and Han (206 BC–220 AD) Dynasties, South China was conquered by the mainstream Chinese civilization, based on the lower course of Huang He (Yellow River), and immigrants began to come in who exerted a variety of influences on the indigenous population. Soldiers were also sent in to protect trade in salt, pearls, and incense – the three most valued products of the area. However, the physical environment was too harsh to attract large-scale settlement. During the Tang Dynasty (618–907 AD), more soldiers were sent to this area to protect the imperial salt monopoly and coastal trades. Many of these soldiers later settled down, married the native inhabitants, and took up farming. By clearing the forests and ploughing the land, using the new technology of the north, they transformed the harsh environment of the south into a more hospitable one.

The next wave of large-scale Chinese immigration occurred at the close of the Northern Song Dynasty in 1127 AD when the Chinese capital was forced to shift southwards as a result of the Tartar invasion. Chinese civilians moved south with the government and gradually penetrated as far as the coast. It was about this time that clustered villages sprang up on the coastal plain around Deep Bay in the northwestern part of the present New Territories (Lo, 1968). These villagers were farmers and were locally known as the Poonti in Cantonese (or bendi in pinyin Chinese) which means the 'Local People'. The Song Dynasty was brought down by the Mongol invaders in 1278 AD and established the Yuan Dynasty (1279–1368 AD). This event generated another wave of immigration into the area. Another group of people known as Hakka (or kejia) or the 'Guest People' who spoke a different dialect moved into South China. Offshoots from this mainstream came to the present Hong Kong area and occupied the narrow river valleys in the hilly regions found mostly in the eastern part of the present New Territories.

Finally, during the early Qing dynasty, a policy of coastal evacuation was ordered by Emperor Kangxi in 1662 AD in order to clear the coast from the threat of pirates. This policy required the removal of all coastal people and settlements inland in Shandong, Jiangsu, Zhejiang, Fujian and Guangdong provinces. As a result, the whole of Xinan District of which Hong Kong is part was affected and the entire population moved inland for about 32 km (Ng, 1961; Lo, 1966). In 1664 AD another evacuation was ordered and the boundary was placed even further inland. About 24 villages in the New Territories were affected by the second evacuation. The evacuation ended in 1669 AD after having caused great suffering to the coastal people. They were later allowed to return. In the Xinan District alone about 16,000 people were driven away but only 1,648 returned after the evacuation. The two important industries of incense and salt-making suddenly came to an end. The evacuated area became barren. In order to rehabilitate the coastal area, the Chinese government set up fields on the abandoned land, and the Hakka people from Eastern Guangdong were called in to farm them. It was at this time that another stream of Hakka people came in and occupied the better farm land in the New Territories (Barnett, 1957). The settlements spread gradually from the more fertile alluvial plain in the northwest to the hilly regions in the east between 1100 and 1900 AD.

Apart from the Poonti and Hakka peoples who made up the bulk of the rural land population in the New Territories, there were also the 'Water Peoples', the Tanka and the Hoklo. The Tanka who now speak the Cantonese dialect are thought to be descendents of the Yue people, the indigenous inhabitants of the area. The Hoklos came from the coastal regions of Fujian and were found mostly in the eastern coast of the New Territories. Both the Tanka and Hoklo are fishermen and live on boats. Today, they are all grouped under the category of marine population in the government census, and many of them have now been resettled onshore.

Population growth 1841–1991

The analysis of Hong Kong's population growth is facilitated by the excellent census statistics collected by the government in the series of decennial population censuses which began in 1881 (Fan, 1974). The picture of Hong Kong's spectacular population growth since 1841 is best

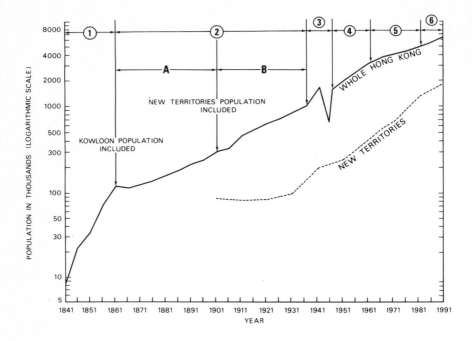

Figure 2.1 Population growth trend, 1841–1991

portrayed by the graph in Figure 2.1, from which six distinct stages of growth can be detected. The full data for this graph are also shown in Table 2.1.

Stage one (1841–1860)

When the British first took over Hong Kong Island from China, the Government Gazette of May 15, 1841 reported a population of 7,450 people, which included 3,200 people in villages and 2,000 people on boats in the harbour. There were also 300 labourers from Kowloon and 800 people in the bazaar (market). These people were all Chinese. This first 'census' revealed the economic characteristics of the Chinese population as farmers, fishermen, pedlars, merchants, and manual labourers. Apart from the farmers and fishermen who were native to the region, the other groups of people just moved in to take advantage of the economic opportunities created by the new colony. Many labourers were required in road building and other construction projects and the daily needs of the populace were served by the retailers and merchants. The political

22

Demographic transition and economic development

Table 2.1 The population growth of Hong Kong, 1941–1991

Year	Population	Increase(+)/ decrease(−)	Annual growth rate (%)	Remarks
1841	7,450	—	—	
1846	21,835	+14,385	38.6	
1851	32,983	+11,148	10.2	
1856	71,730	+38,747	23.5	
1861	119,321	+47,591	13.27	Kowloon included
1866	115,098	−4,223	−0.7	
1871	124,198	+9,100	1.6	
1876	139,144	+14,946	2.4	
1881	160,402	+21,258	3.1	Census
1886	181,720	+21,318	2.7	
1891	217,936	+36,000	4.0	Census
1896	239,419	+21,483	2.0	
1901	300,660	+61,241	5.1	Census, New Territories included
1906	329,038	+28,378	1.9	Census (partial)
1911	456,739	+127,701	7.8	Census
1916	528,010	+71,271	3.1	
1921	625,166	+97,156	3.7	Census
1926	710,000	+84,834	2.7	
1931	840,473	+130,473	3.7	Census
1936	988,190	+147,717	3.5	
1941	1,639,337	+651,147	13.2	Unofficial census by Air Raid Wardens
1945	650,000	−989,337	−12.1	Japanese occupation, 1941–5
1946*	1,550,000	+900,000	138.5	
1951*	2,015,300	+465,300	6.0	
1956*	2,614,600	+599,300	5.0	
1961*	3,129,648	+515,048	3.9	Census
1966*	3,708,920	+579,272	3.7	By-Census
1971*	3,936,630	+227,710	1.2	Census
1976*	4,402,990	+466,360	2.4	By-Census
1981*	4,986,560	+583,570	2.7	Census
1986*	5,395,997	+409,437	1.6	By-Census
1991*	5,522,281	+126,284	0.5	Census

Note: * Mid-year population.

Sources: Historical and Statistical Abstract of the Colony of Hong Kong (1932); Davis (1949); Saw and Chiu (1976); Census and Statistics Department (1969); Census and Statistics Department (1981); Hong Kong Government (1990); Census and Statistics Department (1991).

stability afforded by the British in the colony attracted Chinese immigration. Despite virulent diseases and typhoons which were fatal to the early settlers, the population grew rapidly at an annual rate of 38.6 per cent between 1841 and 1846 (Saw and Chiu, 1976). By June 1845, the population was estimated to be 23,817 which included 595 Europeans, 362 Indians, and 300 visitors (Fan, 1974). Between 1851 and 1864 there was the Taiping Uprising in China which drove more Chinese into Hong

23

Kong in search of peace and order. By 1859 the population grew to 86,941, which represented an average annual growth of 17.7 per cent since 1845. Thus, the main thrust of growth of Hong Kong throughout this stage was rapid growth generated by massive immigration. Predictably this population was highly transient in nature during the early days of the colony.

Stage two (1861–1936)

This stage was a long period of consolidation marked by the expansion of Hong Kong's territory from the island, across the harbour and to the mainland, thus giving Hong Kong the complete control of the harbour and a buffer between itself and China. Because of the acquisition of Kowloon Peninsula and the New Territories the population grew to 119,320 (including 116,335 Chinese) in 1861 and to 300,660 in 1901. The growth of population at this stage can be described as steady with a mean annual growth rate of about 3 per cent. Two sub-stages can be discerned: Stage two (A) which lasted from 1861 to 1900 showed a slight decline in population with −0.7 per cent annual growth rate registered in 1866 (Figure 2.1 and Table 2.1), probably caused by a mild commercial recession in the 1860s. But the speed of growth soon picked up and became steady again, thus indicating the gradual emergence of a more stable society. Stage two (B) which lasted from 1901 to 1936 displayed faster growth, probably because of the intensified political instability in China which drove more people into Hong Kong. In 1911 the Qing Dynasty was replaced by the Republic of China, but civil wars continued in China particularly between the Nationalists and the Communists. Hong Kong provided the haven for many of the Chinese refugees. Immigration continued to be an important factor of population growth in Hong Kong.

Stage three (1937–46)

This stage is a particularly eventful decade because of the hostilities between China and Japan which eventually culminated in the Second World War (1939–45). During this stage very rapid population changes occurred in a very short time. The period from 1937 to 1941 marked a very large influx of population into Hong Kong, hence the 13.2 per cent annual growth in 1941 when the Japanese invaded China and occupied the city of Guangzhou (Canton) in 1939. From 1941 to 1945 the Japanese invaded and occupied Hong Kong, thus resulting in a dramatic decline of population. The Chinese population was reduced to

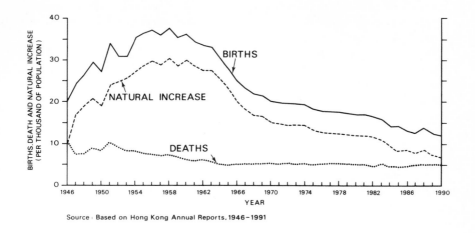

Source: Based on Hong Kong Annual Reports, 1946-1991

Figure 2.2 Rates of birth, death, and natural increase, 1946-1990

about one-third of its pre-war total. The occupation ended with the defeat of the Japanese on August 14 1945. There were only about 650,000 people in Hong Kong. Immediately, the Chinese population began to return, and by early 1946 it was estimated that they were coming in at the rate of 100,000 per month, hence the 138.5 per cent annual growth rate registered in 1946 when the population reached well above 1.5 million.

Stage four (1946–60)

This was a period of rehabilitation and adaptation to the new world order for Hong Kong. It was also a period of a large population influx brought about by the 1949 defeat of the Nationalists by the Communists during the Chinese civil war which caused many Chinese to flee to Hong Kong. This time a geographically more diverse group of Chinese refugees came to Hong Kong, many of whom were well educated or capital rich. At the same time the birth rate increased rapidly from 20.1 per 1,000 in 1946 to 37.0 in 1956 and was still as high as 36.0 in 1960: a result of the post-war baby boom. This was accompanied by a steady drop in death rates from 10.8 per 1,000 in 1946 to 6.2 in 1960 as a result of better sanitation and greatly improved medical facilities (Figure 2.2). Because the Communist Chinese government and the Hong Kong government had an agreement on restricting the immigration of the mainland Chinese into Hong Kong, immigration became less important than natural increase as a factor of population growth in Hong Kong. In

25

terms of the demographic transition model, Hong Kong was at the early expanding stage (or stage two) with high birth rates and declining death rates.

This was also a period of economic hardship for the Hong Kong people. The Korean War (1950) brought about a United Nations embargo on trade in strategic articles with China. The embargo stifled Hong Kong's entrepôt function and led to a decline in external trade. The Hong Kong government was faced with the increasingly difficult problem of where and how to cater for the growing numbers of people. According to Rostow's model for economic development (Rostow, 1971), Hong Kong entered the second stage of development, 'the preconditions for take-off' stage, as the government began to encourage industrial development. Not surprisingly, this was a period of increased government intervention. This was particularly evident in the area of public housing, the provision of which remains as an important controlling factor in the redistribution of Hong Kong's population today.

Stage five (1961–80)

By this time, natural increase had become the major component of population growth in Hong Kong and the population became more and more stable. Hong Kong also successfully completed its industrial transformation. In 1961 the population reached about 3.2 million. Despite some early uncertainties caused by the banking crisis of 1964–5 and the political impact of China at the start of its Cultural Revolution in 1965, the standard of living in Hong Kong continued to improve. The birth rate declined dramatically while the death rate was low and stable. By 1980 the birth rate was 17.1 per 1,000 and the death rate was 5.0. The decline in births during the 1960s was the result of the decrease in the number of women of child-bearing age caused by the extremely low birth rate during the 1941–5 Japanese occupation of Hong Kong (Freeman and Adlakha, 1968). In the 1970s the declining birth rate was probably the result of delayed marriage and the genuine preference for small families in the face of the ever rising cost of housing. This put Hong Kong at the third or the late expanding stage of the demographic transition model. Again, using Rostow's economic model, Hong Kong has attained the stage of take-off to sustained growth with increased rates of investment and the establishment of new industries. During this stage, the government vigorously pursued its population decentralization policy in an effort to improve the quality of life of the population by building new towns and public housing. But this stage ended with a renewed wave of immigration from China and an influx of refugees from Vietnam (Hong Kong Government, 1980). At this stage of development, Hong

Kong had no desire for a large increase in population. Unfortunately, its long coastline is difficult to guard against illegal immigration. In April and May 1962 there was a dramatic influx of illegal immigrants from China as a result of the relaxation of emigration restrictions. Over 60,000 people were arrested and returned to China in six weeks. It was estimated that about 100,000 illegal immigrants managed to settle in Hong Kong in 1962 (Podmore, 1971). Such occasional bursts of immigration from China are quite common, and represent a temporary distortion of Hong Kong's demographic cycle. The government took drastic action to discourage illegal immigration from China by ending the so-called 'touch-base' policy in October 1980, which allowed all those who succeeded in reaching the urban area of Hong Kong (i.e. the base) to stay. On the other hand, Vietnamese refugees presented a more serious problem to Hong Kong than illegal Chinese immigrants. The end of the Vietnam War brought political changes in Indo-China in 1975 which triggered off an emigration stream of Vietnamese, some of whom came to Hong Kong. They waited in Hong Kong for resettlement to other countries, but the number of refugees able to be resettled was much fewer than the number coming in. This problem could be solved only with the help of the United Nations and other countries such as the United States and United Kingdom.

Stage six (1981–90)

In 1981 the population of Hong Kong had grown to about 5 million. During this decade the birth rate continued to decline and by 1991 the population had increased to 5.5 million (Table 2.1). The annual growth rate averaged 1.6 per cent over the period 1981–6, and 0.5 per cent over the period 1986–91 (Census and Statistics Department, 1991). This was very slow growth. It was estimated that in 1990 the birth rate had dropped to 11.8 per 1,000. The death rate remained low and stable. It fluctuated between 4.6 and 5.0 per 1,000. The result was a continuing decline in the natural increase rate which fell from 12.0 per 1,000 in 1981 to 6.8 per 1,000 by 1990. A figure below the 7.1 per thousand for the United States in 1988. In fact, Hong Kong has much lower birth and death rates than the United States. Therefore, Hong Kong is now at the beginning of stage four, or the low stationary stage, of the demographic transition model. This demographic development has been closely associated with Hong Kong's economic achievement during this decade. Within a very short time Hong Kong has attained the drive to maturity stage of Rostow's model with diversification in its economy, although, with its limited natural resources, Hong Kong cannot achieve the self-sufficiency in its economy required at this stage. On the other hand, as a free port,

Hong Kong has the edge over other countries in reaching the stage of mass consumption in an advanced economy. The quality of life of the people has been further improved. This is also a stage marked by a high degree of residential mobility and the further spread of the population to the New Territories, made possible by extensive development of public transport including a modern underground mass transit system.

This period was marked by a major political event – the signing of the Sino–British Agreement relating to the future of Hong Kong on December 19, 1984 (Hong Kong Government, 1985). The impact of this sovereignty change on the population is very great. The most obvious effect is the increased population movement between Hong Kong and China for both commercial and non-commercial purposes. The other major impact is Hong Kong residents' declining confidence in the future of Hong Kong after 1997 despite China's promise of maintaining the existing capitalist system for fifty years according to the policy of 'one country two systems'. Emigration by the Chinese population from Hong Kong has intensified since 1984 and was further increased by the Chinese government's bloody crack-down on the Tiananmen Square Pro-democracy Movement in June 1989. It was estimated that 62,000 people have left Hong Kong every year since 1987 (Skeldon, 1991). Large numbers of these people are members of the educated, professional middle class (Barbara Basker, 'Hong Kong Increases Emigration Estimate', *New York Times*, September 9, 1990.) The most favoured destination for emigrants is Canada. During 1989 the number of Vietnamese refugees coming to Hong Kong has increased from 3,395 in 1987 to 34,116 in 1989. The Governor, Sir David Wilson, pointed out in his address to the Legislative Council on October 11 1989 that the problem of Vietnamese refugees represented a great strain on Hong Kong's resources (Hong Kong Government, 1990). This stage is therefore characterized by a lot of anxieties and uncertainties about the future of Hong Kong after 1997.

Population composition

Population composition which refers to such demographic characteristics as ethnicity, age, sex, marital status, language and education shows changes reflecting migration history and stages of economic development.

Ethnicity

The majority of the population in Hong Kong (between 97 and 98 per cent) is Chinese with ancestors originating from different parts of China. Most of them (about 90 per cent) came from the province of Guangdong,

Table 2.2 Place of birth of population

Place of birth	1911	1921	1931	Percentage 1961	1971	1981	1991
Hong Kong	31.5	26.7	32.5	47.7	56.4	57.2	59.8
China	62.2	70.1	64.3	50.5	41.6	39.6	35.6
Elsewhere	6.3	3.1	3.1	1.8	2.0	3.2	4.6
Total	100.0	100.0	99.9	100.0	100.0	100.0	100.0
(Population in thousands)	456.7	625.2	849.8	3,129.6	3,936.6	4,986.6	5,522.3

Sources: (1) Fan, 1974; (2) Census and Statistics Department, 1991

particularly around the areas of Guangzhou and Macao, while the remaining 10 per cent or so came from other parts of China. Despite its small size, the non-Chinese population in Hong Kong originates from a great number of countries in the world. The leading countries are Southeast Asian countries, United Kingdom, India, Pakistan, Bangladesh and Sri Lanka. As a British colony, Hong Kong's largest number of single country nationals are from the United Kingdom (25,703 by origin according to the 1981 Census). If the birthplace of the population is examined, the proportion of the population born in Hong Kong has increased tremendously during the post-war period (beginning from stage 4 of population growth mentioned above). In 1911 only 31.5 per cent of the population was born in Hong Kong, but by 1971 it was well over half (56.4 per cent) (Table 2.2). The 1986 By-Census indicated that 59.4 per cent of the population was born in Hong Kong. On the other hand, the percentage of the population born in China has decreased from 62.2 per cent in 1911 to 41.6 per cent in 1971 (Table 2.2). All these are the result of a more settled society and the growing importance of natural increase rather than immigration as the major component of population growth in Hong Kong since 1949.

The predominantly Chinese population has upheld its traditional philosophy of Confucianism in Hong Kong which emphasises filial duties, ancestor worship, the value of learning, frugality and diligence. All this is inculcated upon the population with the aid of a modern education system modelled after the British system. Mixing with people from different countries of the world makes the Hong Kong Chinese adopt a highly cosmopolitan outlook and Hong Kong has become one of the most westernized cities in the Orient. The economic transition from one stage to another would not have been possible without the hard work and endurance of the Chinese population.

Demographic transition and economic development

Table 2.3 The age structure of the population, 1911–91 (percentage of whole population)

Age group	1911	1921	1931	1961	1971	1981	1986	1991
0–14	21.3	25.8	27.4	40.6	35.8	24.8	23.1	20.9
15–64	74.8	71.6	70.2	56.4	59.7	68.6	69.3	70.4
65 +	2.2	1.8	1.9	2.8	4.5	6.6	7.6	8.7
Not stated	1.8	0.8	0.5	—	—	—	—	—
Dependency ratio	31.2	38.5	41.5	77.3	67.5	45.7	44.2	42.0
Index of Ageing*	10.3	7.0	6.9	6.9	12.6	26.6	32.8	41.8

* Index of Ageing = $(\dfrac{\text{No } 65+}{\text{No } <15} \times 100)$

Sources: Barnett (1964), Vol. 2, p. 24; Census and Statistics Department (1973), p. 21; Census and Statistics Department (1982), pp. 6–7, Census and Statistics Department (1991), p. 33

Age–sex structure

The most dramatic change in population composition occurs in its age–sex structure. As Hong Kong's early stage of growth was based on immigrants from China, and migration is selective by age and sex, the age–sex structure was extremely unbalanced. Because young males tended to migrate more than other groups in the population, there was a large proportion of the population aged between 15 and 50, often exceeding 60 per cent, reported in the censuses between 1881 and 1901. The sex ratio, which is normally expressed as the number of males per 1,000 females, was particularly high during this early period. In 1881 the sex ratio was 2,413 which increased to 2,654 in 1901.

From 1911 onwards there are signs that the population in Hong Kong became more and more settled, and after the end of the Second World War, Hong Kong had entered a stage of economic development that brought about prosperity, thus further promoting social stability. In addition, after 1949 the Communist government in China controlled, with the cooperation of the Hong Kong government, Chinese immigration into Hong Kong. Table 2.3, which shows the changes in the age structure of three groups in the population namely, infants and adolescents (0–14), adults (15–64) and the elderly (65 and over), bears this out. There was a slow decline in the adult group from 74.8 per cent in 1911 to 70.2 per cent in 1931, followed by a rapid decline to 56.4 per cent in 1961 at the end of the post-war period. However, since 1971 the proportion of this adult group has increased again so that by 1991 it rose to 70.4 per cent. This can be explained first in terms of the declining birth rate as Hong Kong moves towards stage four, or the low stationary stage, of the demographic transition, and, second, the occurrence of sporadic

Demographic transition and economic development

Table 2.4 Sex ratios of Hong Kong, 1911–86

Year	Sex ratio (number of males per 1,000 females)
1911	1,844
1921	1,580
1931	1,348
1961	1,056
1966	1,029
1971	1,033
1976	1,046
1981	1,093
1986	1,057
1991	1,038

Sources: Hong Kong Census Reports, various years

immigration from China during the years 1978–80. The sporadic immigration is the result of changes in the political climate in China which either loosens or tightens emigration controls. The declining birth rate is reflected by the decreasing proportion of the group of infants and adolescents (0–14) in the population (from 40.6 per cent in 1961 to 23.1 per cent in 1986) accompanied by a corresponding increase in the proportion of the elderly (65 and over) (from 2.8 per cent in 1961 to 7.6 per cent in 1986) (Table 2.3). In the years before 1931, although the proportion of the 0–14 age group of the population was even lower, there was no corresponding increase in the proportion of the 65 years and older age group and the 15–64 age group was over-represented. The index of ageing, computed as the ratio of the number of persons aged 65 and over to the number of persons aged under 15, best revealed the ageing of Hong Kong's population since 1961. From 1921 to 1961 the index of ageing was low (around 7.0), but by 1986 this has increased to 32.8 and by 1991, 41.8 (Table 2.3). The median age of the population in 1986 was found to be 28.6 years, up from 23.9 years in 1976 (Census and Statistics Department, 1986). By 1991, the median age increased to 31.5 years (Census and Statistics Department, 1991).

The sex ratio has also changed to reflect the more settled conditions in Hong Kong. Although by 1931 the sex ratio has dropped to 1,348, which was still high, indicating the over-dominance of males in the population, it is only since 1961 (1,056) that a more even sex ratio began to appear (Table 2.4). But this sex ratio fluctuated, having declined to 1,033 in 1971 and risen to 1,093 in 1981 and dropped again to 1,057 in 1986 and 1,038 in 1991. These changes reflected the sporadic immigration (which was male-dominated) from China during the years 1978–80 as well as the improved mortality rate of the elderly male population in recent years. In 1990 the life expectancy at birth for males was 74.6 years compared with 80.3 years for females.

31

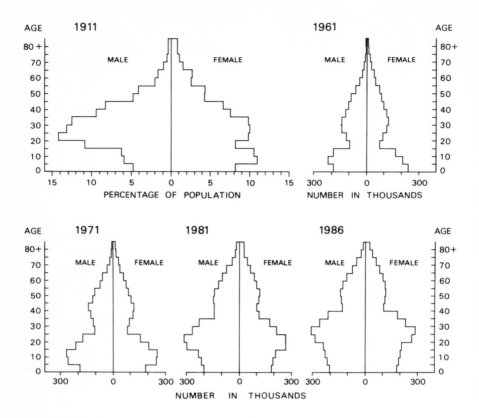

Figure 2.3 Changes in population pyramids, 1911–1986

The changing age and sex characteristics are best portrayed by the population pyramids of the pre- and post-war years (Figure 2.3). The 1911 population pyramid shows the over-dominance of young male adults. In 1961 the population pyramid reveals a bulge in the 0–9 age group and a gap in the 15–24 age group of both males and females. The former reflects the post-war (1954–60) baby boom and the latter the result of the greatly lowered birth rate during the Japanese Occupation period. By 1971 the population pyramid shows a much narrower base than that for 1961 as a result of a declining birth rate. The bulge moves upwards and continues to dominate the population pyramid while the gap became partially filled up as immigrants in the 25–35 age group moved in. The 1981 population pyramid shows a narrower base as a result of the continuing fall in the birth rate and a wider top because of higher life expectancy, especially for the female population. The baby boomers who moved up with the bulge to the 20–30 age group became

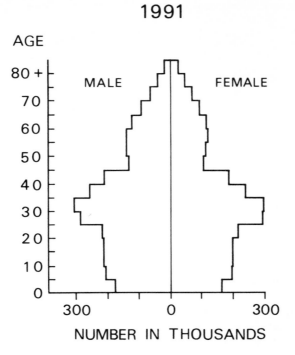

Figure 2.4 Population pyramid, 1991

the most important economically active labour force for Hong Kong in 1981. Apart from the narrower base, a much wider top and the continuing upward shift of the baby boomer bulge, the 1986 population pyramid has not deviated much from that for 1981. From the results released from the 1991 census, the under 15 age group has continued to decline and the 65 and over age group has continued to increase, thus resulting in a population pyramid with an even narrower base but much wider top (Figure 2.4).

Marital status

Marital status is affected by the age structure of the population. As Hong Kong's early growth was due to the Chinese immigrants who were predominantly male, young and single, it was not surprising to find a large proportion of unmarried men in the population. There were also a large number of married male immigrants who did not bring their wives along to Hong Kong in order to lessen their financial burden

Demographic transition and economic development

Table 2.5 Marital status of population

Year	Never married	Married	Crude percentage Widowed & divorced/separated	Total % ('000)
1931	46.7	48.4	4.7	100.0 (821)
1961	27.2	64.9	7.9	100.0 (1,853)
1971	36.2	58.6	5.3	100.1 (2,529)
1976	37.7	56.9	5.4	100.0 (3,708)
1981	38.2	55.0	6.8	100.0 (3,749)
1986	35.2	57.2	7.6	100.0 (4,149)
1991	32.8	60.0	7.1	99.9 (4,370)
		Standardised percentage*		
1976	32.8	61.5	5.7	100.0
1981	33.5	59.1	7.4	100.0
1986	35.2	57.2	7.6	100.0

Notes: (1) The figures exclude persons aged below 15
(2) * Using the 1986 age and sex distribution of the population aged 15 and above as standard

Sources: (1) Fan, 1974; (2) Census and Statistics Department, 1986

during the initial period of job-hunting. The 1931 census indicated that 46.7 per cent of the Chinese population in Hong Kong were recorded as single and 48.4 per cent as married. In 1961 the proportion of married people in the population increased substantially to 64.9 per cent while the proportion of the never married population decreased to 27.2 per cent. However, since 1971 the proportion of married population began to decline (58.6 per cent) with a corresponding increase in the percentage of the never married group (36.2 per cent). This trend continued. The 1986 By-Census discovered that after discounting the difference in the age structure of the population, the decrease in the proportion of married people and the increase in the proportion of the never married became obvious from 1976 onwards (Table 2.5). The increase in the proportion of the never married was particularly strong among females of marriageable ages, thus indicating a tendency towards delayed marriage. The sporadic immigration of predominantly young single males during the preceding fifteen years is another reason for the increasing percentage of never married population. All these trends have helped to lower the birth rate and family size in Hong Kong in recent years.

Education

Socio-economic changes in Hong Kong depends on educational level and attainment of the population. In the early days of the colony, the level

34

of education of the Chinese population was low. Even in 1961 about one-third of the population aged 15 and over had no formal schooling, 40 per cent received primary school education, and just over one-quarter had secondary education or higher. Of those without any formal schooling, over 70 per cent were female, and only about one-quarter of the university students were female. In 1971 the proportion of the population attaining secondary school or higher increased to 33 per cent, and one-third of the university students were females. Education for the 6–11 age group was made compulsory from September 1971. Since then significant improvements in educational opportunities occurred. Nearly 100 per cent of the population in the 15–24 age group received primary or higher education. Most significantly, educational opportunities in the higher levels also improved. In 1976, 7 per cent of the population aged 15 and above had matriculation or tertiary education, and 33 per cent had secondary education. In 1986, these figures were 14 per cent and 43 per cent respectively. The first three years of secondary education, namely Form I to Form III, was made compulsory for 12–14 year olds from September 1978. There was also a discrepancy in the level of educational attainment between males and females. In general, males were better educated than females, but the gap has been narrowing since 1961. Between 1976 and 1986, the number of females receiving technical education or tertiary education has increased by 1,245 per cent! (Census and Statistics Department, 1986). Hong Kong's economic development has therefore kept pace with educational improvement for both sexes and has succeeded in creating a well educated, reasonably prosperous middle class in the 1980s.

Population distribution

Spatial distribution of population in Hong Kong reflects clearly the stages of terrestrial expansion and the government's redistribution policy as Hong Kong's economy advances. Hong Kong's population distribution is also greatly affected by the mountainous terrain, innumerable islands and long winding coastline which combine to promote concentration and clustering of population. Four major mountain masses, namely, Victoria Peak in Hong Kong Island, Kowloon Peak in Kowloon Peninsula, Tai Mo Shan in the mainland New Territories and Lantau Peak in Lantau Island are effective physical barriers that restrict population movement, hence deterring the integration of these different terrestrial units into one. Only in recent years has expensive engineering, such as tunnelling, achieved much better integration for Hong Kong.

When the British first took over Hong Kong Island on January 26 1841, there were only a few villages and hamlets such as Stanley,

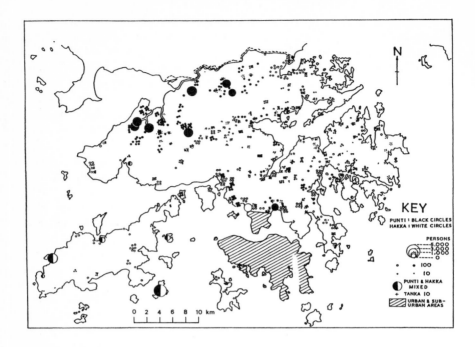

Figure 2.5 Distribution of population in the New Territories, 1898
Source: Lo, 1968

Aberdeen and Shaukiwan situated in sheltered west-facing bays. The site of the new settlement of Victoria was selected on the narrow northern coastal strip of the more sheltered western part of the island (Figure 1.2). Because of the importance of Victoria Harbour as the mainstay of Hong Kong's economy, and the difficulty of the terrain inland (Victoria Peak), the settlement spread along the coast and extended seawards through reclamation. Such reclamations were plagued by controversy and financial problems (Tregear and Berry, 1959). Some development inland was also carried out as witnessed by the development of the Mid-Levels and the Peak areas. On the whole, the major population concentration in the early period was along the coast with an eastward direction of growth. After the acquisition of Kowloon Peninsula in 1861 extensive coastal reclamation was carried out and the coastal orientation of the population became firmly established. Victoria and Kowloon developed into twin port cities separated by the harbour. When the New Territories were leased from China in 1898, they were treated more as a rural appendage to Hong Kong and little development took place before the Second World War. The rural population lived in village clusters found on the extensive alluvial plain in the northwest of the New Territories or at the head of the bays along the coast (Lo, 1968). Adjacent to Kowloon Peninsula there were major population clusters in villages along the coast (Figure 2.5). Such a pattern clearly reflects the control of relief.

The coastal orientation of the population in the twin cities of Victoria and Kowloon was particularly important in the past because proximity to the harbour was essential to the success of Hong Kong's economic activities. Because of space limitation and the difficulty of commuting imposed by the mountainous terrains, people invariably lived close to their places of work and so tended to cluster around the harbour on Hong Kong Island. This resulted in overcrowding. The preference was for the northern coastal strip between Kennedy Town in the West and Causeway Bay in the East. From Table 2.6, it is clear that over 50 per cent of the population lived on Hong Kong Island and 12–18 per cent in Kowloon Peninsula in 1911 and 1921. With the population growth and the continued development of Kowloon Peninsula, the population gradually spread out from the urban area of Hong Kong Island. In 1931 the population living on Hong Kong Island declined to 49 per cent while that in Kowloon Peninsula increased to 28 per cent. New Kowloon – the portion of land between Boundary Street and Kowloon Peak – recorded only 3 per cent of the population (relatively unchanged as compared to 1911 and 1921). It is interesting to note that the New Territories have exhibited a declining trend in population from 1911 to 1931. The decline may be explained by the population movement to the twin cities of Hong Kong and Kowloon. The marine population notably Tanka, who lived on boats, also showed a drastic drop from 14 per cent in 1911 to 8 per cent in 1931. Again, this reflected the resettlement of some of the fishing peoples on shore.

The first scientific census carried out after the war in 1961 revealed a more even population spread in Hong Kong. Although Hong Kong Island remained ahead with 32 per cent of the population, it represented a sharp drop from 49 per cent recorded in 1931. The population in Kowloon decreased to 23 per cent while that in New Kowloon increased to 27 per cent (Table 2.6). Clearly the metropolitan area of Hong Kong spread across the harbour to cover the whole of Kowloon and became better integrated due to a more efficient network of land and sea communications. It is also interesting to note that the population in the New Territories increased by 2 per cent over the 1931 figure. On closer examination of the population distribution pattern in the New Territories, certain large population clusters emerge in a number of market towns, namely, Tsuen Wan, Yuen Long, Tai Po, Sheung Shui and Fanling (Figure 2.6). These market towns provided the key links in a ring road system which circled the central portion of the New Territories.

As Hong Kong became more economically advanced the demand for

Table 2.6 Population distribution by area, 1911–86

Area	1911 ('000)	1911 %	1921 ('000)	1921 %	1931 ('000)	1931 %	1961 ('000)	1961 %	1971 ('000)	1971 %	1981 ('000)	1981 %	1986 ('000)	1986 %
Hong Kong Island	244	53	347	56	409	49	1,500	32	996	25	1,184	24	1,176	22
Kowloon	56	12	114	18	240	28	725	23	716	18	799	16	691	13
New Kowloon	13	3	10	2	23	3	853	27	1,479	38	1,651	33	1,609	30
New Territories	81	18	83	13	98	12	410	14	666	17	1,303	26	1,883	35
Marine	62	14	71	11	70	8	137	4	80	2	50	1	37	0.7
Total	457	100	625	100	841	100	3,130	100	3,937	100	4,987	100	5,396	100

Sources: Barnett (1964), Vol. 2, p. 24; Census and Statistics Department (1973), p. 21; Census and Statistics Department (1981), Vol. 2, p. 22, and Census and Statistics Department (1986), p. 8

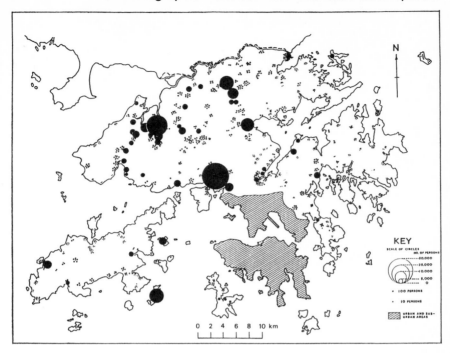

Figure 2.6 Population distribution in the New Territories, 1961

Source: Lo, 1968

higher quality of life, such as the adequacy of personal living space, became intensified. The government had to deal with the problem of overcrowding which had been endemic since the founding of the Colony. As population continued to grow by both natural increases and immigration (legal and illegal) in the post-war years, squatters proliferated and population density in urban areas rose. In 1954 the government became committed to the provision of housing which involved the resettlement of squatters and the construction of low-rent public housing for middle-income families (Wong, 1986). Rapid industrialization demanded large land sites which could no longer be found within the existing built-up area on Hong Kong Island and Kowloon. In the early 1960s the government adopted the strategy of building new towns in the New Territories in an attempt to solve these problems of housing and industrial needs (Leung, 1986). It is noteworthy that by the 1970s the New Territories were no longer regarded as a rural appendage and a buffer zone between Hong Kong and China. The New Territories became an invaluable asset capable of providing relief to the congestion in the traditional urban areas of Hong Kong. Such developments have resulted in massive population dispersal from the major urban areas on Hong Kong Island and in

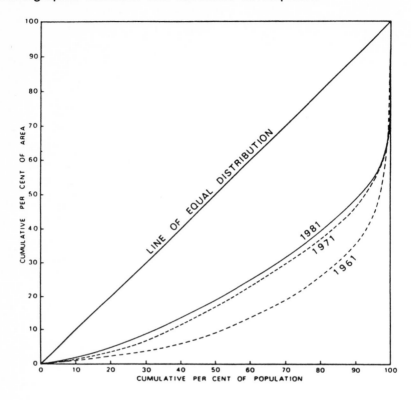

Figure 2.7 Lorenz curves showing population distribution in Hong Kong, Kowloon, and New Kowloon, 1961–1981

Source: Lo, 1986

Kowloon, as seen in the loss of dominance in population concentration on Hong Kong Island, which were superseded by New Kowloon in 1971 (Table 2.6). New Kowloon and Kowloon together attracted 56 per cent of the total population in 1971 while the percentage of population in the New Territories increased to 17 per cent. With the creation of more new towns in the New Territories the population percentage there rapidly jumped to 26 per cent by 1981. Most of the population came from New Kowloon although both Kowloon and Hong Kong Island also lost population moderately (Table 2.6). One should note that the new towns were based on the major market towns found along the ring road such as Tsuen Wan, which has now grown into an integral part of the New Kowloon metropolitan area. The 1986 By-Census revealed that 35 per cent of Hong Kong's population lived in the New Territories while only 22 per cent and 13 per cent lived on Hong Kong Island and in Kowloon respectively. New Kowloon came second with 30 per cent (Table 2.6).

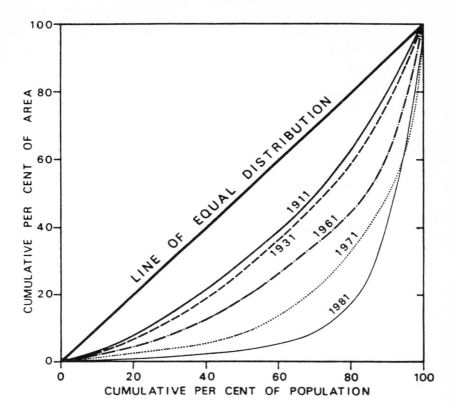

Figure 2.8 Lorenz curves showing population distribution in the New Territories, 1911–1981

Source: Lo, 1986

In other words, the New Territories were gaining population at the expense of Kowloon and New Kowloon. Today the population of Hong Kong is more evenly spread spatially, with the centre of population shifting north towards New Kowloon and the New Territories, thus attesting to the success of the government's decentralization policy. Plotted Lorenz curves reveal a trend towards a more even population distribution in Hong Kong, Kowloon and New Kowloon (Figure 2.7) but a more concentrated population distribution for the New Territories (Figure 2.8). In the 1991 Census the marine population was found to dwindle to a mere 0.3 per cent which indicates the near-complete resettlement of the fishing population on land.

Despite the recent overall trend towards a more even distribution of population, high population densities continue to prevail. Between 1981 and 1986 the overall population density increased by 8 per cent from

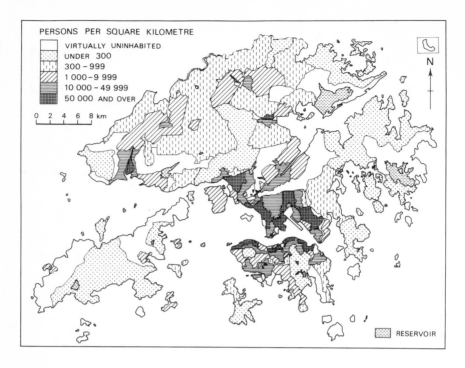

Figure 2.9 Population density in Hong Kong and the New Territories, 1986

Source: Census and Statistics Department, 1987

4,760 persons per sq km to 5,130 persons per sq km (Census and Statistics Department, 1986). Population density has increased substantially in the New Territories, especially in the new town areas. The three major increases were found in Sha Tin (203 per cent), Tuen Mun (137 per cent), and Tai Po (88 per cent). In the main urban areas of Hong Kong Island, Kowloon and New Kowloon, population density tended to decline. However, because of the small size of the urban districts, highest population densities continued to be found in these main urban areas. In 1971 Sham Shui Po Tertiary Planning Unit (TPU) recorded a population density of 196,915 persons per sq km; the highest in Hong Kong. This same Unit maintained the highest population density of 165,445 persons per sq km for 1981 and 147,624 persons per sq km for 1986, although the densities did decline by about 11 per cent between 1981 and 1986. Overall, population densities of 50,000 per sq km and over were found along the northern coastal strip of Hong Kong Island, the western and eastern coastal strip of Kowloon, the New Kowloon area to the north and east of the airport (namely; San Po Kong, Ngau Tau Kok and Kwun Tong – the main industrial and public housing areas of Hong Kong), and

URBAN AREAS   NEW TOWNS

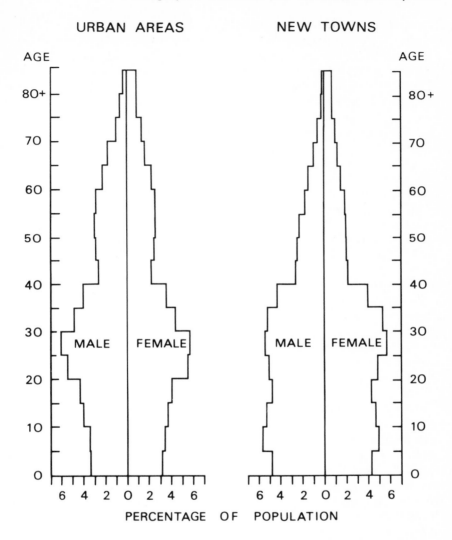

Figure 2.10 Population pyramids of the urban areas of Hong Kong and new towns (1986) compared

Source: Census and Statistics Department, 1986

the major towns in the New Territories (namely; Tsuen Wan New Town, Tuen Mun New Town, Tai Po Town and Fanling-Sheung Shui Town) as revealed by the population density map of 1986 (Figure 2.9).

The huge development programme in the New Territories stimulated by the creation of new towns and industry since the 1970s has tended to polarize the population characteristics into two types: the main urban areas versus the new towns. The 1986 By-Census found that a higher proportion of the population in the new towns was under fifteen than in the main urban areas and that the male population aged 15–44 in the new towns had a higher labour force participation rate than those in the main urban areas (Census and Statistics Department, 1986). There were also more elderly people in the main urban areas. These age differences are clearly revealed by the population pyramids for the main urban areas and new towns in 1986 (Figure 2.10). There were more simple nuclear families in the new towns than in other areas. On average, households in the new towns were worse off than those in the main urban areas. It is also not surprising that there were more workers in manufacturing industries in the new towns than in the main urban areas.

Two other characteristics of the distribution of population have been noteworthy in recent years. First, there is a predominance of children aged five and under in the peripheral regions of Hong Kong, notably in North, West and Northeast New Territories and on the more remote and rural East and West Lantau Island than in the main urban areas around the harbour. Second, there is also a greater percentage of people aged 65 and over in the more-or-less similar peripheral area. These characteristics indicate out-migration in this peripheral region where young and economically active people have left to seek better employment in the core area. These migrants return to their home villages during holidays and other occasions.

Internal movement of population

The population in Hong Kong has exhibited a high degree of longer term mobility since 1961. It was found that between 1961 and 1966 no less than 52 per cent of the total population had changed their address (Barnett, 1969). Between 1971 and 1976 36 per cent of the total population had moved. This percentage had declined to 16 per cent between 1976 and 1981. The 1986 By-Census showed that about 24 per cent had moved in the past five years (Census and Statistics Department, 1986). The lower percentage is an indication of a decreasing number of people being resettled in the new towns' public housing as the demand for better housing is gradually met.

The 1986 By-Census revealed that about 38 per cent of the total number of people who moved was within the main urban areas of Hong Kong Island, Kowloon and New Kowloon. About 35 per cent of people moved from the main urban areas to the new towns in the New Territories. Less than 3 per cent of people moved from the main urban areas to the rural part of the New Territories (Table 2.7). Despite a general move towards the new towns from the main urban areas, there

Table 2.7 Internal movement and population by areas of origin and destination, 1986

Area of origin	Hong Kong Island, Kowloon and New Kowloon	New Towns	Rural New Territories	Total
		Area of destination		
Hong Kong Island, Kowloon and New Kowloon	444,731 (38.5%)	401,597 (34.7%)	30,639 (2.6%)	876,967 (75.8%)
New Towns	62,489 (5.4%)	118,706 (10.3%)	15,603 (1.3%)	196,798 (17.0%)
Rural New Territories	18,830 (1.6%)	44,030 (3.8%)	4,102 (0.4%)	66,962 (5.8%)
Marine	5,768 (0.5%)	8,078 (0.7%)	2,527 (0.2%)	16,373 (1.4%)
Total	531,818 (46.0%)	572,411 (49.5%)	52,871 (4.5%)	1,157,100 (100.0%)

Source: Census and Statistics Department (1986), p. 26

had been also quite a lot of population movement within the main urban areas. The population movement between new towns accounted for about 10 per cent. There was a higher proportion of workers in the high-income professional, administrative and managerial occupations among the movers, particularly in the case of those moving within the main urban areas. Clearly, as Hong Kong becomes more advanced in its economic development, the level of residential mobility in the main urban area increases.

Conclusions

The growth of Hong Kong was characterized by the influx of Chinese immigrants in the early stage of the colony's development. The demographic cycle progressed in step with the economic growth of Hong Kong. Despite some setbacks in the Japanese Occupation Period (1941–45) and in the Korean War (1950), Hong Kong recovered quickly and transformed itself from an entrepôt port into an export-oriented industrial centre, benefiting from the large pool of labour, capital and skills brought to Hong Kong by Chinese entrepreneurs fleeing the Communist regime from 1949 onwards. Communist restrictions on migration within China also lessened the importance of immigration as a factor of population growth for Hong Kong, and natural increase assumed a more important role. Economic prosperity in Hong Kong brought about a decline in birth rates and death rates as the population became more stable. Hong Kong is now at stage four of demographic transition with both low birth and death rates.

The population of Hong Kong has traditionally concentrated in the twin cities of Victoria and Kowloon around the harbour where the population density is usually very high. The New Territories were treated more as a rural appendage until Hong Kong's economic advances meant a greater demand for industrial land and better quality housing. New towns were therefore developed in the New Territories from the 1960s onwards. A policy of population decentralization was vigorously pursued and population redistribution carried out with the help of a public housing programme which provided low-rent housing to the middle-income group. The squatting population was also resettled by the public housing project. The result was a greater population spread in the New Territories where new towns occupy specific points on a ring road. The rate of internal migration also increased with more and more people moving out from the main urban areas towards the new towns although population movement within the main urban areas also intensified. Population characteristics in the main urban areas and in the new towns became quite distinct with a younger population predominating in the new towns.

Recently, the demographic cycle has been interrupted by people's anxieties about Hong Kong's future because of the impending transfer of power in 1997. Emigration by Hong Kong's Chinese professionals to Canada, the United States, Australia and other countries intensified in the latter half of the 1980s, especially after the Tiananmen Square incident in June, 1989. People's level of confidence continues to be eroded by the iron grip and antagonistic attitude of the hardline regime in China. One can predict further increases in the emigration rate as 1997 draws near. Paradoxically, Hong Kong is still viewed as a haven, no matter how short-lived, for many mainland Chinese who want to flee from Communist China. Apparently the Vietnamese feel the same and have been arriving in Hong Kong in droves over recent years. It is interesting to note that while Hong Kong people are shrewd, well educated and hard working, their sense of belonging is weak. The latter is probably an effect of their government's policy of discouraging any participation in local politics until the late 1980s. The present generation of Hong Kong people still exhibit the immigrant attitudes of their forebears and retain a high degree of passivity.

References

Barnett, K.M.A. 1957. The people of the New Territories. In *Hong Kong Business Symposium*, J.M. Braga (ed). Hong Kong: South China Morning Post Press, pp. 261–266.

Barnett, K.M.A. 1964. *Hong Kong report on the 1961 census, vol. 2*. Hong Kong: Government Printer.

Barnett, K.M.A. 1969. *Hong Kong: report on the By-Census 1966, vol. 1*. Hong Kong: Government Printer.

Census and Statistics Department, 1969. *Hong Kong statistics 1947–67*. Hong Kong: Government Printer.

Census and Statistics Department, 1973. *Hong Kong population and housing census, 1971: main report*. Hong Kong: Government Printer.

Census and Statistics Department, 1981. *Hong Kong 1981 census: Tertiary Planning Unit population by age*. Hong Kong: Government Printer.

Census and Statistics Department, 1982. *Hong Kong 1981 census: basic tables*. Hong Kong: Government Printer.

Census and Statistics Department, 1986. *Hong Kong 1986 By-Census: summary results*. Hong Kong: Government Printer.

Census and Statistics Department, 1991. *Hong Kong 1991 population census: summary results*. Hong Kong: Government Printer.

Chang, Kwang-chih 1986. *The archaeology of ancient China*. New Haven: Yale University Press.

Davis, S.G. 1949. *Hong Kong in its geographical setting*. London: Collins.

Fan, S.C. 1974. *The population of Hong Kong*. Hong Kong: Swindon Book Co.

Freeman, R. and Adlakha, A.J. 1968. Recent fertility declines in Hong Kong: the role of the changing age structure. *Population Studies*, 22: 181–97.

Hong Kong Government, 1980. *Hong Kong 1980 – a review of 1979*. Hong Kong: Government Printer.

Hong Kong Government, 1985. *Hong Kong 1985 – a review of 1984*. Hong Kong: Government Printer.

Hong Kong Government, 1990. *Hong Kong 1990 – a review of 1989*. Hong Kong: Government Printer.

Hong Kong Government, 1991. *Hong Kong 1991 – a review of 1990*. Hong Kong: Government Printer.

Leung, W.T. 1986. The new towns programme. In *A geography of Hong Kong*, T.N. Chiu and C.L. So (eds). Hong Kong: Oxford University Press, pp. 251–78.

Lo, C.P. 1966. Some geographical aspects of demographic change in the New Territories, Hong Kong, from 1911 to 1961. Unpublished M.A. thesis, University of Hong Kong, Hong Kong.

Lo, C.P. 1968. Changing population distribution in the Hong Kong New Territories. *Annals of the Association of American Geographers*, 58: 273–84.

Lo, C.P. 1986. The population: a spatial analysis. In *A geography of Hong Kong*, T.N. Chiu and C.L. So (eds). Hong Kong: Oxford University Press, pp. 148–84.

Ng, Y.L.P. 1961. *The 1819 edition of the Hsin-an Hsien-chih: a critical examination with translation and notes: Hong Kong, Kowloon and the New Territories*. Hong Kong: University of Hong Kong.

Podmore, D. 1971. The population of Hong Kong. In *Hong Kong: the industrial colony, a political, social and economic survey*, K. Hopkins (ed). Hong Kong: Oxford University Press, p. 23.

Rostow, W.W. 1971. *The stages of economic growth: a non-communist manifesto*. Cambridge: Cambridge University Press.

Demographic transition and economic development

Saw, S.H. and Chiu, W.K. 1976. Population growth and redistribution in Hong Kong, 1841–1975. *Southeast Asian Journal of Social Science*, 4: 124.

Skeldon, R. 1991. Emigration, immigration and fertility decline: demographic integration or disintegration? *The Other Hong Kong Report*. Hong Kong: The Chinese University Press, pp. 233–58.

Tregear, T.R. and Berry, L. 1959. *The development of Hong Kong and Kowloon as told in maps*. Hong Kong: Hong Kong University Press.

Wong, L.S.K. 1986. Urban housing and the residential environment. In *A geography of Hong Kong*, T.N. Chiu and C.L. So (eds). Hong Kong: Oxford University Press, pp. 279–304.

3
Economic growth and structural change

... it is preferable to describe our attitude to the economy as one of positive non-interventionism: this involves taking the view that, in the great majority of circumstances it is futile and damaging to the growth rate of the economy for attempts to be made to plan the allocation of resources available to the private sector and to frustrate the operation of market forces which, in an open economy, are difficult enough to predict, let alone to control

Sir Philip Haddon-Cave, 'Introduction' to *The Business Environment in Hong Kong*, ed. by David Lethbridge, 1984

The character of Hong Kong's economy has been strongly influenced by its physical environment. Because of its small size, rugged terrain and the lack of natural resources, Hong Kong has to depend on other countries to supply it with food, fuels and raw materials. In order to earn its living, Hong Kong has to provide services to other countries. Hong Kong is fortunate in being endowed with one of the best natural harbours in the world which facilitates trade with other nations. As Chiu (1973) observed, Hong Kong was occupied by the British for diplomatic, military and commercial purposes. Diplomatic and military purposes were the means to an end which was commerce. Before 1949 Hong Kong functioned mainly as an entrepôt and trading centre between Britain and China but political changes in China have also dictated Hong Kong's direction of economic growth. The United Nations embargo imposed during the Korean War period in 1950 and the closed economic policy of Communist China during the reign of Chairman Mao Zedong resulted in the decline of the entrepôt trade. On the other hand, the large influx of refugees fleeing from China between 1948 and 1951 brought Hong

Kong labour, capital and entrepreneurial skills, all of which favoured the growth of industry. The entrepôt function of Hong Kong was revived in 1979 when China, under the control of Deng Xiaoping, adopted an open-door policy with an emphasis on foreign trade. Meanwhile, between 1969 and 1979 Hong Kong gradually emerged as an international financial centre by virtue of its British connection, a sound legal system and political stability. The opening up of China in the late 1970s elevated Hong Kong into an important gateway to China for the West. But, with the political upheavals caused by the Tiananmen Square incident of June 4 1989 and the impending restoration of Hong Kong's sovereignty to China by Britain in 1997, Hong Kong's economy will certainly undergo further structural changes. In the following sections, changes in the course of Hong Kong's economic growth will be examined and explained in more detail.

Primary economic sector

Included in the primary sector are economic activities related to agriculture, forestry, hunting, fishing, mining and quarrying. Before the arrival of the British, Hong Kong's sole livelihood was agriculture with a little fishing (Davis, 1949). But the hilly topography of Hong Kong does not favour agriculture on a large scale. Indeed, most of the agricultural activity on Hong Kong Island, Kowloon and the New Territories was restricted to pockets of river valleys or riparian lowlands. Only in the northwestern part of the New Territories around Deep Bay where an alluvial plain occurs is there extensive arable land. It was estimated by Davis (1949) that at most only about 18 per cent of the total land area of Hong Kong could be put into cultivation. In 1955 a land use survey carried out by Tregear (1958) determined that about 133 sq km or about 12.9 per cent of the total land area were cultivated. The most important crop grown was rice which occupied 71.4 per cent of the cultivated land while vegetables accounted for only 6.9 per cent. Because of the favourable climatic conditions, two crops of rice were normally grown a year. The rice produced was consumed locally but the quantity was insufficient to supply the total need of Hong Kong residents (Lai, 1964).

The influx of refugees from mainland China dramatically affected agricultural activities in Hong Kong. Among these refugees were skilled farmers who rented land in the New Territories and started intensive cultivation in the form of market gardening and poultry farming. They had a growing domestic market as the population in Hong Kong increased and became more wealthy. As these agricultural activities brought in more profit even the local farmers learned and adopted the technology of intensive market gardening. The result was a rapid increase in vegetable cultivation at the expense of rice cultivation. By 1961 rice land declined to only 57 per cent while vegetable land increased to 17.8 per cent (Wong, 1964). But in terms of the actual value of production, vegetables exceeded rice by 2.7 times because they could be grown throughout the year (Census and Statistics Department, 1969). This trend continued and by 1971 rice land had dropped to 34.2 per cent while vegetable land had increased to 30.4 per cent. However, the overall area of cultivated land in Hong Kong had also shown a decline to 124 sq km. The 1971 census showed that farmers comprised only 2.1 per cent of the total economically active population of Hong Kong, produced about 44 per cent of the vegetable consumed, some 48 per cent of the total live chicken requirements and about 16 per cent of all pigs slaughtered (Hong Kong Annual Report, 1977). This reveals the efficiency of agriculture in Hong Kong and the trend towards more specialization in agricultural production. As income increased Hong Kong people had more money to spend on other goods, and the improved agricultural productivity released surplus farm labour to industries and the secondary economic sector expanded.

Despite the natural limitations on agricultural activities, the Hong Kong government has encouraged the highest possible level of self-sufficiency in food production through extending the services of its Agriculture and Fisheries Department. In 1976 cultivated land declined further to 103.6 sq km or about 9.9 per cent of the total land area of Hong Kong. Rice land shrank to a mere 11.3 sq km. Accompanying this change was the continuing shift towards farming poultry, pigs and pond fish in response to the decline in rice consumption when the Hong Kong population became more affluent. In other words, intensive commercial agriculture replaced the subsistence rice-based agriculture of the past. In 1988 there was less than one hectare (0.01 sq km) of rice land and by 1989 rice cultivation had given way completely to intensive vegetable and flower cultivation. However, local agricultural production is highly efficient and has managed to supply 34 per cent of the fresh vegetables, 37 per cent of the live poultry, 18 per cent of the live pigs and 13 per cent of the freshwater fish consumed in Hong Kong from only about 8 per cent of the total land area and with only 2 per cent of the workforce. In cash terms the value of crop production in 1989 amounted to US$62.3 million, of which vegetables contributed 74 per cent. The vegetable crops exhibit great diversity in both Chinese and Western species including white cabbage, flowering cabbage, lettuce, kale, radish, watercress, leaf mustard, spring onion, chives, water spinach, string beans, Chinese spinach, green cucumber and many species of Chinese gourd. Straw mushrooms are also produced, using industrial cotton waste as the growing medium.

Another primary activity of importance in Hong Kong is marine fishing because of Hong Kong's location on the Pacific Rim. Over 150 fish species of commercial importance are caught. As the affluence of the population increased, the demand for fish, particularly fresh marine fish, rose. It is therefore not surprising that there was a constant increase in marine fish catches despite a dwindling number of fishermen. Indeed, the demand for marine fish was so great that culture of marine fish was developed in the 1970s. This involves the growing of marine fish from fry or fingering stages to marketable size in cages suspended in the sea in various bays throughout the New Territories. The total marine fish catch (including marine culture fish) increased from 2,467 tonnes in 1947 to 41,882 tonnes in 1957 and 55,720 tonnes in 1967. By 1976 it was 113,400 tonnes and reached 178,640 tonnes in 1989. The number of people engaged in fishing was about 40,446 in 1961 and increased to 45,080 in 1966. This number remained quite constant until the late 1970s when the 44,000 fisherfolks in 1976 were reduced to 24,000 in 1986 and then to 23,400 in 1989. The number of fishing vessels also declined from 5,500 in 1976 to 4,900 in 1989. In order to maintain high productivity, the majority of vessels is mechanized with trawling as the most important type of fishing being carried out. The fishing ground covers the continental shelf extending between the Gulf of Tonkin and the East China Sea. Supplementing the marine fish catch is the pond fish farming being practised in the New Territories and covering 1,380 hectares in 1989. These fish farms concentrate on highly intensive cultivation of carp.

Despite its small size, Hong Kong does possess some rocks and minerals of commercial value which have been quarried or mined. Iron ore was the most important mineral and was mined for export to Japan until 1976. Hong Kong is also well endowed with high quality granite which has been quarried for building use locally. Closely associated with granite are kaolin, feldspar and quartz which are mined for export to Japan and Taiwan. But mining and quarrying are not as important as agriculture and fishery in their economic impact on the primary sector. The number of people engaged in mining and quarrying is very small and has shown a continued decline from 8,860 in 1961 to 4,518 in 1971. It was down to 1,556, or less than 0.1 per cent of the working population, in 1981. In 1986 it fell to 812 which makes it a highly insignificant type of economic activity.

The importance of the primary sector as a whole to the Hong Kong economy is revealed by the trend graph in Figure 3.1, which measures the percentage contribution of primary economic activity to the Gross Domestic Product (GDP) between 1970 and 1988. It is clear that the primary sector contribution to the economy has always been extremely small and declined from 2.2 per cent in 1970 to 0.4 per cent in 1988.

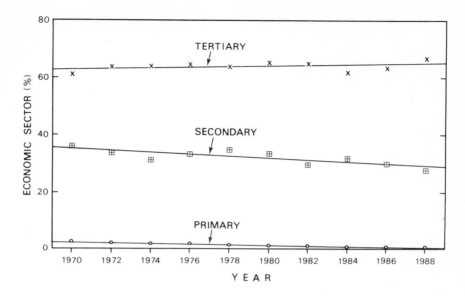

Figure 3.1 Economic sector trends, 1970–1988

Table 3.1 Gross domestic product by economic activity (in per cent)

Type	1970	1974	1978	1982	1986	1989
I. Primary	2.4	1.7	1.4	0.9	0.6	0.3
1. Agriculture*	2.2	1.6	1.3	0.7	0.5	0.3
2. Mining and quarrying	0.2	0.1	0.1	0.2	0.1	—
II. Secondary	36.0	31.3	34.8	29.7	30.1	25.9
3. Manufacturing	30.8	25.0	26.5	20.6	22.3	18.3
4. Electricity+	1.9	1.6	1.4	1.8	3.0	2.3
5. Construction	3.3	4.7	6.9	7.3	4.8	5.3
III. Tertiary	61.0	63.9	63.7	64.9	63.3	67.5
6. Wholesale#	21.9	21.5	21.2	19.1	21.3	23.9
7. Transport@	7.4	6.2	7.2	7.7	8.1	9.2
8. Financing$	14.5	18.0	20.4	22.5	17.3	19.7
9. Community**	17.2	18.2	14.9	15.6	16.6	14.7

Notes: * including hunting, forestry, and fishing
     + Electricity, gas, and water
     # Wholesale, retail, and import/export trades, restaurants and hotels
     @ Transport, storage, and communication
     $ Financing, insurance, real estate, and business services
    ** Community, social and personal services

Sources: (1) Chen, 1984; (2) *Hong Kong Government Annual Reports*, 1985–1991

In other words it is virtually negligible in the overall economy (Table 3.1).

Secondary economic sector

The secondary sector includes manufacturing, utilities (electricity, gas, and water) and construction. The rise of the secondary sector in Hong Kong was rapid from 1949 onwards (Table 3.1) but it should be noted that this was not stimulated by improved agricultural productivity as the sector model of Clark and Fisher postulated for a normal country (Clark, 1940). When the British colony was first founded, the primary sector lost its importance because Hong Kong's prime economic function was to be an entrepôt and trading centre. Hong Kong also managed to develop some industries associated with its port functions. These were ship-building, cement works, rope making and sugar refining and were all owned or controlled by Europeans (Davis, 1949). There were also local small-scale Chinese factories housed in the highly congested tenement districts which produced cheap textile goods for export to Southeast Asian countries. The Hong Kong goods could not compete with Chinese goods in the home market because China had imposed heavy tariffs on imported goods since 1925. However, industry managed to grow in Hong Kong, albeit slowly. In 1939 there were 948 factories of all types and in 1941 this number rose to 1,200. The Japanese Occupation inter-rupted the growth and after the Second World War in 1946 there were only 900 factories (Davis, 1949).

The rise in the importance of manufacturing industries in Hong Kong came about after 1949 when the communist regime was established in China. A combination of factors occurred at the right time to trigger off industrialization in Hong Kong. Communist China preferred to trade with the Soviet Union and Eastern Europe. The United Nations trade embargo imposed on China during the Korean War in 1950 further damaged Hong Kong's entrepôt trade. The large number of Chinese immigrants strained the social resources of Hong Kong to their limit. All these compelled Hong Kong to re-orientate its economy. Hong Kong took advantage of the cheap labour pool and the capital and skills provided by some of these Chinese immigrants, particularly those from Shanghai, to develop industries. Institutional factors such as the advantages of Common-wealth preference, membership of the Sterling Area by virtue of Hong Kong's British connections, the *laissez-faire* government philosophy and a free port status with no foreign exchange control and low tax also helped to promote an export-orientated industrialization. Again, because of Hong Kong's small size and limited natural resources, the types of industries developed had to be light, export-oriented and dependent on

Table 3.2 Percentage share of major industries in domestic exports

Industry type	1959	1964	1970	1974	1978	1982	1986	1990
Textiles & clothing	52.9	52.6	45.4	50.1	45.7	39.0	41.0	39.4
Plastics	7.0	11.0	11.3	9.1	8.7	8.4	8.3	0.6
Electronics	—	2.4	9.5	12.0	12.7	10.7	21.7	25.9
Footwear	4.3	3.9	2.4	1.4	1.0	0.9	—	—
Watches & clocks	—	—	—	2.2	6.7	9.0	7.6	8.5
Electrical appliances	—	—	—	—	—	—	3.1	1.5

Sources: (1) Chen, 1984; (2) *Hong Kong Government Annual Reports*, 1985–1991

imported raw materials. The industries developed at the initial stage in the 1950s had to be labour-intensive in order to take advantage of Hong Kong's pool of cheap labour. These concentrated on textiles and clothing and still remain important even today. But textile products were subjected to increasing trade restrictions imposed by Hong Kong's trade partners. In 1959 the United Kingdom imposed restrictions on Hong Kong textile exports under the Lancashire Pact. In 1961 the General Agreement on Tariffs and Trade (GATT) Long Term Cotton Textile Agreement (CTA) limited Hong Kong's textile exports to the United States and the European Economic Community (EEC) by a quota. This later also extended to clothing exports. The Multi-Fibre Arrangement (MFA) replaced the CTA in 1974 and imposed limitations on the export of non-cotton textiles as well. In face of these restrictions the Hong Kong industrialists tried to develop other industries. Two became important – plastics and electronics – and their rapid growth compensated for the decline in textiles. In the 1950s and 1960s the footwear industry became important but declined in the early 1970s. The wig industry was very important during the late 1960s and early 1970s but falling world demand means that it is no longer important today. During the 1970s Hong Kong began to shift its attention to watches and clocks and became extremely important in this area by the 1980s (Table 3.2).

It is clear from this brief survey that Hong Kong specialised in labour-intensive industries producing consumer goods to meet the demand of the world market. Hong Kong exhibited an amazing degree of adaptability to the world market by rapidly shifting from one type of industry to another. This type of flexibility in industrial production has been made possible by the very small-scale factories which employed less than 20 workers. These were the 'sweat shops' which have been responsible for many of the Hong Kong success stories during the early stages of industrialization. This type of 'sweat shop' could only operate under the Hong Kong government's non-interventionist policy. Another observation is that the number of industries developed was in fact very small.

Economic growth and structural change

Table 3.3 Percentage employment in manufacturing industry

Type of manufacturing industry	1951	1961	1971	1982	1990
1. Food products	8.2	4.5	2.7	2.8	3.4
2. Textiles, wearing apparel and leather	37.3	48.8	46.8	43.6	45.2
3. Wood and cork products incl. furniture	1.5	2.7	1.8	1.9	1.1
4. Paper and paper products	7.0	4.8	4.5	4.7	7.3
5. Chemicals, chemical products, petroleum, coal, rubber and plastic products	10.2	5.1	14.9	11.1	8.6
6. Non-metallic mineral products except petroleum & coal	2.4	1.0	0.6	0.5	0.5
7. Basic metal industries	1.4	1.2	0.5	0.5	0.4
8. Fabricated metal products, machinery and equipment	30.2	21.7	23.1	26.3	25.0
9. Professional and scientific equipment and photo and optical goods	—	—	—	5.2	4.4
10. Others	1.9	10.3	5.3	3.4	4.0
Total no. of persons employed in manufacturing	86,136	215,914	564,370	856,137	730,217

Sources: (1) Census and Statistics Department, 1969; (2) *Hong Kong Government Annual Reports,* 1985–1991

Although over 90 per cent of the industrial products are exported, an over-dependence on a few industries can be dangerous in periods of world recession. As Hong Kong became economically more developed labour costs correspondingly increased and it lost its cheap labour advantage as a result of competition from other newly industrializing Asian countries. To remain competitive in the world market, Hong Kong had to diversify its products in the 1960s and 1970s within its limited number of industries. But there is a limit to product diversification. Since the 1980s Hong Kong has turned to the more capital- and technology-intensive industries, such as metal products, electrical appliances, photographic and optical goods. Hong Kong's age-old shipbuilding industry has been modernized, and the aircraft engineering industry has developed a high international reputation. All these industrial structural changes have been accomplished with the minimal amount of government intervention. The government's prime industrial policy has been to maintain an efficient infrastructure, to provide services that will increase industrial productivity and to encourage technology transfer through an inward investment promotion programme.

Despite the change in the economic structure of Hong Kong, the manufacturing employment pattern remained relatively unchanged. It should be noted from Table 3.3 that textiles, wearing apparel and leather products were the most important employers from 1951 onwards when they employed 37.3 per cent of the manufacturing workers. This rose to 45.2 per cent in 1990 although the peak year was 1961 with 48.8 per cent. The second major group of manufacturing industries was fabricated metal products, machinery and equipment which employed 30.2 per cent of the manufacturing workers in 1951 but declined to 25 per cent in 1990. The third category is chemicals and chemical products, petroleum, coal, rubber and plastic products which employed 10.2 per cent of the manufacturing workers in 1951 and declined to 8.6 per cent in 1990, again without changing its rank. A new manufacturing category generally known as professional and scientific, measuring and controlling equipment and photographic and optical goods appeared in the late 1970s as a result of an attempt to diversify into high-technology. The total population engaged in manufacturing increased from 86,136 in 1951 to a peak of 856,137 in 1982, but dropped to 730,217 (about 26 per cent of the 2.8 million-strong workforce) in 1990. There has been tremendous growth in employment in manufacturing industries since 1951. However, in terms of Gross Domestic Product (GDP) by economic activity, the secondary sector, which is primarily influenced by the manufacturing industry, reveals a downward trend as Hong Kong's economy advances (Figure 3.1).

Tertiary economic sector

The tertiary economic sector includes commerce, finance, transport, communications and services of all kinds. In Figure 3.1 one sees the important contribution of the tertiary sector to the Gross Domestic Product of Hong Kong since 1970. It has accounted for no less than 60 per cent of the GDP of Hong Kong (Table 3.1). This percentage increased to 67.5 per cent in 1989. The most important component of the tertiary sector is wholesale, retail and import/export trades, restaurants and hotels followed by financing, insurance, real estate and business services. In 1989 the former contributed 23.9 per cent and the latter 19.7 per cent to Hong Kong's GDP. The financing sector reached as high as 22.5 per cent in its GDP contribution in 1982 but declined since then, probably reflecting the concerns relating to 1997.

The importance of the tertiary sector is not surprising in view of Hong Kong's long tradition as an entrepôt and trade centre. More important was the emergence in 1969 of Hong Kong as a major financial centre for the Asian–Pacific region which set it apart from other world ports. According to Jao (1980) there are readily observable characteristics in Hong Kong which indicate its importance as a regional financial centre.

First, there is a large and increasing number of international banking institutions and other non-bank financial intermediaries. These institutions engage not only in business transactions in Hong Kong's financial markets, but also in the channelling of funds to and from other countries. In other words, Hong Kong's rapid rise as a financial centre has been the result of the phenomenal growth of loans and advances to countries in the Asian-Pacific region, including Indonesia, South Korea, Taiwan, Malaysia, Japan, Australia, Philippines, Thailand, India and New Zealand as well as Latin America (Brazil and Mexico) and Europe (Ireland). Second, Hong Kong's banks can offer deposits of various maturities in foreign currencies. Third, Hong Kong shows financial deepening indicated by increased accumulation of financial assets and increased banking density as well as increased relative share of financial sector in GDP and in total labour force. Fourth, Hong Kong has an active stock market, a gold market and a Commodity Exchange. Hong Kong's rise as a regional financial centre is the result of a number of geographical and political factors. Finally, Hong Kong has developed efficient sea-land transport and telecommunications which keep it in touch with the world 24 hours a day.

In the 1970s multinational banks were compelled to follow a strategy of international diversification and to expand their overseas business. Hong Kong's efficient workforce, excellent infrastructure, British legal system, political stability, absence of foreign exchange control, low corporate and income taxes and favourable geographical location as the gateway to China, all helped to lure multinationals. After the death of Chairman Mao Zedong in 1976 and the rise to power of Deng Xiaoping, China proclaimed a modernization policy and adopted a free market economy. In 1978 China even went so far as to issue a specific invitation to the West for investment. Hong Kong benefited from all these changes and its entrepôt trade revived and grew in importance. The multinational banks found it convenient to establish themselves in Hong Kong in order to finance China's modernization programme. Proximity to China gives Hong Kong a major advantage over Singapore as the choice site for an Asian–Pacific financial centre. Clearly, it is this special relationship with both China and Britain that makes Hong Kong a unique haven for foreign bankers and industrialists. Despite the important contribution to Hong Kong's economy by the financial sector only about 7.3 per cent of the total workforce, or about 200,000 people, were engaged in it in 1990 (Hong Kong Government, 1991).

Hong Kong's changing foreign trade pattern

Foreign trade has always been important to Hong Kong's survival from

Economic growth and structural change

Table 3.4 Growth in volume of trade, 1966–1985*

Year	Domestic exports	Index	Re-exports	Index	Imports	Index
1966	16,655	100	5,126	100	27,235	100
1971	30,846	185	7,853	153	45,888	168
1976	44,690	268	13,842	270	62,092	228
1981	73,716	443	38,598	753	125,336	460
1985	91,146	547	70,255	1370	163,417	600

* HK$ million at constant 1980 prices

Source: Hong Kong Government Annual Report, 1987, p. 5

the very first day the Crown Colony was founded. The three major components of foreign trade are domestic exports, re-exports and imports. Hong Kong is obviously a strong protagonist of free trade and its economic success would be greatly hampered by protectionism practised by importing countries.

Domestic exports

Domestic exports became important to Hong Kong only after the mid-1950s when Hong Kong started its export-orientated industrialization. Before then, re-exports were much larger than exports. It was estimated that up to 90 per cent of Hong Kong's manufacturing output was eventually exported. In 1960, the value of domestic exports increased dramatically to HK$2,867 million. By 1989 this value reached HK$224,104 million. A more realistic comparison which takes inflation into account is shown in Table 3.4. It is clearly revealed, using constant 1980s prices, that domestic exports in 1985 were 5.5 times larger than those in 1966.

In early years, the major products exported were those industrial products locally produced, such as, clothing, textiles, plastics, and footwear. After 1973 when Hong Kong's industrial pattern changed, the types of export also changed. Electronics caught up with plastics and textiles, while watches and clocks became important. Clothing remains important all the time as Hong Kong has become either the world's largest or second largest exporter of clothing since 1973 (Table 3.2). Hong Kong is also the world's second largest exporter of electronics and the world's largest exporter of watches. The plastic products exported are mainly toys and household goods. In 1990 the five commodity groups of textiles and clothing, electronic products, watches and clocks, plastic products, and electrical appliances constituted 73 per cent of the total value of domestic exports for Hong Kong. This amazingly small

59

Economic growth and structural change

Table 3.5 Major countries of domestic exports (as percentages of total values)

Countries	1960	1964	1968	1972	1976	1980	1984	1988	1990
USA	26.0	27.7	41.4	40.2	34.4	33.2	44.5	33.5	29.4
United Kingdom	20.4	21.9	15.9	14.4	10.1	10.0	7.6	7.1	6.0
Federal Rep. of Germany	3.7	6.6	5.9	10.0	12.2	10.8	6.9	7.4	8.0*
Australia	3.0	2.6	2.9	2.9	4.2	2.9	2.8	1.9	—
Canada	2.7	2.6	3.4	3.3	4.3	3.0	3.3	2.7	2.4
Japan	3.5	2.7	2.8	3.1	4.3	3.4	3.9	5.3	5.3
China	0.5	0.9	0.1	0.1	0.1	2.4	8.2	17.5	21.0

*With the unification of Federal Republic of Germany and German Democratic Republic in October 1990, the figure includes exports to both countries.

Sources: (1) Census and Statistics Department, 1969; (2) Chen, 1984; (3) *Hong Kong Government Annual Reports*, 1985–1991

number of products is matched by an equally amazingly small number of importing countries: the United States, China, the United Kingdom, the Federal Republic of Germany, Japan, Australia and Canada (Table 3.5). Collectively these countries imported about 72 per cent of the total domestic exports from Hong Kong in 1990. The major characteristic of the direction of trade has been China's rapid growth in importance since 1982 in receiving Hong Kong's domestic exports (from 0.5 per cent in 1960 to 8.2 per cent in 1984 and to 21 per cent in 1990) while the United Kingdom's importance has dwindled considerably (down from 20.4 per cent in 1960 to 6.0 per cent in 1990). The United States has been and remains as the number one market for Hong Kong's products and accounted for 29.4 per cent in 1990 and 26 per cent in 1960. Another noteworthy development is that Hong Kong has also succeeded in increasing its exports to the Federal Republic of Germany and Japan in recent years. Relying heavily on a few markets can cause problems during economic recessions like the one between 1974 and 1975. Some economists have observed that Hong Kong could recover quite rapidly after an economic setback probably because of a built-in self-regulating mechanism (Chen, 1984). However, Hong Kong has tried to expand its market to the Asian–Pacific region and must continue to do so if it wants to maintain its competitiveness, rate of growth and stability. Hong Kong's continued reliance on textiles and clothing as its major domestic exports makes it vulnerable to competition from other Asian nations with much lower labour costs as well as to the restrictive effects of protectionist regulations practised by United States, the United Kingdom and other economically advanced European countries. Industrial diversification into high-tech products requiring a better educated labour force and more capital investment is crucial if Hong Kong wishes to continue to flourish as an export-orientated economy.

Re-exports

Re-exports are products which have been previously imported and which are subsequently re-exported without having undergone a manufacturing process to permanently change the shape, nature, form or utility of the product. As an entrepôt, Hong Kong handles a lot of re-exports and these were also its major source of income before the mid-1960s. It was estimated that in 1950 89 per cent of the total exports were re-exports. In 1966 the proportion of re-exports declined to 23.5 per cent of total exports and then to 20.3 per cent in 1971. In 1976, the year when China began to implement a modernization policy, re-exports increased to 23.6 per cent. Since then, re-exports have grown in importance because of China's open economic policy which necessitated overseas imports. Once again, Hong Kong recaptured its entrepôt function, and became an important port for China. This was witnessed by the increase of re-exports in 1985 to 13.7 times that for 1966 (Table 3.4). In 1990 re-exports made up 64.8 per cent of the total exports and were once again larger than domestic exports. The principal re-exported commodities have traditionally been textiles. These are still the most important re-export items and make up between 10 and 15 per cent of total re-exports. The other commodities are clothing and electrical machinery, apparatus and appliances. The major origins of these re-exports are China, Japan, the United States, Taiwan and the Republic of Korea (South Korea), while the largest re-export markets are China, the United States, Japan, Taiwan and the Republic of Korea. It is quite obvious that Hong Kong acts as a middleman for trade between China and Taiwan as well as between China and South Korea.

Imports

Because of its lack of natural resources, Hong Kong has to rely heavily on other countries for foodstuffs and raw materials. Hong Kong in fact imports more commodities from other parts of the world than the combined total of its domestic exports and re-exports. (This is very clearly shown in Table 3.4.) In fact, as Hong Kong has increased its total exports in recent years, it has also increased its imports. There are five principal groups of commodities imported by Hong Kong, namely: raw materials and semi-manufactured goods; capital goods comprising machinery, transport equipment, and computers; mineral fuels, basically petroleum; foodstuffs consisting of fish, vegetables, fruit, and meat; and consumer goods comprising mostly consumer electronics such as television sets, radios and hi-fi audio items, toys, games, sporting goods, travel goods, watches and diamonds. The most important imports

Economic growth and structural change

Table 3.6 Major imports of Hong Kong (as percentages of total values)

Year	Foodstuffs	Raw materials	Fuels	Capital goods	Consumer goods
1960	25.0	52.5	3.4	10.2	7.4
1964	24.7	44.3	2.8	8.5	19.7
1968	20.7	43.8	3.1	8.6	23.9
1972	17.5	41.0	2.8	12.8	25.8
1976	16.0	44.1	5.9	12.6	21.4
1980	10.8	41.6	6.8	14.4	26.4
1984	9.0	45.0	5.0	15.0	26.0
1988	6.0	43.0	2.0	15.0	33.0
1990	6.0	39.0	2.0	15.0	39.0

Sources: (1) Chen, 1984; (2) *Hong Kong Government Annual Reports*, 1985–1991

are the raw materials for Hong Kong's industries which have remained consistent at around 40 per cent of the total imports since 1964 (Table 3.6). Imports of foodstuffs have declined considerably since 1964 from 24.7 per cent down to 6 per cent in 1990. This is because as the level of income increases the demand for foodstuffs will normally increase less than proportionately. On the other hand, imports of consumer goods have risen considerably from 19.7 per cent in 1964 to 39 per cent in 1990 to meet the demands of a more affluent population and to sell to tourists. Imports of capital goods remained quite stable in recent years at about 15 per cent. Investment in capital goods is important if Hong Kong is to advance further in its industrial development, particularly in high technology. Fuel imports have also declined and remained at a stable 2 per cent in recent years. In contrast to the pattern of domestic exports, Hong Kong imports a wide spectrum of goods.

The principal suppliers of imports are China, Japan, the United States, the United Kingdom, Singapore and Taiwan. China has always been an important supplier of foodstuffs and supplied 36 per cent of Hong Kong's total imported foodstuffs in 1990. Japan and the United States are the major suppliers of consumer and capital goods. However, China and Japan were respectively responsible for providing 37 per cent and 16 per cent of the total imports in 1990. China has caught up with Japan as Hong Kong's number one supplier. Taiwan, which supplied textile products, electrical appliances, fruit, vegetables and plastic products ranked third, providing about 9 per cent of the total imports. Singapore is the principal supplier of crude oil. The United Kingdom has declined in importance as a supplier and accounted for only 2.2 per cent of the total imports in 1990 as compared with 9.8 per cent in 1964. Both the United Kingdom and the Federal Republic of Germany supplied machinery and transport equipment. With the rise in the importance of the newly industrializing countries in the Asian–Pacific region, obviously it is to Hong Kong's advantage to import its goods from them. It also indicates that despite Hong Kong's close political affiliation with Britain, trade between Hong Kong and Britain has declined in recent years.

Nature of Hong Kong's economy

The trade pattern described above reveals an interesting characteristic of Hong Kong's economy: excess of imports over exports. Either a deficit exists on visible trade or there is an imbalance of payments. This is quite normal for Hong Kong. According to the government (Hong Kong Government, 1987), in the whole period between 1947 and 1987 there has been a surplus in only one year, 1985. Hong Kong's economy thrives on exporting the goods which it makes from the imports. After all, most of the imports are raw materials or semi-manufactured goods (40 per cent) which will be exported again after they have been transformed. In other words, value and services are added. Even in the case of imported consumer goods, over a half are re-exported. This is why as Hong Kong's economy grows, both its imports and exports also grow. Thus, Hong Kong exports to live, but lives on imports.

Hong Kong's advances in the tertiary activities, particularly in the services provided by shipping, aviation, tourism, financial services and other invisible transactions, have consistently run a balance-of-payments surplus. Most importantly, Hong Kong has attracted long-term and short-term capital from outside either for direct investment or as a safe haven because of Hong Kong's political uniqueness in the Asian–Pacific region. All these factors help offset the deficit on visible trade.

Hong Kong's highly open economy means that it is conducive to foreign investment. An important form of foreign investment is the establishment of transnational corporations (TNCs) by both developed and developing countries. According to a study by Chen (1988), these TNCs invest both in the manufacturing and non-manufacturing sectors. In the manufacturing sector the United States, which invested US$725.5 million (or 36.4 per cent) in 1986, is the largest investor, Japan follows with a US$419.7 million or 21.1 per cent investment, China with US$365.5 million or 18.4 per cent and the United Kingdom with US$134.5 million or 6.8 per cent. Other foreign investors in manufacturing industries include the Netherlands, the Philippines, Switzerland, Singapore, Australia, Denmark, the Federal Republic of Germany, Taiwan and France. They invest mostly in electronics, textiles and clothing, electrical products, metal products, watches and clocks and chemical products. Most of the investors from developed countries tended to favour wholly-owned subsidiaries while those from developing countries tended to favour joint ventures with local Hong Kong people.

They are attracted to Hong Kong by the availability of lower cost skilled and technical labour and the colony's geographical location as a springboard to China and other Asian countries. For the non-manufacturing sectors, most of the foreign investment is in retail and wholesaling, banking and financial services and consultancy services. The most important foreign investors are the United States, Japan, the United Kingdom, Australia, Canada and China. China is a newcomer but its importance is increasing. All these foreign investors benefit Hong Kong in technology transfer and in assisting its industrial restructuring. Local investors generally tend to be hesitant about commitments to long-term investment in view of the uncertainties after 1997. On the other hand, it should be noted that local Hong Kong investors have also invested heavily overseas. In fact, Hong Kong is the largest foreign direct investor among developing countries. Therefore, the success of Hong Kong's economy after 1997 depends on the extent to which foreign investors continue to be attracted to it.

Trends in economic development

What will Hong Kong' economic policy be in view of the rapid technological change and keen competition among the export-orientated economies in the world market? Is the *laissez-faire* or the non-intervention policy going to work after 1997 when Hong Kong's sovereignty will revert back to communist China? To answer these questions, one has to compare Hong Kong's structure of production with that of economically advanced countries (Table 3.7). It is obvious that Hong Kong's economic structure closely resembles that of the United States where a policy of free trade is also emphasised. For such an advanced stage of economic development, a greater degree of government intervention becomes necessary in order to satisfy the rising expectations of a more affluent population. This is clearly demonstrated by examining the changes in government expenditure in recent years. According to economic theories, government expenditure increases as a country's economy advances because of the increasing pressure for 'social progress' (Ho, 1980). Table 3.8 illustrates the changes in the composition of government expenditure in the two periods 1975–6 and 1985–6. It is worth noting that the major item (over 40 per cent) of expenditure is 'Social Services' which include education, medicine, housing, social welfare and labour. Indeed, it has increased from 44.1 per cent in 1975–6 to 44.8 per cent in 1985–6. The next important item (over 20 per cent) of government expenditure is 'Community Services', which comprise transport, land and civil engineering, water, public safety, recreation and environmental protection. These represent development of

Table 3.7 Comparison of the structure of production between Hong Kong and other economically advanced countries of the world (by percentage of distribution of Gross Domestic Product) for 1985

Country	Agriculture*	Industry#	(Manufacturing)	Services+
Hong Kong	1	31	24	68
United States	2	31	20	67
United Kingdom	2	36	22	62
Federal Republic of Germany	2	40	31	58
Japan	3	41	30	56

Notes: * The agricultural sector comprises agriculture, forestry, hunting, and fishing
Industry comprises mining, manufacturing (for which subgroup data are entered in a separate column), construction, and electricity, water, and gas
+ Services include all other branches of economic activity

Source: World Bank, 1987

Table 3.8 Changes in the composition of government expenditure in Hong Kong (per cent of total expenditure)

Item	1975–76	1985–86
I. General services	15.0	15.6
II. Economic services	8.4	3.5
III. Community services	23.6	23.2
IV. Social services	44.1	44.8

Note: I. General services include administration, law and order, defence, public relations, revenue collection and financial control
II. Economic services include food supply, aviation and shipping, trade and industry, posts and telecommunications
III. Community services include transport, land and civil engineering, water, public safety, recreation, culture and amenities, environmental protection
IV. Social services include education, medical, housing, social welfare, labour

Sources: (1) Ho, 1980; (2) *Hong Kong Government Annual Report*, 1988

the infrastructure needed to maintain an efficient environment for industry and commerce. This category has slightly declined in recent years. The category of 'General Services' includes the provision of general administration, internal security and law and order, and should be kept low. However, in recent years, some growth has occurred. Finally, the category of 'Economic Services' which includes food supply, aviation and shipping, trade and industry and post and telecommunications has shown a drastic drop from 8.4 per cent in 1975–6 to 3.5 per cent in 1985–6. This small share of 'Economic Services' suggests limited direct government involvement in economic activities and is a good indicator of a *laissez-faire* policy. Therefore, it appears that the non-intervention policy has been upheld by the government in recent years. However, it is also obvious that the government had to spend more money on housing and education. It is through this investment in human capital that most government intervention is seen. The development of public housing has been carried out in conjunction with the new towns programme, and has brought about a re-distribution of population and industry over Hong Kong. It is through the allocation of land that the government can control the type of industry that is developed or the kind of foreign investment desired. By investing in education the government recognises the need to compete with other countries in the provision of better trained and educated labour force and to prepare for diversification into technology-intensive industries. Investment in university education is particularly urgent to fill the talent-gap created by the brain drain at a time when confidence in Hong Kong's future is low. During the 1990s it will be increasingly difficult for the British Hong Kong government to maintain effective administration without any interference from China. At the time of writing, the controversy between China and Britain over the US$16.3 billion port and airport development project, which has been designed to prepare Hong Kong for the 21st century, has not yet been settled. While Hong Kong, with the support of the British government, is prepared to launch this massive project, the Chinese government, suspicious that all the Hong Kong treasury's cash reserves will be emptied before 1997, vehemently opposes it. The outcome of the argument will have a great impact on the economic policy of Hong Kong because, by implementing this project, the Hong Kong government will increase its expenditure on 'Economic Services' in an unprecedented manner, thus assuming a greater responsibility in providing for the economic development of Hong Kong in the future.

References

Census and Statistics Department, Hong Kong. 1969. *Hong Kong statistics*. Hong Kong: Government Printer.

Chen, E.K.Y. 1984. The economic setting. In *The business environment in Hong Kong*, D.G. Lethbridge (ed.). Hong Kong: Oxford University Press, pp. 1–51.

Chen, E.K.Y. 1988. The role of TNCs in Hong Kong's economic development. Paper presented to the International Conference on the Changing Role of TNCs in Asia-Pacific Development, Sydney, Australia, July 14–15, 1988.

Chiu, T.N. 1973. *The port of Hong Kong*. Hong Kong: Hong Kong University Press.

Clark, C. 1940. *The conditions of economic progress*. London: Macmillan.

Davis, S.G. 1949. *Hong Kong in its geographical setting*. London: Collins.

Ho, H.C.Y. 1980. Government expenditure and economic development in Hong Kong. In *Hong Kong, dilemmas of growth*, C.K. Leung, J.W. Cushman, and G. Wang (eds.). Canberra: Australian National University, pp. 195–205.

Hong Kong Government. 1985–91. *Annual Reports* (for various years). Hong Kong: Government Printer.

Jao, Y.C. 1980. Hong Kong as a regional financial centre: evolution and prospects. In *Hong Kong, dilemmas of growth*, C.K. Leung, J.W. Cushman, and G. Wang (eds.). Canberra: Australian National University, pp. 161–94.

Lai, C.Y. 1964. Rice cultivation, distribution and production in Hong Kong. In *Land use problems in Hong Kong*, S.G. Davis (ed.). Hong Kong: Hong Kong University Press, pp. 81–7.

Lethbridge, D.G. 1984. *The business environment in Hong Kong*. Hong Kong: Oxford University Press.

Tregear, T.R. 1958. *Land use in Hong Kong and the New Territories*. Hong Kong: Hong Kong University Press.

Wong, C.T. 1964. Changes in agricultural land use in Hong Kong. In *Land use problems in Hong Kong*, S.G. Davis (ed.). Hong Kong: Hong Kong University Press, pp. 60–9.

World Bank. 1987. *World development report 1987*. New York: Oxford University Press.

4
Land use and transportation

The main objective of the internal transport policy is to maintain and improve the mobility of both people and goods through an integrated, multi-modal transport system.
Commissioner for Transport: *Hong Kong Annual Departmental Report*, Transport Department, 1986

As has already been explained in Chapter 3, a major role of the Hong Kong government has been to maintain efficient infrastructures so that economic growth can be supported. This is why government expenditure on Community Services has always been maintained at a high level. The most important component of the infrastructure is undoubtedly an internal transport system which can provide a high degree of mobility for passengers and freight. To achieve this is no mean feat for the transport planners because Hong Kong's steep slopes, limited flat land, complex multiple land use characteristics and high population density tend to hamper such an effort. As Thomson (1977) observes, the buildings in a city and the activities within them do not exist independently of the transport which serves them. Indeed, the physical structure of a city, its size and spread, its way of life and character are all dependent on the nature and quality of its transport system. In other words, different types of land use can generate demands for different types of transport, and transport planning in turn has played an important role in shaping the land use development of a city.

Land use characteristics

Land use represents human activities on land which are directly related to the land (Clawson and Stewart, 1965). In Hong Kong, human

Table 4.1 Land use/cover in Hong Kong, 1990

Class	Area (sq. km)	Percentage
A. Developed land		
Commercial	1	0.1
Residential	48	4.4
Industrial	9	0.8
Open space	14	1.3
Government institution and community facilities	16	1.5
Vacant development land	34	3.2
Roads/railways	22	2.0
Temporary housing areas	2	0.2
Sub-total	146	13.5
B. Non-built-up land		
Woodlands	220	20.5
Grass and scrub	519	48.3
Badlands, swamp and mangrove	44	4.1
Arable	69	6.4
Fish ponds	17	1.6
Temporary structures/livestock farms	13	1.2
Reservoirs	26	2.4
Other uses	21	2.0
Sub-total	929	86.5
Total	1,075	100.0

Source: Hong Kong Government (1991), *Hong Kong Annual Report 1991*, p. 445

activities in the secondary and tertiary sectors predominate and are strongly related to the area immediately surrounding the harbour. Because of the scarcity of flat land, both the steep hills and the sea had to be developed for commercial, industrial and residential uses. The restrictive nature of the topography resulted in a highly concentrated but diverse juxtaposition of land uses within small areas. Again because of the shortage of land for development, the land use in Hong Kong tends to be multi-purpose and three-dimensional in nature. Such intensive use of land is made necessary by its high cost and the expenses involved in building site formation. Since the early 1960s, the Hong Kong government has been engaged in building new towns in the more rural areas, notably the New Territories, with the aim of alleviating the high population density and land use in the old established urban areas. Despite this effort, land developed for commercial, industrial, residential and institutional uses in 1990 amounted to only about 146 sq km or 13.5 per cent of the total land area of Hong Kong (Table 4.1). From the spatial perspective, the main urban built-up area continues to be contained within Kowloon Peninsula and the northern coastal strip of Hong Kong

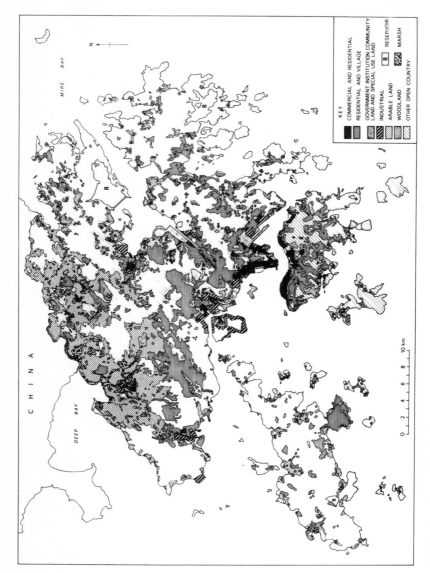

KEY

COMMERCIAL AND RESIDENTIAL

RESIDENTIAL AND VILLAGE

GOVERNMENT INSTITUTION COMMUNITY
LAND AND SPECIAL USE LAND

INDUSTRIAL

ARABLE LAND

WOODLAND

OTHER OPEN COUNTRY

R RESERVOIR

MARSH

CHINA

DEEP BAY

MIRS BAY

N

0 2 4 6 8 10 km

Figure 4.1 A simplified land use map of Hong Kong and the New Territories, 1982

Island while the new towns occupy individual spots along the major ring road in the New Territories (Figure 4.1).

Hong Kong has a substantial portion of rural land for a city state, found mainly in the New Territories. In 1990, only about 69 sq km or 6.4 per cent of the total land area of Hong Kong were put under cultivation, while the majority of the land, around 519 sq km or 48.3 per cent was being used as grass and scrublands. Woodlands took up a further 220 sq km or 20.5 per cent (Table 4.1 and Figure 4.1). About 413 sq km of these woodlands, grass and scrublands have been designated as country parks within which no urban development is allowed and vegetation and wildlife are protected. These country parks provide important recreational areas for Hong Kong's citizens living in overcrowded urban areas. In fact, Hong Kong people are quite fortunate in being able to go to a beach or a mountain from any point in the main metropolitan area in about half an hour by public transport.

Hong Kong published its first land use map in 1955 at a scale of 1:80,000 under the World Land Use Survey project directed by Professor L. Dudley Stamp (Tregear, 1958). In 1966 the Planning Division of the then Crown Lands and Survey Office, Public Works Department of Hong Kong, published a more detailed land use map of Hong Kong at a scale of 1:100,000 (Planning Division, 1968). The land use map continued to be updated by the Planning Division at regular intervals, and detailed land use statistics were extracted for town planning applications. A generalised land use map at the scale of 1:200,000 was published by the Lands and Survey Department in 1976 and was included as the endpaper in the Annual Report for 1977. A very detailed land use map covering only Hong Kong Island and Kowloon at the scale of 1:30,000 was published in 1987 by the Town Planning Office, Buildings and Lands Department. In 1988 a land use map covering the whole of Hong Kong and the New Territories was published at the scale of 1:75,000. Hong Kong planners have therefore been very conscious of the need to maintain accurate and up-to-date land use statistics to guide them in planning an efficient and desirable environment in which people can live and work.

Land use patterns

It is obvious that the most complex land use pattern occurs in the main metropolitan area which consists of the northern coastal strip of Hong Kong Island and the whole of Kowloon Peninsula (Figure 4.2). The complexity is caused by mixed land usages in both horizontal and vertical directions, a characteristic shared by many other cities in the developing world.

Land use and transportation

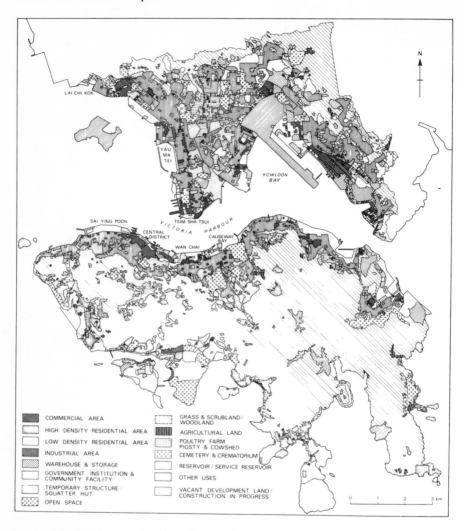

Figure 4.2 Land use in the Hong Kong and Kowloon metropolitan area, 1988

Commercial land use

Commercial land use encompasses a wide range of human activities from the retailing and wholesaling of goods to the provision of services. The scale of these activities can also vary greatly because both the formal and informal sectors typically occur side by side. It is quite common to find pedlars on the sidewalk or along specially designated streets located just adjacent to the large modern department stores or financial institutions. The greatest concentration of such commercial activities is found in the

Plate 4.1 Eastern part of the Central District where major banks tend to concentrate. This plate shows the old China Bank and the new Hong Kong and Shanghai Bank behind it

Plate 4.2 Old Chinese shophouses in Sheung Wan, to the west of the Central District. Many of these shophouses have been demolished to give way for new buildings under government's urban renewal programme

Plate 4.3 Hotel complex developed over the ocean terminal in Tsim Sha Tsui, Kowloon

Central District of Hong Kong Island, where the original city of Victoria was started, and in Tsim Sha Tsui at the southern tip of Kowloon Peninsula. The Central District is the traditional Central Business District of Hong Kong where the major banks (both local and foreign) have their headquarters in its eastern part (Plate 4.1). Many large office buildings, including the Stock Exchange, are located here. It also has a very important informal sector in the western part closely related to a food market. This includes some Chinese shophouses and hawkers of food products and clothing (Plate 4.2). However, much development has occurred in recent years in the eastern part of Tsim Sha Tsui where a great number of tourist hotels, speciality shops, department stores, restaurants and shopping malls in the formal sector have been added. All of these were developed on the old wharf area which was important in the old days before the development of the container terminal in Kwai Chung in the northwestern part of Kowloon Peninsula in 1972. The western shore of Tsim Sha Tsui still has a modern ocean terminal for passenger liners to berth, and indeed the whole ocean terminal complex is a multi-storey shopping mall linked up to hotels and orientated towards tourists (Plate 4.3).

In a similar vein, the Central District of Hong Kong Island has continued to extend eastwards along the coast with the construction of

Plate 4.4 New commercial development in the Queensway area symbolizing the eastern extension of the Central District. Three new hotels, Merriot, Conrad, and Shangri-La Island, with associated shopping facilities are now standing side by side with the government office buildings in the area

a new suite of government buildings, which, among other government offices, house the new Supreme Court and the Transport Department. Three new hotels, namely, the Merriot, Conrad, and Shangri-La Island, together with the prestigious Lane Crawford department store, which was built as a part of a fancy shopping complex, strengthens such a development (Plate 4.4).

There are more retailing activities of both modern and traditional types found throughout the high density districts such as Sai Ying Pun, Wan Chai, Causeway Bay, North Point on Hong Kong Island, Yau Ma Tei, Mong Kok, Sham Shui Po, Cheung Sha Wan and To Kwa Wan in Kowloon. It is noteworthy that Causeway Bay is the centre of Japanese department stores and an important tourist district. In the lower density areas such as the Peak and Mid-Levels on Hong Kong Island and Kowloon Tong in Kowloon, which are high-class residential areas, retail activities are much less abundant.

On the whole, retail use of the land is very widespread and important throughout Hong Kong and in the new towns such as Tsuen Wan, Tuen Mun, and Sha Tin. Apart from the high-class residential areas mentioned above, retail and residential use tend to be mixed in multi-storey buildings in the high density districts.

Industrial land use

Industrial land use occurs on both a large and a small scale throughout Hong Kong. Large-scale industrial estates are found in the new towns of Tsuen Wan, Tuen Mun and Tai Po in the New Territories (Plate 4.5), but, within the main metropolitan area, large-scale industrial use occurs mainly in Kowloon at Kwun Tong, To Kwa Wan, San Po Kong and Cheung Sha Wan. Large-scale industrial use is found in Wong Chuk Hang in the southern part of Hong Kong Island but not in the main urban area in the north. Because of Hong Kong's emphasis on light manufacturing industries, small industrial units can occur anywhere in the main urban area (Plate 4.6). These units have played an important role in the economic development of Hong Kong as discussed in Chapter 3 (Dwyer and Lai, 1967). Because of their high degree of adaptability and their use of cheap labour, the manufactured products from these small industrial units are highly competitive in the world market. Many also operate as sub-contractors to the large factories. Some of these industrial units are mixed with residential units, particularly in the high density areas. However, being dictated by the need for industrial links, many of these small industrial units occur in close proximity to the large factories.

Hong Kong's traditional shipbuilding and repairing industries continue

Land use and transportation

Plate 4.5 Modern factories in Tai Po Industrial Estate in the New Territories

to be important, but the location of the shipyards has shifted from Hung Hom in the south-eastern coast of Kowloon and Quarry Bay in the north-eastern coast of Hong Kong Island to Tsing Yi Island across from Tsuen Wan New Town in the New Territories. This move freed highly prized urban land for residential development – a most profitable venture for the corporations involved.

Warehouse and storage use

This type of use is closely associated with commercial and industrial land use. But because of the high value of land in the main urban area of Hong Kong and Kowloon, many of the warehouses have been replaced by more profitable residential and commercial developments. However, warehouse and storage use can still be found in Kwun Tong, Yau Tong and Cheung Sha Wan in the Kowloon urban area and in Aberdeen in the south-western shore of Hong Kong Island. The main warehouse and storage areas are found in the new towns.

Plate 4.6 Small industrial units housed in government-built multistoried industrial buildings in Cheung Sha Wan, Kowloon

Residential land use

The most important and widespread land use in the main urban areas and the new towns is residential (Figures 4.1 and 4.2). There are basically two main types of residential use in Hong Kong: private and public (Wong, 1978). Private residential use can be high density or low density, depending on the location and price. High density residential use is more common in the main urban area because people still prefer to live close to their work. In order to maximize the use of a plot of land, multi-storey buildings (up to twenty or more storeys high) partitioned into as many small (500 to 600 sq feet) flats as possible on each floor are typical. They tend to be located near the coast and combine commercial and industrial uses (Plate 4.7). On the other hand, low density residential use is characteristically found outside the main urban area and is located at a much higher level from the coast so that it can command a good view of the harbour. This type of residential use can be multi-storey or villa-style housing. The size of each residential unit is well over 1,500 sq feet and there are two units at most on each floor while the villa-style housing can be single enclosed units with gardens. On Hong Kong Island, the Peak District is famous for many types of low-density

Plate 4.7 A high-density private residential building mixed with commercial uses in Causeway Bay, Hong Kong

Plate 4.8 High-class residential buildings of varying styles climbing uphill from the Mid-Levels to the Peak in Hong Kong

high-class residential housing and has the prime residential properties in the whole of Hong Kong (Plate 4.8). Other low-density residential areas of repute on Hong Kong Island are Repulse Bay, Stanley, Shouson Hill, Jardine Lookout and Happy Valley. In Kowloon, the low density residential area is confined to Kowloon Tong in the north. Because of its location on the flight path for Kai Tak International Airport, the height of residential buildings has to be restricted to a maximum of four storeys and so many villa-style houses with gardens are found there. In 1990, there were 892,800 private housing quarters inhabited by a population of about 2.6 million.

Public residential use refers to the government housing programme which began in 1953 when there was a great influx of Chinese refugees into Hong Kong. Since then, the public housing programme has expanded and is responsible for the dispersal of population from the main urban area into the New Territories. The importance of the public housing programme can be appreciated from the fact that by 1990 2.8 million people, or about half of the total population of Hong Kong, were living in public housing. The programme is responsible for the concept of high density living and most of the public housing estates are found in the peripheral regions of the main urban area or in the New

Plate 4.9 A public housing building of the early stage in Wong Tai Sin, Kowloon. To its left is the famous Wong Tai Sin Temple, and to its right are the more modern but much higher public housing buildings

Territories. The northern edge of Kowloon Peninsula (e.g. Shek Kip Mei, Wang Tau Hom, and Wong Tai Sin), the eastern shore of Kowloon Bay (e.g., Ngau Tau Kok and Sau Mau Ping) and the eastern extremity of the urban strip on Hong Kong Island (Chai Wan) were typical sites for these public housing estates at the early stage of the programme (Plate 4.9). In later stages, public housing became an integral part of the new town programme. Tsuen Wan, Tuen Mun, and Sha Tin are the three major new towns which have had a high concentration of public housing in recent years (Plate 4.10). It is noteworthy that public housing policy has been changing all the time because as the economy improves the population expects the standard of public housing to rise accordingly. There is always the issue of social justice that needs to be addressed by the government. Public housing is generally welcomed by the low- and middle-income people who cannot afford expensive private housing. It is normally accepted that public housing in Hong Kong has been responsible for the high degree of stability in society. On the other hand, the government is trying to encourage those whose incomes have improved since they first moved into public housing to move into private housing in order to make room for a more needy household. The alternative is

Plate 4.10 New public housing estates in Sha Tin, the New Territories, in a much nicer environmental setting

for them to pay more for the heavily subsidized public housing. There is a government programme which encourages those living in public housing to buy the housing units from the government if they become better off. In 1990 there were 763,800 public housing quarters accommodating 2.76 million people. In other words, about half of Hong Kong's population live in public housing. All these public housing developments would not have been possible without efficient public transport support because their peripheral locations are not particularly convenient for places of work. Transportation will be discussed in greater detail in the second part of this chapter.

Despite the large-scale public housing programme, Hong Kong still has squatters occupying land illegally. They can be found both in urban and rural areas. In the urban areas they can be found occupying the rooftops of buildings, particularly in areas with tenement buildings. In the rural area of the New Territories they occupy hillsides and villages. In 1990 it was reported that there were still 100,000 domestic structures occupied by squatters. This indicates a squatter population of about 300,000, with 65,000 in the urban areas and 235,000 in the New Territories (Hong Kong Annual Report, 1990).

Plate 4.11   Market gardening land in Tai Po

Agricultural land uses

Most agricultural land use is found in the New Territories. This takes
three forms: cultivating crops, raising livestock and poultry and
cultivating pond fish. The most extensive arable land occurs in the
alluvial plain at Tuen Mun, Yuen Long, Kam Tin and San Tin in the
north-western part of the New Territories around Deep Bay (Figure 4.1).
This plain also extends north-eastwards to Sheung Shui-Fanling region
and down to Tai Po. This area covers the important villages of the New
Territories which used to specialize in paddy cultivation. But today the
paddy land has been changed into market gardening land specializing in
the cultivation of vegetables, fruit and flowers for the big urban market
nearby. In 1990 about 69 sq km or 6.4 per cent of the total land area
of Hong Kong was used for this type of market gardening (Plate 4.11).

The next category of agricultural land use – livestock and poultry –
tends to be more widespread. This involves the raising of cattle for milk,
pigs for meat and chicken, ducks, pigeons and quail for meat and eggs.
The cattle is found in more restricted areas where there is suitable grass.
The final category – fish ponds – are found mainly in the low-lying
alluvial plain in north-west New Territories mentioned above,
particularly near the coast. The livestock, poultry and fish pond use of

the land amounted to 30 sq km or 2.8 per cent of the total land area (Table 4.1).

Woodland, grass and scrubland

Despite its economic development, Hong Kong still retains some forests in isolated patches on Hong Kong Island, Kowloon and the New Territories. The term 'forest' used in the land utilization context by the Hong Kong government refers to shrubs and trees over 2.4 metres in height with interlocking canopies (Planning Division, 1968). The most common forest genus in Hong Kong is *Pinus*, represented by the native *Pinus massoniana* (Southern or China Red Pine) and the introduced *Pinus elliotti* (Slash Pine) from Australia (Catt, 1986). Most of the forests are associated with the catchment areas of reservoirs which are built by the government to supply the Hong Kong population with water. Thus, the most extensive forest is found around Tai Lam Chung Reservoir extending all the way to Shek Kong in the New Territories. Other extensive forest sites are found around Shing Mun Reservoir and Kowloon Reservoirs. The Chi Ma Wan Peninsula at the south-eastern tip of Lantau Island also has a large forest cover. In Hong Kong Island, good forest cover is found in the Peak District and the southern part of the island in close association with the high-class low density residential areas (Fig. 4.1). Most of these forests were planted to prevent soil erosion. Natural forests, however, can be found only in small areas around villages in the New Territories. These small forests are known as 'fung-shui' (wind and water) trees and are very well guarded by the villagers because of their belief that the destruction of the 'fung-shui' trees would affect the prosperity of their villages. The study of 'fung-shui' belongs to the pseudo-science of geomancy but its overall effect is environmental protection. According to Catt (1986), 'fung-shui' woods represent relics of the original woodland with the addition of trees planted by the villagers. These additions include such plants of economic value as *Aquilaria sinensis* (Joss Stick Tree), *Litchi chinensis* (Litchi), *Canarium album* (Chinese White Olive), *Psidium guajava* (Guava) and *Bambusa and Dendrocalamus spp.* (Bamboo). All these forests form the woodlands which accounted for 220 sq km or 20.5 per cent of the total land area in 1990 (Plate 4.12). It should be noted that the area of woodland has increased tremendously since the first land use survey in 1955 (32.8 sq km) and the second land use survey in 1966 (136.5 sq km) as a result of intense afforestation by the government.

Where there are no trees, the hillslopes are invariably covered by grass and scrub. Together these account for the most extensive land cover in Hong Kong spreading over an area of 519 sq km or 48.3 per cent.

Plate 4.12 Forests near Sha Tin Railway Station. Despite Hong Kong's high degree of urbanization, forests can be seen everywhere

Grassland refers to land covered with grasses and low scrub generally under 0.3 metres in height (Planning Division, 1968). It can be found on slopes in the higher areas (typically over 300 metres) such as on the upper slopes of Tai Mo Shan and the hillslopes of Lantau Island. The dominant grasses belong to the genera *Ischaemum* and *Arundinella*. The grasses are formed because they are subjected to wind exposure, poor soil conditions and rapid runoff. There are also grasses on lower slopes with poor soil conditions and they owe their origin to human interference. Typically, they are found in areas formerly used for paddy cultivation or vegetable cultivation under irrigation. The dominant grasses are *Isachne globosa, Panicum repens* and *Imperata cylindrica* (Wolly Grass). Scrubland refers to land with a fairly continuous cover of shrubs and bushes from 0.3 metres to 2.4 metres in height (Planning Division, 1968). Scrubland appears to be the transitional zone between grassland and forest. The most characteristic types of vegetation associated with scrubland in Hong Kong are *Rhodomyrtus tomentosa* (Rose Myrtle) and *Raphiolepis indica* (Hong Kong Hawthorn). They are found on hillslopes with infertile soils and where burning or interference by humans has taken place. The grass and scrubland area has shown some changes: it increased from 588.8 sq. km in 1955 to 612.7 sq km in 1968 and 616.4 sq km in 1976, but then decreased to 533 sq km in 1986. It decreased further to 519 sq km in 1990. Much of this loss was the result of afforestation and urban encroachment. Forests, grasses and scrubs are all found in the so-called 'country parks' designated by the government within which urban development is prohibited. Thus, these land covers are closely associated with recreational uses.

Wetland

This category of land use includes low-lying marshy areas usually found in association with lakes, estuaries, rivers and along the coast. It has an area of about one sq km with the most extensive occurrence being the mangrove swamp in San Tin and along the coast of Deep Bay in the New Territories. This has also been protected by the government as a site for ecological conservation.

Transportation development

The high concentration of commercial, industrial and residential land use in small areas has greatly influenced transport development strategy in Hong Kong. The government conducted two comprehensive transport studies, one in 1973 and one in 1986. These aimed to develop analytical tools to evaluate transport proposals and to devise a balanced programme of transport projects and transport policies (Wilbur Smith and Associates, 1976; Transport Department, 1989). The second study attempted to 'achieve and maintain an acceptable level of mobility for passengers and freight by road, rail and ferry up to 2001' (Transport Department, 1989). Therefore, the government has continuously monitored the development of transportation in Hong Kong in order to keep up with the rapid economic growth.

Transport systems had to be developed in line with the government's policy of decentralization seen in the new towns' programme and the provision of public housing. All these changes can be examined under two perspectives: the land communication system and the public transport system.

Evolution of a land communication system

Because of the rugged topography, the development of roads has been constrained by steep slopes. The initial road development was necessarily focused on the original settlement site, the city of Victoria, on the northern coast of Hong Kong Island. The first road laid out was Queen's Road which skirted the waterfront in 1843. After a period of unco-ordinated growth, reclamation along the coast was proposed by the governor in 1851 in the form of a praya running continuously from west to east. Despite some setback, a more or less continuous praya running along the present site of Des Voeux Road was completed in 1873. The coastal reclamation continued in a piecemeal manner. In 1931 reclamation between Causeway Bay and Quarry Bay was completed (Tregear and Berry, 1959). Thus the entire stretch of the coast from east to west was reclaimed. Today, coastal reclamation is still being vigorously pursued by the government in conjunction with urban development and road construction. At a very early stage of development roads were also extended uphill from the heart of the city, located between Ice House Street and Possession Point. Bonham Road and Caine Road were constructed in 1851, and Robinson Road and the Peak Road were laid out in 1861. All these roads were narrow and winding and were only suitable for use by carriages. Modern transportation technology requires much better and wider roads which can only be built in Hong Kong's extremely restricted and congested environment by using new engineering techniques. By 1930 an island road ringing the whole of Hong Kong Island from Shaukiwan to Kennedy Town was completed.

By contrast, the development of Kowloon Peninsula proceeded in a more orderly manner. The two major roads running north-south, Nathan Road and Canton Road, were built in 1865. Reclamation was carried out in the Yau Ma Tei and Tsim Sha Tsui district as well as to the east of Canton Road. All roads were laid out in a regular geometric pattern totally unlike those on Hong Kong Island. After the lease of the New Territories in 1898 road development was extended into the northern part of the Kowloon Peninsula. The north-south running Nathan Road was extended and a regular layout of roads and streets was constructed on reclaimed land along the coast both to the east and the west. A single-track railway to Guangzhou (Canton) was also constructed in 1906 and came into operation in 1910. The railway terminus was originally located at Tsim Sha Tsui, the tip of Kowloon Peninsula where the clock tower, the remnant of the terminus, still stands today. With the shift of the population into the New Territories there came an increasing demand on the railway services. Double tracking between Kowloon and Sha Tin took place in 1973 and in 1975 the terminus was re-situated in a reclaimed area of Hung Hom Bay in Kowloon. In 1978, as trade between Hong Kong and China increased, the government proceeded with the modernization and electrification of the whole railway line from Kowloon to Lo Wu. In July 1983 the electrification and double-tracking of the Hong Kong section of the Kowloon-Guangzhou (Canton) Railway was completed and became the important commuter railway for the new towns that it still is today. In 1936 an airport was constructed at Kai Tak on a piece of reclaimed land in Kowloon Bay. This is still the site of Hong Kong international airport, now greatly enlarged, with a long runway which was extended out into the sea in the 1960's to cater for the new jumbo jets. Vigorous road development has taken place in Kowloon ever since, particularly after the Second World War when Hong Kong became more industrialized. The old and new parts of Kowloon have become better integrated.

Development of the New Territories was slow during the early years of the lease. Roads and railways were developed in the area after the land titles were sorted out. Initially, many of the road developments were military in nature but they later became integrated into the modern road network for civilian use, such as sending produce to the urban markets and for the spread of industries into the area. In 1904 the first section of a main road to Guangzhou was built to Tai Po. This was a partial ring road running along the coast to the west through Tsuen Wan, Tuen Mun, Yuen Long, San Tin, Sheung Shui, Fanling, Tai Po and Sha Tin. The circuit was finally completed in 1919. The Kowloon hills presented a formidable physical barrier which hampered the linking of the Kowloon roads with the roads in the New Territories. Through the construction of road tunnels such as the Lion Rock Tunnel (built from a single tube in 1967 and with a second tube added in 1978) and more recently the Tate's Cairn Tunnel (1991), the problem was alleviated temporarily. New problems arose when the tunnels became traffic bottlenecks during the rush hour. Another road tunnel of importance is the Aberdeen Tunnel opened on Hong Kong Island in 1982, which links the north and south side more directly. The enhancement of the ring road in the New Territories continued and further construction was carried out in the 1980s on the Circular Road to support the rapid urbanization of the area.

This problem of connecting different pieces of land of varying sizes separated by sea remains a major challenge to transportation planners especially if the population decentralization policy is to succeed. An important accomplishment by the government in promoting better integration was the construction of the Cross-Harbour Tunnel which was opened in 1972 (Plate 4.13). The tunnel runs beneath the harbour between Hong Kong Island and Kowloon Peninsula and was built by private enterprise with government participation. It immediately assumes an important north-south linkage role between Hong Kong Island and the New Territories. In 1983 it became the world's busiest four-lane facility with an average of 110,000 vehicles using it per day. Unfortunately, approaches to the Cross-Harbour Tunnel entrances, located near the Central Business District on Hong Kong Island and the Railway Terminus in Hum Hom in Kowloon Peninsula, have become congested

Plate 4.13 Hong Kong Cross-Harbour Tunnel, a vital land link between Hong Kong Island and Kowloon

with traffic, particularly during rush hours. The government approved the construction of a second cross-harbour tunnel located in the east, known as the Eastern Harbour Crossing and linking Quarry Bay on Hong Kong Island and Cha Kwo Ling in Kowloon, which was opened on September 21, 1989. But this tunnel has not attracted as much traffic as was hoped because it does not provide such a direct or central route as the Cross-Harbour Tunnel which links the main north-south strategic road. These two tunnels have displaced the ferries, particularly the vehicular ferries, which before 1972 provided the only link for people and cars between Hong Kong Island and Kowloon Peninsula. The amount of time saved is quite considerable. On the other hand, as the economy of Hong Kong advances further, the mobility of people and the flow of goods increase. All these tunnels are potential bottlenecks and when they reach saturation point the whole land communication system will be paralysed. This is why the government imposed a special passage tax in June 1984 on all vehicles except public and private buses, disabled drivers and members of the consular corps, using the Cross-Harbour Tunnel. Finally, another tunnel of note is the Airport Tunnel in Kowloon which provides direct access from the central area of Kowloon to Hong Kong (Kai Tak) International Airport.

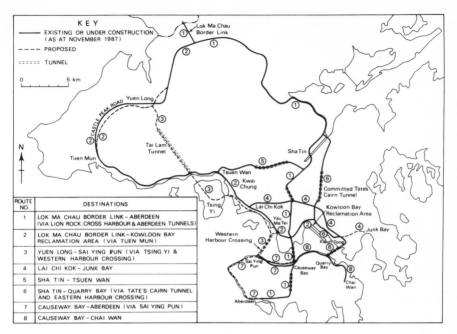

Figure 4.3 Strategic road network of Hong Kong

At the end of 1990, the land communication system consisted of 1,484 kilometres of roads – 403 km on Hong Kong Island, 379 km in Kowloon, and 702 km in the New Territories – which provided the basis for a Strategic Road Network comprising of eight routes (Figure 4.3 and Table 4.2).

These eight routes represent the major expressways that will connect different components of Hong Kong in the most efficient manner. They all display ingenious engineering designs to overcome many of the limitations imposed by the terrain and the overcrowded conditions of high density development. A commonly observed characteristic is three-dimensional development with the construction of flyovers for the roads. Leading from these major roads are a large number of streets and feeder roads in the main urban area. Those in Hong Kong Island tend to be narrow and winding as they negotiate the steep slopes. Streets in Kowloon are much straighter and exhibit more regular patterns. Those in the new towns are wider and better planned. Overall, the land communication system and its environmental setting in Hong Kong is not particularly conducive to speedy movement of vehicles. In 1990 there were 363,520 licenced vehicles on the road in Hong Kong, thus averaging about 245 vehicles per kilometre of road. Therefore, Hong Kong's roads have one of the highest vehicle densities in the world.

Land use and transportation

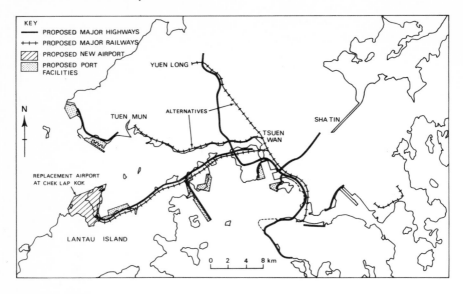

Figure 4.4 Proposed major highways and railways

In view of the importance of the Hong Kong–China trade, movement of people and anticipated 1997 sovereignty change, Hong Kong's road and rail network has to be planned for better links with China. There are now rail links with China at Lo Wu and road connections at Lok Ma Chau. The passenger and vehicle capacity at the border crossing is expected to grow rapidly. This road and rail network has to be planned in conjunction with the whole port development of Hong Kong which will be discussed in the last section of this chapter.

All the development of the transport infrastructure in Hong Kong was guided by the First Comprehensive Transport Study completed in 1976 which set the transport development policy for Hong Kong up to 1991. The Second Comprehensive Transport Study, commissioned in 1986 and completed in 1989, projected the growth in transport demand up to 2001 and a White Paper was produced from it in January 1990 (Transport Branch, 1990). The recommendations for road development were made in conjunction with the relocation of the airport to Chek Lap Kok. These included the North Lantau Expressway and Lantau Fixed Crossing which were designed to provide a direct expressway link to the replacement airport at Chek Lap Kok, Route 3 to provide a third harbour crossing and major north-south road link connecting the border with the existing container port and the urban area, the Hung Hom bypass and the Kai Tak connector to provide new east-west road links in Kowloon, Route 16 to provide a new expressway connecting Sha Tin and West Kowloon and Route 7 and Central-Wan Chai bypass to

Table 4.2 The eight routes of the Strategic Road Network for Hong Kong as shown in Figure 4.3

Route 1 Runs from Aberdeen in South Hong Kong Island via Aberdeen Tunnel, Cross-Harbour Tunnel, Kowloon Peninsula and Lion Rock Tunnel to Lok Ma Chau Border Control Point in the northern New Territories.

Route 2 Runs from Kowloon Bay reclamation via the Airport Tunnel, East and West Kowloon Corridors (flyovers), Tsuen Wan Road, Tuen Mun Road and Yuen Long Northern Bypass to Lok Ma Chau Border Control Point.

Route 3 Runs from Yuen Long in the north-western New Territories via Tai Lam Tunnel, Tsing Yi Island, West Kowloon Expressway, and the Western Harbour Crossing to Sai Ying Pun in the western part of Hong Kong Island. This is being proposed. Both Tai Lam Tunnel and Western Harbour Crossing have not yet been constructed.

Route 4 Runs along the base of the Kowloon Hills between Lai Chi Kok in the west and Kwun Tong in the east of Kowloon.

Route 5 Runs from Sha Tin to Tsuen Wan, completed in April 1990, thus filling up the gap in the ring road in the New Territories (officially known as the New Territories Circular Road System).

Route 6 Runs from Quarry Bay on Hong Kong Island via the Eastern Harbour Crossing, Kwun Tong Bypass in Kowloon, and Tate's Cairn Tunnel to Tolo Harbour in the eastern part of the New Territories.

Route 7 On Hong Kong Island, runs from Causeway Bay via Sai Ying Pun to Aberdeen in the South. The section between Causeway Bay and Sai Ying Pun was completed in 1990.

Route 8 Runs from Causeway Bay near the Cross-Harbour Tunnel along the northern shore via the Island Eastern Corridor to Shau Kei Wan and Chai Wan in the east.

Source: Transport Department, 1986

provide a continuous expressway along the northern and western shores of Hong Kong Island. The Mass Transit Railway is to be extended to Junk Bay, and a railway will connect Tsuen Wan with the New North West Territories (Figure 4.4). Thus, by 2001 even Lantau Island, the most remote component of Hong Kong, will have been connected to the main metropolitan area by a total land communication system.

Multi-modal public transport system

Another important characteristic of Hong Kong's transportation is its multi-modal public transport system which successfully serves the needs of the people living in this highly congested but fragmented city. Despite Hong Kong's tradition of 'positive non-intervention', the public transport system has been heavily regulated by the government through its Transport Department. It has been government policy to give priority to public transport and to allow healthy competition among different modes of public transport to promote efficiency in order that no direct subsidy need be given (Pang and Lee, 1988). The entire public transport system has expanded considerably since 1947 with the most rapid development taking place between 1966 and 1978. The provision of efficient and reliable public transport was essential to the day to day functioning of the city in the course of economic development and became crucial for the successful implementation of the government's public housing and new towns programmes. The cost of public transport has also to be kept low and government policy has been to provide people with a wide choice in terms of speed, cost, level of comfort and accessibility (Transport Department, 1986). Private car ownership has been kept low by heavy taxes on car registration, driver's licences and fuel because increased affluence has meant an increased desire for car ownership. In 1985 it was estimated that only about 12 per cent of households owned a car (Leung, 1986) and so there is obviously a great reliance on public transport. A daily average of 9.1 million passenger on public transport were recorded over recent years.

The modes of public transport available in Hong Kong are extremely varied. Specifically, they are: rail transport in the form of the Mass Transit Railway (MTR), the Kowloon-Guangzhou (Canton) Railway (KCR), Hong Kong Tramways, the Peak Tramways and the Light Rail Transit (LRT) system; bus transport in the form of franchised bus companies including the Kowloon Motor Bus Company operating in Kowloon, the China Motor Bus Company operating on Hong Kong Island and the New Lantao Bus Company operating on Lantau Island, public light buses (PLB), and the Residents' Coach Services; personalised taxi transport; and ferry transport in the form of Star Ferry and the Hongkong and Yaumati Ferry Companies for both passengers and vehicles. All these different modes of public transport did not come into existence at the same time and each has an importance in relation to a particular stage of Hong Kong's economic development, as reflected by changes in land use and the accompanying territorial expansion. For two decades since the 1950s, when Hong Kong strove towards industrialization, buses and ferries were the most important modes of public transport. The vehicular ferries operated by the Hongkong and Yaumati Ferry Companies were particularly important in transporting goods between Hong Kong and Kowloon. In recent years, with Hong Kong's economic advancement, there has been an increasing emphasis on rail transport ever since the opening of the Mass Transit Railway (MTR) in 1979/80. Rail transport is well suited for fast transportation links between the main urban area and the outlying residential and industrial districts in New Kowloon and the New Territories. However, buses have remained the most important form of passenger transport over recent years and accounted for about

43 per cent of the total 9.1 million passenger journeys taken in 1986. This is because the MTR, KCR and the tramway run on fixed rails and so are not as flexible as buses or taxis in reaching those out of the way places (Table 4.3). Typically, the mixed land use and the compact and high-density development gave rise to urban public passenger travel patterns which are multi-modal, multi-purpose, and relatively short in distance (Leung, 1986). With the opening of the Cross-Harbour Tunnel for bus and the MTR services, many of the multi-modal trips have been reduced. The important role played by ferry transport in linking Hong Kong Island with Kowloon Peninsula has declined considerably in recent years. However, ferry transport still complements all forms of land transport very well because of its lower cost. Also, it provides an essential link to the outlying islands. The ten minute cross-harbour ride on the Star Ferry between Tsim Sha Tsui in Kowloon and Central District in Hong Kong Island is cheap (US$0.13) and most enjoyable for both residents and tourists.

The Mass Transit Railway (MTR) has, in conjunction with the buses, succeeded in integrating different components of Hong Kong, i.e. Hong Kong Island, Kowloon Peninsula and the New Territories better than any other mode of transport managed to do in the past. Its success illustrates the foresight of the Hong Kong government's transport planners who advocated its construction as early as 1967. The mass transit system relies largely on underground railways and so avoided the purchase of expensive properties in the prime urban area for its route. Another advantage was that it was not restricted by the steep terrain and overcrowded conditions of the main urban area. After consultants' recommendations in 1970 for the construction of a four line mass transit system 52.7 km in length, the government approved the construction of the first line, known as the Initial System, in 1972. The government initially negotiated and obtained a single fixed price contract with a Japanese consortium for the construction in 1973. However, in December 1974, the Japanese withdrew. Immediately, the Hong Kong government modified the Initial System into a reduced version and abandoned the single contract. The construction work was subdivided into a number of civil, electrical and mechanical contracts for which tenders were invited. The government also created the Mass Transit Railway Corporation (MTRC) to supervise the work. The MTRC is wholly owned by the government with instructions to operate according to prudent commercial principles, in other words, to be self-supporting. The Modified Initial System which is 15.6 km long with 15 stations was a single line from Kwun Tong in Kowloon to Central District on Hong Kong Island (Figure 4.5). In 1977, an extension of the Modified Initial System, running from Prince Edward Station in north Nathan Road in Kowloon to Tsuen Wan New Town in the New Territories with a length

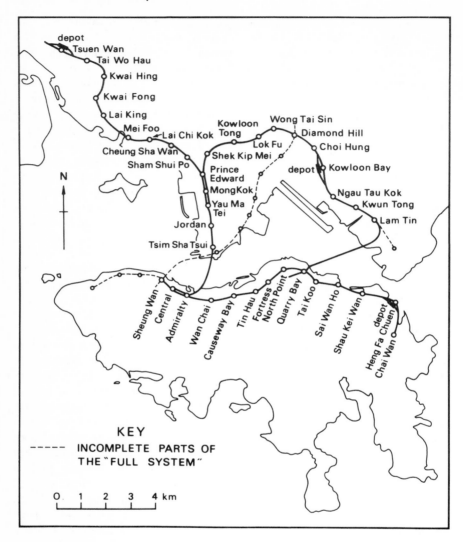

Figure 4.5 The mass transit railway (MTR) network

of 10.5 km and 10 stations was approved. This Modified Initial System began operation in 1979/80 and the extension line was opened in 1982. At the end of 1980 the government also decided to build an Island Line running along the north shore of Hong Kong Island, the traditionally overcrowded but important commercial–residential mixed area. The total length of this line was 12.5 km with 13 stations from Chai Wan in the east to Kennedy Town in the west. In May 1985 the section between Chai Wan and Central started operating and in May 1986 the westward extension to Sheung Wan also opened for use. In August 1989 the Eastern Harbour Crossing extension between Kwun Tong and Quarry Bay, together with a new station at Lam Tin, began operation, thus providing a second cross-harbour railway link. Therefore, at the time of writing, the MTRC is operating a three-line metro system with a 43 km route with 38 stations served by 671 cars formed into eight-car trains and running at two-minute intervals during peak morning hours (Figure 4.5). The total construction cost for the whole system was about HK$30 billion (US$3.85 billion at the current exchange rate). One sees here the government's strong determination to provide efficient public transport irrespective of cost and, despite the high cost, the MTR has been a great success. Through the use of interchange arrangements between lines and connections with other modes of transport, such as the interchange with the electrified Kowloon-Guangzhou (Canton) Railway at Kowloon Tong station, the New Territories are now much more easily accessible by residents in the main urban area and, in turn, residents of the new towns in the New Territories can go to the main urban area easily. In fact, it also greatly facilitates links with China. It is possible for anyone to board the MTR train in Central Hong Kong and go directly to Shenzhen across the border in China where one can take a train to Guangzhou. In 1990, the MTR carried 2.1 million passengers a day which, in relation to its length, made it the busiest underground railway in the world.

The Kowloon–Guangzhou (Canton) railway which completed its electrification and double-tracking in July 1983 assumes the role of a commuter train for the residents in the new towns located along this north-south line. It is also an important freight carrier between Hong Kong and China. There are now direct train services between Hong Kong and Guangzhou operated by the Chinese authorities which have attracted both local and international passengers. Because the Kowloon–Guangzhou (Canton) railway (KCR) focused only on the eastern part of the New Territories, the government started a 23 km Light Rail Transit (LTR) system in the north-western New Territories in September 1988 and invited KCR to operate it. This system now consists of 70 light rail vehicles running on six routes linking Yuen Long and Tuen Mun. Feeder buses are needed to ensure the success of this system. The system will have been extended to the Tin Shui Wai New Town by late 1992, thus lengthening it to 30 km.

Despite the success of the underground MTR, electric trams continue to operate on the north shore of Hong Kong Island. The tramway dates back to 1904, and has more or less become a symbol of Hong Kong. There are six overlapping services over 13 kilometres of double track between Kennedy Town in the west and Shau Kei Wan in the east. There is also a single 3 km line around Happy Valley where Hong Kong's horse-racing course is located. It is slow but cheap at US$0.13 per

Land use and transportation

Table 4.3 Public transport passenger journeys by mode (in thousand journeys)

Mode	1976	%	1980	%	1986	%	1990	%
Bus	2,592	45.3	3,251	46.3	3,917	43.1	3,504	35.7
Public Light Bus	1,595	27.9	1,495	21.3	1,513	16.6	1,743	17.7
Taxi	591	10.3	822	11.7	1,198	13.2	1,237	12.6
Ferry	508	8.9	509	7.2	338	3.7	274	2.8
Tram	350	6.1	440	6.3	342	3.8	359	3.7
Railway	34	0.6	511	7.3	1,775	19.5	2,666	27.1
Public Hire Car*	47	0.8	—	—	—	—	—	—
Total	5,717	99.9	7,028	100.0	9,098	100.1	9,826	100.0

*Reclassified as taxis completed on June 27, 1978

Source: Hong Kong annual reports for 1976, 1986 and 1990

person and has many short stops, thus making it ideal for short-distance commuting. On the other hand, it occupies valuable road space and can obstruct the flow of traffic, particularly during rush hours. Equally as famous as the trams is the funicular railway. Known locally as the Peak Tram it runs up the steep slope of Victoria Peak for 373 metres between the Central District and the Peak District, a high-class residential area for local and foreign government officials as well as rich bankers and merchants. It began operating in 1888 and is largely used by tourists although it also caters for some commuters.

Buses remain as the most important means of public transport in Hong Kong (see Table 4.3). As has been observed, the MTR is too inflexible to reach every nook and cranny of Hong Kong. Buses have to be relied on not only as feeder services to more outlying areas but also to provide a lower cost alternative to the MTR. An important characteristic of Hong Kong's bus system is its great variety. There are the larger, mostly double-decker, red buses operated by two franchised bus companies: one on Hong Kong Island and one in Kowloon and the New Territories as well as a third but much smaller franchised bus company on Lantau Island – and the smaller 14- or 16-seater minibuses which can operate either freely without controlled fares and routes ('yellow light buses') or have been licensed to operate only on fixed routes ('green light buses'). The minibuses are more comfortable but also more expensive than the franchised buses. They therefore provide feeder services to areas which are more remote or where the demand for public transport is less. They accounted for 17.7 per cent of the total public transport passenger journeys in 1990 (Table 4.3). The two franchised bus companies are still heavily relied on to provide the much needed and cheaper public transport for the masses in Hong Kong, having accounted for the highest percentage of public transport passenger journeys (35.7 per cent) in 1990. The complexity of the bus services is reflected by the fact that in

1990 Kowloon Motor Bus Company ran 260 bus routes in Kowloon and the New Territories, carrying 966 million passengers while the China Motor Company on Hong Kong Island ran 87 routes carrying 281 million passengers. Both companies jointly ran 22 cross-harbour routes. The Hong Kong government imposed very strict control on the operation of the bus companies through the Transport Department.

The most expensive form of public transport in Hong Kong is taxis, the main role of which is to provide a quick service to anywhere in Hong Kong desired by the passengers. There are basically three types of taxis: First, taxis which can operate anywhere within Hong Kong Island, Kowloon and the New Territories but which primarily serve the urban areas. Second, taxis which operate only in permitted areas in the New Territories and third, Lantau taxis which can operate only on Lantau Island. The government strictly controls the number of taxis, particularly in the urban areas, through a quota system. The limit on the number of taxi licences is approved by the Executive Council of the Hong Kong government because the government beli;ves that taxis are not the most efficient users of the limited road surface. However, the demand for taxis is quite high in Hong Kong because fares are low compared to other cities. For urban taxis the fare in 1990 was US$1.03 for the first two kilometres and US$0.12 per subsequent metre. The New Territories and Lantau taxis have cheaper fares of US$0.90 for the first two kilometres and US$0.10 per subsequent metre. Taxi licences are in great demand and, their issuance is controlled by the government. They are sold through public auction. Because of the shortage of supply, their value can be bid up very high. By the end of 1990, there were 14,588 urban taxis, 2,442 New Territories taxis and 40 Lantau taxis. Collectively they carry out 12.6 per cent of the total public transport passenger journeys (Table 4.3). Clearly, despite the availability of many other cheaper modes of public transport many people in Hong Kong, particularly the middle classes who cannot bear the government inflated costs of private car ownership, prefer the convenience of taxis.

From this brief discussion, it is quite clear that Hong Kong's transport planners have developed one of the most efficient public transport systems in the world through an integrated multi-modal approach in conjunction with ingenious engineering to make the best of a physically restricted network. In addition, the government's Transport Department introduced an element of competition among the different modes of public transport which drove down prices and balanced the power among the competitors. The government will not hesitate to promote a certain mode of public transport if it feels justified to do so. One exam-ple is the promotion of the mass transit railway during the early stage of its development. However, in recent years when the mass transit railway became too popular and began to endanger public safety through overcrowding, the government allied with the bus companies to provide an alternative. Air-conditioned bus services were set up to run along the most popular routes across the harbour in order to attract those passengers who would normally have preferred the mass transit railway. Here, one sees the highly pragmatic nature of the Hong Kong government which will not hesitate to intervene where necessary in the area of public transport. Admittedly, it is an extremely difficult task to control the growth of private car ownership and to satisfy the rapidly rising demand for high-quality public transport from an increasingly affluent population.

Finally, there is one area of transport in which Hong Kong could be considered to be weak: internal freight transport. An increasing number of trucks are being used to transport industrial goods to and from factories and docks. Facilities for freight transport are totally inadequate even in the largest and well planned new town of Tsuen Wan (Leung, 1986). The problem is the availability of parking space for loading and unloading. It is not uncommon to see trucks parked illegally on the pavement to load or unload. The increase in the number of trucks has caused traffic congestion on the roads.

International transport and port development

The economic growth of Hong Kong is dependent on its successful export-orientated strategy of industrial development and its role as a centre for world finance, both of which hinge on efficient transportation links with the major world markets. The container port and the international airport have successfully fulfilled this very important role. Hong Kong's deep-water harbour, high standard of shipping services, and age-old experience as a port are its major advantages.

In the beginning, when Hong Kong started as a port, only a few quays with sufficient depth of water for ocean-going vessels were constructed. Cargo handling took place at moorings and anchorages and lighters were used to transport cargo from ship to shore. Cargo working areas were developed along the shore where cargo from the lighters was transferred on to trucks. As Hong Kong became increasingly industrialized during the 1950s and 1960s this method was no longer able to cope with the rising amount of cargo shipments. Also, since the mid-1960s the container has become widely accepted and Hong Kong was compelled to modernize its cargo-handling methods. By 1972 the government had constructed three specialized container berths at Kwai Chung, an area just north of the main urban area of Kowloon (Chiu, 1986). The development of container facilities consolidated Hong Kong's importance as a port and more transhipment cargoes were attracted. As a result

Hong Kong added three more container berths to Kwai Chung in 1975 and 1976. The container terminals were all operated by private companies. In 1978 the average number of TEUs (20-foot equivalent units) handled per berth per year had reached 188,000. By 1984, this had risen to 300,307 TEUs. The tremendous increase overloaded the access road to the container terminals and interfered with traffic between the urban area of Kowloon and the new towns of Tsuen Wan and Tuen Mun. Further expansion of the Kwai Chung container facilities has been carried out in recent years and new terminals have been added. By 1990 Hong Kong was handling 5.04 million TEUs of containerized cargo. Two more new terminals are being planned but, in view of the congestion of the existing Kwai Chung site, one of these will be constructed on new reclaimed land adjoining Stonecutter Island, and the other one will be located on reclaimed land on south-east Tsing Yi island. In co-ordination with the airport development proposed in the Port and Airport Development Strategy (PADS) Studies initiated in 1988, new container terminals will be located in the future on the east of the Tsing Chau Tsai Peninsula at the north-eastern tip of Lantau Island where the water is deepest (Hong Kong Government, 1989).

Hong Kong's link with the outside world relies heavily on its airport located at Kai Tak at the north-eastern part of Kowloon Peninsula. The airport had very modest beginnings as a grass runway in 1925. At that time, the site of the airport was quite remote from the main metropolitan area concentrated on the northern coast of Hong Kong Island and the southern tip of Kowloon Peninsula. Even by 1936 when the first scheduled flights began operating, the airport site was still a rural area. After the Second World War air traffic increased rapidly and by 1948 there were about 25 scheduled flights a day and 250,000 passengers using the airport. However, with the rapid industrialization of Hong Kong and the declining cost of air travel, air traffic became more and more important. The present runway, opened for commercial traffic in September 1958, was extended from 2,540 metres to 3,390 metres in 1975. The extension of the runway into the sea is a famous Hong Kong landmark which signifies its characteristic high intensity and its environmental constraints. By 1975, the urban area of Kowloon had already engulfed the airport. On a fine day when one flies in to the airport, one sees the magnificent harbour view as well as the multi-storey buildings as the airplane wings pass within inches of them. Although the urban location of the airport is extremely convenient for travellers, the airport presents environmental problems in terms of noise pollution and traffic congestion in the area. The height of buildings in and around the airport has to be controlled. In 1990, despite the impact of China's crack-down on the pro-democracy movement in June 1989, the airport handled 18.7 million passengers and some 800,000 tonnes of air cargo.

Land use and transportation

Hong Kong's exports, imports and re-exports all make significant use of air transport. In anticipation of the rapid growth of passenger and cargo traffic (about 5 to 6 per cent increase per annum), the Hong Kong government has decided to build a replacement international airport at Chek Lap Kok off the northern coast of Lantau Island, far removed from the urban area. This was recommended by Hong Kong's Port and Airport Development Strategy (PADS) as a way of restoring the confidence of Hong Kong citizens in face of the 1997 changeover to Communist China. By opening up a new site in Lantau Island, Hong Kong's planners have expanded urban development into the largest, and essentially rural, island in the New Territories. Much reclamation will take place on its northern coast and the airport will be built on reclaimed land joining the island of Chek Lap Kok with Tung Chung on the main island. The airport will occupy an area of 1,000 hectares and will have two runways. It will have the capacity of handling 80 million passengers, 320,000 aircraft and over 4 million tonnes of air cargo annually. The first runway will be commissioned in early 1997, just before the sovereignty change. The construction of this new airport on Lantau Island requires a lot of infrastructural support, such as roads, highways, bridges and tunnels to link it up with the main metropolitan area on Hong Kong Island and in Kowloon. The total investment cost was estimated to be US$16.3 billion at 1989 prices and it is hoped that this project will attract private investment. For this to happen, the Hong Kong government needs strong support for this expensive project from the Chinese. Local people believe that the British Hong Kong government is attempting to develop a 'rose garden' before its departure. There are also concerns that the large sum of money required for this development will unnecessarily strain Hong Kong's exchange reserve to such an extent that it will be impoverished at the time of its turnover to China. The Chinese authorities, guided by the hardline policy of Premier Li Peng, have vehemently objected to the construction of the new airport. After numerous meetings between British and Chinese officials, the Chinese government finally agreed in July 1991 to support the construction of the new airport on the condition that they should be consulted on all financial matters that the Hong Kong government is committed to beyond 1997. This agreement was signed by the British and Chinese Premiers in September 1991, and became an addendum to the 1984 Sino–British joint declaration on the future of Hong Kong. The implication is that the British Hong Kong government will clearly be subjected to more Chinese control before 1997.

The relocation of the airport to Lantau Island will leave a large piece of land vacant at the site of the existing Kai Tak airport (about 230 hectares). There is also new land obtained by reclamation (1,250 hectares) as well as other old sites of public housing requiring redevelopment. Altogether, there will be 3,270 hectares of land waiting to be developed. How this will be done affects the overall development and redevelopment of the main metropolitan area concentrated on the northern coast of Hong Kong Island and the Kowloon Peninsula. The government's planners have started a Metroplan study to discover the best strategy for development and redevelopment which will also complement the port and airport development strategy. More about the Metroplan will be discussed in Chapter 5.

Conclusions

As a small city state, Hong Kong's land use exhibits both urban and rural characteristics and a great deal of diversity. The main metropolitan area of Hong Kong is concentrated around the harbour area because people have traditionally preferred to live close to their work. The resulting overcrowding is a commonly observed phenomenon in the primate cities of developing countries and, because of the hilly topography, Hong Kong displays this feature vividly with numerous high-rise buildings erected on steep slopes. Transportation development takes a wide variety of forms because of Hong Kong's highly fragmented configuration. Hong Kong has focused on the most efficient movement of goods and people to meet the needs of export-orientated industrialization and cope with the great diversity of land usage. As trade with China increases, air, land or sea links with China become increasingly important. Hong Kong's transport planners have been successful in implementing eight strategic road routes to integrate the city's different components most efficiently. The efficiency of road, rail, ship, air transport and telecommunications facilities in Hong Kong has no comparison with other similarly sized cities in Asia. It is not surprising therefore, that Hong Kong has emerged as the favourite city for corporations to establish their headquarters in Asia.

Hong Kong's planners have displayed excellent foresight in planning both the transportation and the future development strategy. The most interesting aspect of Hong Kong's public transport policy is its multimodal competition to bring down costs by market control. The planners' foresight is displayed by their decision to construct the expensive mass transit railway in the 1970s and to build the cross-harbour tunnels. These two have effectively expanded Hong Kong beyond the confines of the harbour area in line with the decentralization policy spearheaded by the new towns programme. The planners' control of private car ownership is also laudable in view of the need to use the limited road surface most efficiently. In the matter of transportation, the government applies strong regulations and the usual *laissez-faire* attitude has been dispensed with. Such pragmatic policy-making is also seen in the on-going

103

development of the port facilities, notably container terminals, and the international airport. Hong Kong has been able to emerge as a world city because of far-sighted and successful planning, made possible by a close-knit team of government administrators unaffected by local politics. However, as Hong Kong moves closer to 1997, stronger and stronger political influences will be felt, not only from ordinary citizens who are very concerned about their own future, but also from China who is always suspicious of any supposed British plot, like the construction of the new international airport on Lantau Island, to empty the treasury. Nevertheless, the ambitious airport project will certainly transform the internal structure of the whole city state of Hong Kong in the year 2000.

References

Catt, P. 1986. Vegetation. In *A geography of Hong Kong*, T.N. Chiu and C.L. So (eds). Hong Kong: Oxford University Press, pp. 118–47.

Chiu, T.N. 1986. The port. In *A geography of Hong Kong*, T.N. Chiu and C.L. So (eds). Hong Kong: Oxford University Press, pp. 328–49.

Clawson, M. and Stewart, C.L. 1965. *Land use information. A critical survey of US statistics including possibilities for greater uniformity.* Baltimore, Md.: The Johns Hopkins Press for Resources for the Future, Inc.

Dwyer, D.J. and Lai, C.Y. 1967. *The small industrial unit in Hong Kong: patterns and policies.* Hull: University of Hull Publications.

Hong Kong Government, 1991. *Hong Kong 1991, a review of 1990.* Hong Kong: The Government Printer.

Hong Kong Government, 1989. *Gateway to new opportunities, Hong Kong's port and airport development strategy.* Hong Kong: The Government Printer.

Leung, C.K. 1986. Urban transportation. In *A geography of Hong Kong*, T.N. Chiu and C.L. So (eds). Hong Kong: Oxford University Press, pp. 305–27.

Planning Division, Hong Kong 1968. *Land utilization in Hong Kong as at 31st March 1966.* Hong Kong: The Government Printer.

Pang, H.C. and Lee, E.S.W. 1988. Transit facilities in Hong Kong. Paper presented to the Conference of Institute of Traffic Engineers held in Vancouver, Canada, 1988.

Thomson, J.M. 1977. *Great cities and their traffic.* Harmondsworth: Penguin Books.

Transport Branch, Hong Kong Government, 1990. *Moving into the 21st century: the white paper on transport policy in Hong Kong.* Hong Kong: Transport Branch, Hong Kong Government.

Transport Department, 1986. *Hong Kong annual departmental report by the Commissioner for Transport.* Hong Kong: Government Printer.

Transport Department, 1989. *Hong Kong second comprehensive transport study: final report.* Hong Kong: Government Printer.

Tregear, T.R. 1958. *Land use in Hong Kong and the New Territories.* Hong Kong: Hong Kong University Press.

Tregear, T.R. and Berry, L. 1959. *The development of Hong Kong and Kowloon as told in maps.* Hong Kong: Hong Kong University Press.

Wilbur Smith and Associates, 1976. *Hong Kong comprehensive transport study.* Hong Kong: Government Printer.

Wong, L.S.K. (ed.) 1978. *Housing in Hong Kong, a multi-disciplinary study.* Hong Kong: Heinemann Educational Books (Asia) Ltd.

5
Urban planning: successes and failures

The primary goal for restructuring our city over the long term was . . . to bring about a better organised, more efficient and more desirable place in which to live and work.
Strategic Planning Unit, Planning, Environment and Lands Branch, Hong Kong Government (1990): *Metroplan: Initial Options*, p. 2

. . . it is not town planning which directs development, but development which directs planning.
Cuthbert, A.R. (1987): Hong Kong 1997: the transition to socialism – ideology, discourse, and urban spatial structure. *Environment and Planning D*, Vol. 5, p. 143

Such a lofty goal stipulated by the government suggests the great importance of urban planning in the present day development of Hong Kong. This presents a strong contrast to the traditional image of Hong Kong as a city with the minimal government intervention and a *laissez-faire* philosophy. Indeed, urban planning has a very short history of development in Hong Kong. The Planning Department was only founded on January 1 1990.

History of urban planning in Hong Kong

Planning is the process of preparing a set of decisions for action in the future directed at achieving goals by optimal means (Bristow, 1987, p. 2). This involves drawing out an optimal plan and implementing it. Urban planning or town planning is applying the process to both urban and rural areas. Planning therefore implies government exercising control over the use of land and the intensity of development. Planning is a continuous process which cannot be stopped once started.

At the beginning, when the British Colony of Hong Kong was founded, no grandiose plan for its future development was conceived. The government's main task was to regulate the sale of land with the minimum amount of intervention. The directions of development were dictated by the general economic conditions of the Colony at any one time. The coastal reclamation was carried out in a piecemeal manner and lacked co-ordination (Tregear and Berry, 1959). There was a lot of indiscriminate growth which created tensions between conflicting civil, military and naval claims. Overcrowding was also a problem right at the beginning and squatters appeared as early as 1844. Sanitary conditions were poor and culminated in several outbreaks of the bubonic plague in 1894, 1896, and 1901. The government had to act to control building density through legislation. The Public Health and Buildings Ordinance which was finally passed in 1903 set down requirements for open spaces and scavenging lanes as well as restrictions on building styles, heights and modifications. Developers had to submit plans and drawings for approval to the Building Authority which was specially set up to administer the ordinance (Bristow, 1987). Most of the Hong Kong cityscape was determined for the next fifty years by this particular ordinance, which heralded the beginning of urban planning.

The first major attempt to apply urban planning principles took place in 1922 and was stimulated by the explosive growth of Kowloon Peninsula. A Committee was set up to 'investigate and report regarding a town planning scheme for the Colony'. The result was the production of a plan for Kowloon which laid out building lots for subsequent private development. The government also reserved sites for a wide variety of public services, future communications, reclamations and harbour works but interwar economic difficulties prevented the implementation of much of the scheme. In the early 1920s, Hong Kong enjoyed an economic boom which compelled the government to recommend a programme of works for the future development of the harbour. The resulting plan proposed the construction of a network of enclosed cargo-handling docks at Kowloon Point and Hung Hom Bay but, because of the expense and impact on naval requirements, this was not implemented. By 1941 another plan for the improvement of the harbour was drawn up by Sir David Owen.

With the influx of Chinese into Hong Kong in the 1930s as a result of the Sino–Japanese War, the government was concerned about overcrowding and its impact on public health. The clearance of slums and the provision of adequate housing for the poorer classes became a major issue. A Housing Commission set up in 1935 recommended the formation of a permanent town planning and housing committee to advise the government. The recommendations led to the passing of the Town Planning Ordinance in June 1939, which remains the guiding legislation for urban planning today (Bristow, 1987; Pun, 1986). The most important provision of the Town Planning Ordinance was the establishment of a Town Planning Board, made up of representatives from relevant government departments and members of the general public. Its main responsibility was the systematic preparation of draft plans for the future layout of existing and potential urban areas as directed by the Governor (Pun, 1986). It also provided for public participation in urban planning.

Because of the outbreak of the Second World War and the Japanese Occupation of 1941–5, the first town plan was not prepared until 1947. At the end of the war the most urgent concerns were the rebuilding of Hong Kong and the housing shortage. In August 1947 Sir Patrick Abercrombie, a famous British town planner was appointed to advise the Hong Kong government on planning and development, especially for Victoria and Kowloon. The plan he drew up required a strict policy on population to be enforced in the existing urban area to limit it to a maximum of two million. However, the rapid immigration of mainland Chinese immediately after the war precluded the implementation of such a policy until the 1970s when the new towns and public housing programmes were firmly implemented. However, Abercrombie's plan proposed industrial locations, future reclamations, cross-harbour tunnels, new communications and the likely eventual need of the new towns. His plan therefore provided the model for future plans for Hong Kong's development.

In 1953 the Town Planning Office was established within the Crown Lands and Survey Office, and the Town Planning Board met for the first time in 1954. But the idea to develop a Master Plan for Hong Kong was not readily acceptable to the government because it argued that such a plan would soon become outdated. The government had no desire for too much planning for fear of objections from the public. On the other hand, too little planning would retard growth and cause development to proceed along undesirable lines. The government preferred planning that lay somewhere between these two extremes. Here one clearly sees the Hong Kong government's pragmatic approach. But economic development and a building boom in the 1960s led to more concern about social justice and the interrelationship between physical planning and its social and economic effects. In view of the need for better central co-ordination of planning and development, the government was forced in 1962 to move towards planning for Hong Kong as a whole. This resulted in the preparation of the Colony Outline Plan. The preparation of the Plan was assisted by a number of government committees and outside experts working in various subject areas such as population, industry, utilities, transport and others. The Plan was completed in 1971 and submitted to the Executive Council for approval in 1972. It became the document on which the government based its provision of facilities in suitable locations in Hong Kong.

In essence, the Colony Outline Plan consisted of two parts: First, a development strategy for the next 20 years and second, the planning standards and guidelines for the provision of infrastructural facilities and services. The Plan was a follow-up to the Abercrombie Plan with updates and substantiations. Thus, a three-tier system of government planning comprising the Colony Outline Plan (long-term territorial development directions), outline zoning plan (broad land-use patterns for particular districts) and departmental development and layout plans (detailed data given on the layouts of individual districts) was firmly established. It is noteworthy that the town planners' main responsibility was land-use planning, which is separate from transport planning by the Highways Office, the public transport planners and the development control responsibilities of the Building Ordinance Office. However, the Building Ordinance was amended in 1959 to specifically empower the Building Authority to reject any building plan which did not conform to the land-use zoning of draft plans. In 1974, the Colony Outline Plan was revised and updated. The task was completed in 1979 and the Plan was renamed the Hong Kong Outline Plan.

Concern for the long-term development of Hong Kong resurfaced in 1980 when the Land Development Policy Committee approved the establishment of the Territorial Development Strategy (TDS) to formulate a comprehensive long-term development strategy for Hong Kong during the 1990s and up to the year 2001. TDS was not only concerned with meeting population requirements for land, services and facilities, but also paid attention to sustaining the growth of key economic activities in Hong Kong (Hong Kong Government, 1985). TDS also attempted to co-ordinate urban development with transport provision, a problem encountered in the development of new towns. For this purpose, Hong Kong was divided into five sub-regions: the Metropolitan Area comprising Hong Kong Island, Kowloon Peninsula, New Kowloon and Tsuen Wan; the north-east New Territories comprising Sha Tin, Ma On Shan, Tai Po and Sheung Shui; the north-west New Territories comprising Tuen Mun, Yuen Long and Tin Shui Wai; the south-east New Territories comprising Junk Bay and Sai Kung, and the south-west New Territories consisting of North Lantau, Peng Chau and Cheung Chau. The long-term development potential of each sub-region was studied and analysed with the aid of quantitative methods such as Land Use-Transport Optimization (LUTO) model (Choi, 1985; Eason, 1985).

With the continued growth and economic development of Hong Kong in the 1970s, further controls on the direction of growth became necessary. The role played by urban planning accordingly assumed

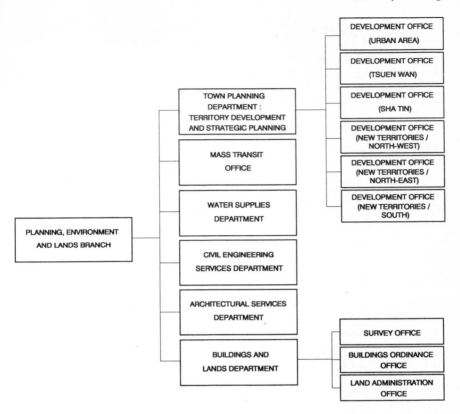

Figure 5.1 The organization of Planning, Environment and Lands Branch, Hong Kong Government, 1990

greater importance and the status of the Town Planning Office was elevated. The administrative structure of urban planning changed as the whole administrative machine of the government changed. The Town Planning Office, located inside the Lands and Works Branch, not only conducted all planning surveys and studies but also participated both in the preparation of the Territorial Development Strategy (TDS) mentioned above and in sub-regional planning matters. On January 1 1990, the Town Planning Office was further elevated to become the Planning Department after the creation of the Planning, Environment and Lands Branch on September 1 1989 (Figure 5.1). This change was aimed at greater integration of all planning functions and activities stimulated by the planning needs of the Port and Airport Development Strategy and the Metroplan – two major future developments for Hong Kong. Finally, the Planning Department was also charged with the review of the 1939 Town Planning Ordinance which was so out of date that it could no longer provide adequate guidance and control for planning and development. With this new administrative change, it became quite clear that the government felt the need to intervene more in Hong Kong's development. This need was prompted by the desire to preserve through more effective planning control Hong Kong's standing as a world city and international finance centre after the political change in 1997.

Major areas of development

The strategy for the development of Hong Kong is pragmatic and consistently promotes economic development based on the harbour and the port facilities. In other words, planning is to serve the needs rather than to restrict the economic activities of the population in Hong Kong. With limited land resources and a large population to support, the harbour has always been the core area of economic activity. This has resulted in a population concentration in the area around the harbour, and high-density living as the norm for most people in Hong Kong. The planners in the past were more concerned about the health impact of high-density living and had tried to control the plot ratio or building volumes on individual sites through the Buildings Ordinance. They also attempted to set a limit on the number of people living in the main urban area. Abercrombie's plan set a maximum of 2 million people for the urban area in 1948. However, as Hong Kong became more industrialized in the 1950s, 1960s and 1970s there were increasing demands for new land for factories and so Hong Kong adopted an ingenious solution of using multi-storey buildings to house the small-scale 'flatted factories'. Another urgent need was to increase the supply and quality of housing. There were many people who preferred squatting, not only because they could not find any affordable housing, but also because they could live in a more spacious environment. They usually occupied the peripheral areas immediately adjoining the main urban areas of Hong Kong Island and Kowloon Peninsula, which were valuable land that could be used for urban expansion. These two areas – provision of industrial land and better quality housing – occupied the attention of the government and the planners and led to the development of the new towns programme in 1960.

New towns programme

The move towards developing new towns implies population decentralization which deviates from the traditional policy of population concentration. At the beginning, the planners were not very sure of the

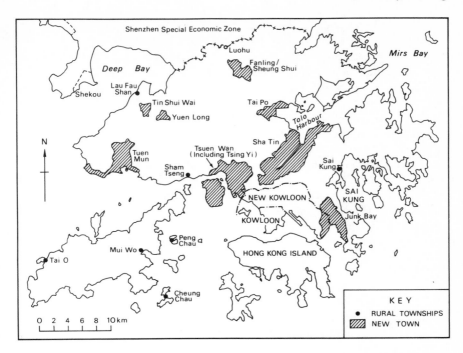

Figure 5.2 The location of the eight new towns in relation to Hong Kong Island, Kowloon and New Kowloon (1991)

appropriateness of such a programme. In 1953, in meeting the need for more industrial land, the site of Kwun Tong on the eastern coast of Kowloon Bay adjoining Kowloon Peninsula and near the airport was developed into an industrial satellite town (Figure 5.2). This was the forerunner of the new towns programme. In the same year, after a disastrous fire in a squatter area in Shek Kip Mei rendered 50,000 people homeless, the government decided to take up a public housing programme to resettle the squatter population after clearance. A new town was considered ideal to house these people. In 1960, Tsuen Wan, located on the coast adjoining the north-western part of the Kowloon urban area and originally picked out for development into an industrial satellite town, was designated as a new town. A new town differs from an industrial satellite town in that it is comprehensively planned and developed into a balanced and self-sufficient community in which people can live and work in pleasant surroundings. Ideally, residents find work within the new town and do not have to commute to work. The new town offered a solution to both the industrial land and housing shortage problems.

The development of new towns requires new land and the predominantly rural New Territories at that time had plenty to offer. Because the New Territories were acquired by the British as a buffer between China and Hong Kong, and on a lease basis, they were treated as a rural appendage and not much urban development took place. With the adoption of a new towns programme, the relationship between the New Territories and the main urban areas on Hong Kong Island and in Kowloon changed. A period of urbanization began in the New Territories which would drastically alter their character and integrate them with the development of Hong Kong and Kowloon.

The development of Tsuen Wan revealed the town planners' vision of a new town modified to suit the needs of Hong Kong at that time. Tsuen Wan was to be developed into a self-contained community with a balanced land-use pattern designed to allow people to live within a reasonable distance from their workplace, with adequate public services, communications and community facilities for the well-being of a population of 1.2 million. This was to be attained by 1978 (Leung, 1986). Unlike the Utopian idea of Ebenezer Howard's 'garden city', which gave birth to the new towns in Britain, Tsuen Wan New Town was a pragmatic compromise which adopted a compact high-density form of development, characterised by high-rise buildings. This became the model for the first generation of new towns in Hong Kong to follow in the future.

Fearing another massive population influx from China in the early 1960s, the planners formalised and consolidated the new towns programme in the period from 1965 to 1972. Two more new towns, Castle Peak (later renamed Tuen Mun) and Sha Tin were proposed and approved. They are located further out in the New Territories. Castle Peak, in particular, is at a great distance from the main urban area in Kowloon. Sha Tin, on the other hand, is on the railway line and is quite close to the main urban area (Figure 5.2). These two new towns were on a much smaller scale than Tsuen Wan. After the 1971 census, it became clear that the population growth in Hong Kong was not as high as had been expected, and as a result, a lower target population was used for the new towns of Tsuen Wan, Castle Peak and Sha Tin. It was also realized at that time that there was a need for better quality housing, communication and community facilities. However, the construction of new towns was still required if a maximum population of 3.8 million in the main metropolitan area of Hong Kong and Kowloon was to be maintained (Wigglesworth, 1971). An estimated growth of Hong Kong's population to 5.8 million in 1986 would mean that the new towns had to absorb two million more people. The new towns programme was reassessed, and it was realized that the demand for housing was increasing. This led to the development of three existing market towns in the New Territories, namely Yuen Long, Fanling/Sheung Shui and Tai Po

(Figure 5.2). They were to be developed into medium-sized settlements which would accommodate 300,000 people resettled from the old urban area of Hong Kong and Kowloon. The continued economic growth of Hong Kong resulted in real income growth among the population whose age and sex structure had changed. After reviewing its housing programme, the government decided to increase the target population for the three market towns to 220,000 for Tai Po, 170,000 for Fanling/Sheung Shui and 95,000 for Yuen Long so that the three combined to accommodate nearly half a million people. These comprise the second generation of new towns located deeper in the New Territories. It should also be noted that the quality of housing in the second generation new towns was higher, and that the objective of the new towns programme had shifted to stress the provision of a better residential environment for the population of Hong Kong. In 1973 the government announced a ten-year housing programme with the establishment of the Housing Branch, thus indicating its strong commitment to the provision of public housing. Meanwhile, some of the initial poorer quality public housing estates would be redeveloped. The new towns have since become an integral part of the government's housing policy. It is therefore not surprising to find a high proportion of public housing tenants in the new towns. By 1984–5 the new towns of Tsuen Wan, Tuen Mun (Castle Peak) and Sha Tin had 75 per cent, 70 per cent, and 57 per cent respectively of people living in public housing compared with 46 per cent for the whole of Hong Kong. The three new towns combined therefore contained 72 per cent of Hong Kong's total public housing population.

The new towns programme underwent further expansion and, in January 1979, the government designated the three market towns as new towns because of an expansion in the scale of development. In view of another possible population explosion caused by legal and illegal immigrants from China, a much larger public housing sector was planned for in these new towns. Apart from extending Sha Tin New Town to the Ma On Shan area, another new town for 300,000 people, Junk Bay (Tseung Kwan O), was proposed. In 1982 one more new town, Tin Shui Wai, was added in the north-west New Territories near the Chinese border. Thus, the development of new towns has gone deeper and deeper into the New Territories. There were eight new towns in Hong Kong with a total population of about 2.2 million (or 38 per cent of the total population of Hong Kong) in 1990. This may be the end of the new towns programme because the recent planning policy seems to favour a return to the development of the main urban area of Hong Kong and Kowloon by means of large-scale reclamations, particularly in the western Victoria Harbour area. The relocation of the airport to Chek Lap Kok off Lantau Island (see Chapter 4) will open up a large piece of land on the eastern coast of Kowloon for urban development and provide an opportunity to reshape the city with the so-called 'Metroplan' project.

The experience of the new towns programme has not been totally positive. The emphasis in the new towns on public housing has resulted in an over-representation of population in the lower social class and failed to produce balanced and self-contained communities. Only in Sha Tin new town can a greater mix of different social classes be found. There was also a delay between the residents moving in and the provision of public and private services such as schools and shops. Much of the infrastructure was not up to the standard of the main urban area and many residents were unable or unwilling to find work in the new towns, either because of the much lower pay or because of the lack of correspondence between their skills and the type of industry established in the new towns. The new towns become dormitory towns and residents had to commute long distances to work in the main urban area. This placed an additional burden on the already congested transport system. Tuen Mun was often cited as an example of this type of problem in the initial stage. On the other hand, the new towns programme succeeded in accommodating a large number of people on low-incomes who would otherwise have been unable to afford housing or would have become squatters occupying valuable land in the metropolitan area. The new towns programme also succeeded in decentralizing the population and industries. It was also instrumental in integrating the New Territories with Hong Kong and Kowloon and so reduced the inequality between the core and the periphery commonly observed in the cities of Third World countries. The new towns programme has also brought about clustered development of the New Territories based on the existing market towns. Together with the main metropolitan area, they produced a hierarchy of settlements which is functionally interrelated and supports the efficient operation of Hong Kong as a world city.

The Metroplan study

Metroplan represents the planners' idea of focusing the development back on the main metropolitan area after the relocation of the airport and it was announced by the government in May 1988. The main purpose was to replan the metropolitan area around the harbour so as to bring about 'a better organised, more efficient and more desirable place in which to live and work' (Strategic Planning Unit, 1990). In essence, Metroplan provides a strategic framework to guide planning and development at a district level. It is made up of five components (1) a broad land use and transport plan; (2) guidelines for urban design, broad planning controls, urban landscape principles and the height and density of building development; (3) a comprehensive landscape strategy for the conservation of major recreational amenities; (4) the broad phrasing of major works for land formation and principal transport links; and (5) a series of development statements to interpret (1) to (4) above. The time frame covered by Metroplan is up to the year 2011, the same design year used for the Port and Airport Development Strategy (PADS) mentioned in Chapter 4. But an important rider for Metroplan is that all proposals will be continuously and carefully monitored to 'ensure that they evolve over time to meet changing needs, demands and problems'.

Basically, the plan sets a maximum population limit of 4.2 million in the metropolitan area. It is projected that from 1986 to 2011 an additional 1.4 million flats will be needed for Hong Kong, of which 80 per cent will arise from the metropolitan area, and 80 per cent of this need will be met by the private sector. Land reclamation and terracing of hillsides will be needed to provide the land required. The old public housing estates developed during the initial stage of the public housing programme will have to be redeveloped. However, such redevelopment cannot satisfy all the projected rehousing needs, and the new towns programme will have to be continued for some years to come. Along with the redevelopment of old public housing estates is the upgrading of obsolete private development areas. All these proposals aim at greatly improving the quality of the residential environment in the metropolitan area. However, the major concern of the plan is to maintain a metropolitan area conducive to business activities. At present the major concentration of business activities is in the Central–Wanchai and Tsim Sha Tsui areas and has created severe traffic congestion. The proposal is to look at the development of 'satellite' office centres at suitably accessible locations. It is envisaged that manufacturing industry will decline in importance as an employer in Hong Kong with the continued industrialization in the Zhu Jiang (Pearl River) delta region where labour costs are much lower even than in Hong Kong. Nevertheless, Hong Kong has much higher labour productivity. Further development of light industry should take place in the new towns rather than in the main metropolitan area. With the completion of the new airport in Chek Lap Kok and the container port developed in Kwai Chung, it is obvious that industry will be attracted to the West Harbour–North Lantau sector and in West Kowloon. In view of Hong Kong's importance as a tourist centre and the gateway to China, further provision of hotels and convention facilities are required in the metropolitan area. In line with Hong Kong's planning tradition, which places planning to serve economic growth, investment in new infrastructure should maximise multiple development benefits. Hence, the Port and Airport Development Strategy is closely co-ordinated with Metroplan.

The plan also mentions environmental protection in the metropolitan area for the first time. In the past, most of the economic development

Figure 5.3 Part of Central and Wan Chai reclamation as they will appear by 2011

Source: Hong Kong Government, 1990

of Hong Kong had paid very scant attention to the problems of water, air and noise pollution. As a result, all of these problems are very severe in Hong Kong today. The planners see these as a result of inadequate land use planning in the past and advocate the use of lower tier plans to reverse the situation where practicable in the future.

Metroplan has emphasized the importance of efficient transport networks (roads and railways in particular) in anticipation of the rising demands in the lead up to 2001. New highway projects and railway extensions have been recommended. These include the Western Harbour Crossing, the West Kowloon Expressway, an east-west road link across

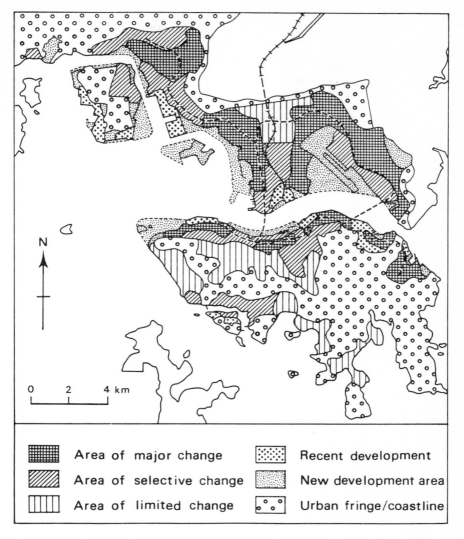

Figure 5.4 Structural land use change required in the metropolitan area of Hong Kong

Source: Hong Kong Government, 1990

urban Kowloon, a Central-Wanchai bypass, an expressway from the north coast of Hong Kong Island West to Hong Kong Island South, an extension of the Mass Transit Railway Kwun Tong Line to Tseung Kwan O (Junk Bay) new town, a new urban rail link between the North West New Territories and the urban area and a possible third harbour rail crossing. Public transport will continue to play an important role in

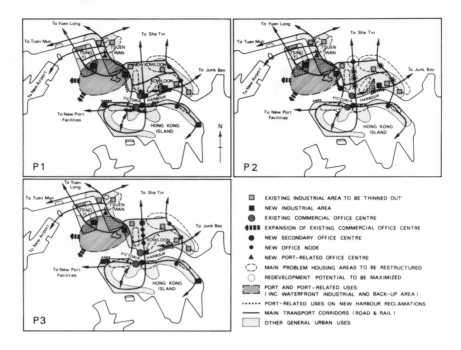

Figure 5.5 Three broad development patterns proposed for the metropolitan area

Source: Hong Kong Government, 1990

meeting all these increasing needs. The pedestrian traffic in the metropolitan area is to be separated from the vehicular traffic on the road. Underground and elevated walkways will be provided in great number to allow freer and less crowded pedestrian traffic.

The planners have also focused on the visual appeal of the metropolitan area, paying particular attention to the three-dimensional urban form. Certain buildings and landscape features should be designed as landmarks to create points of interest and a sense of place. A good mixture of compatible uses is also required to help create a convenient and lively urban environment (Figure 5.3).

Based on the above recommendations, the planners identify areas in need of structural land use change (Figure 5.4) and they also propose three broad development patterns (Figure 5.5). The areas in need of major change cover the old established area where urban renewal will be carried out, such as the areas on the northern coast of Hong Kong Island, eastern and western coasts of Kowloon and Kwai Chung. The broad development patterns, on the other hand, differ according to the scale and disposition of major commercial and industrial activities, the relaxation of current airport height controls in certain areas, the redevelopment of the Kai Tak airport site, and the structure of an urban system of open spaces. Details for each of the three options are summarised for the purpose of comparison in Table 5.1. The most interesting divergence lies in the use of the 230 hectares of land at the Kai Tak airport site. Option 1 envisages the development of light, low to medium density industrial estate, and mixes residential use with open spaces. Option 2 emphasizes light industrial low to medium density industrial estate. Option 3 will develop the site into mixed residential uses with associated community facilities and open spaces. The initial options of Metroplan have been produced for public consultation. Professional and interested bodies have been invited to send in their comments, which will be incorporated in formulating more specific land use transport proposals and various development guidelines.

Urban planning's role in shaping the city of Hong Kong

A comparison between the new towns programme and the Metroplan Study makes it apparent that the government is much more willing to exercise control over the long-term development of Hong Kong in the 1990s than it has been in the past four decades. In the case of the new towns programme, many of the actions taken were on an *ad hoc* basis, and the government appeared to have no long-term plan until the approval of the Colony Outline Plan in 1972. The government has been very careful in ensuring that planning is neither excessively intrusive to local merchants and industrialists, nor detrimental to the economic well-being of Hong Kong. This also explains why environmental protection has never been high on the list of standards and guidelines for planning. The change of heart came gradually but is now being forced upon the government by events beyond its control. The greatest influence of course comes from China and the signing of the joint Sino–British agreement in 1984 relating to the future of Hong Kong. The prospective return of Hong Kong's sovereignty to China by 1997 may have weakened the confidence of some local residents and investors but China's bloody crackdown on the June 4 1989 post-democracy movement in Tiananmen Square devastated them. The Port and Airport Development Strategy and Metroplan are the necessary means to project the economic viability of Hong Kong beyond 1997, or in other words, the creation of a rose garden to restore the badly battered confidence of the population. With the proliferation of plans to be proposed and projects to be executed, the role of the planners has suddenly become very important.

Despite these fluctuations in the importance of planning, Hong Kong's city development has been affected by the integrated new towns and public housing programmes. The planners, the majority of whom studied

Table 5.1 Broad spatial patterns for generation of initial options in the Metroplan

Sector	Pattern P1	Pattern P2	Pattern P3
Industry	Redevelop obsolete industrial zones to reduce congested conditions with relocation of factories within Metro.	As for Pattern P1 but with limited relocation of factories to the new towns.	As for Pattern P1 but with major relocation of factories to the new towns.
	New land for export-related industry provided in proximity to the Kwai Chung container port and expanded West Harbour facilities.	As for Pattern P1.	As for Pattern P1.
	Develop a dispersed pattern in Metro of new, comprehensively designed, low-medium density light industrial estates.	Develop a limited number of major, comprehensively designed, low-medium density light industrial estates.	As for Pattern P1.
Business and Commercial Activities	Expansion mainly around established business centres on H.K. Island and E. Kowloon.	Limited expansion around existing centres with major development of secondary office centres along N–S MTR axis of Kowloon Peninsula.	Limited expansion around existing centres with major development of satellite business centres at key transport nodal points.
	Decentralized major Government office functions within Metro at key transport nodal points.	Centralized major Government office functions.	As for Pattern P1.
Housing	Redevelop obsolete public housing estates to produce a more diverse mix of public and private housing.	As for Pattern P1.	As for Pattern P1.
	Upgrade obsolete private housing areas as fully as possible.	As for Pattern P1.	As for Pattern P1.
	Provide new housing sites to create a more diverse housing mix within each broad district to satisfy locally generated needs as far as possible.	As for Pattern P1.	As for Pattern P1.

Sector	Pattern P1	Pattern P2	Pattern P3
Port Related Activities	Generally as per recommended Port & Airport Development Strategy.	As for Pattern P1.	As for Pattern P1.
Transport Related Development	Concentrate development within walk-in catchments of public mass transit modes and major interchanges.	As for Pattern P1.	As for Pattern P1.
	Develop nodes of major economic activities along Route 3.	As for Pattern P1.	As for Pattern P1.
	Develop nodes of new activities along Route 6 exploiting opportunities for redevelopment of obsolete land uses.	As for Pattern P1.	As for Pattern P1.
Open Space and Landscape	Provide large number of relatively small but interlinked urban open spaces dispersed throughout Metro.	Provide fewer but larger inter-linked urban open spaces dispersed throughout Metro.	Compromise between Pattern P1 and P2.
	All suitable urban fringe areas rehabilitated, developed and managed for public recreation and amenity use.	As for Pattern P1.	As for Pattern P1.
	Conservation and development of Hong Kong Island South and coastline west of Tsuen Wan as low intensity but diverse recreation zones.	As for Pattern P1.	As for Pattern P1.
Use of Kai Tak Site	Develop part of Kai Tak Site for light, low-medium density industrial estate, PCWA's and other port facilities.	Develop most of Kai Tak site for light industrial, low-medium density industrial estate, PCWA's and other port facilities.	Develop most of Kai Tak site for mixed residential uses, associated community facilities and district open space.
	Develop balance of Kai Tak site of mixed residential uses, associated community facilities and district open spaces.		

Table 5.1 continued

Sector	Pattern P1	Pattern P2	Pattern P3
Removal of Airport Height Controls	Redevelopment restrictions imposed by current height lifted to fullest extent possible.	Redevelopment restrictions imposed by current airport height controls lifted mainly around major transport nodes.	Redevelopment restrictions imposed by current airport height controls generally maintained by special development controls.

Source: Hong Kong Government, 1990

Geography, have been trained in Western theories and practices of planning (as represented by those planners with degrees obtained from Great Britain, Australia, New Zealand, Canada and the United States). It is not surprising therefore, that the spatial form developed is very Western in appearance. The debate over centralized or decentralized development echoes the concepts of centripetal and centrifugal forces expounded in geography. The development of new towns brought about a dispersed, multi-centred urban form linked by an efficient road and rail network. The public housing programme did provide a solution to the squatter problem but, because of the very minimal standard of accommodation being proposed for this low-income population in the initial stage, very quickly resulted in slums of its own. The standard of housing in both the public and private sectors did improve with time.

Conclusions

Because of the *laissez-faire* policy urban planning has only become important in recent years. In the past, planning in Hong Kong was *ad hoc* in nature and demand-oriented (Bristow, 1981). It appeared that the government was very much concerned about 'too much' planning which would interfere with the freedom of individual merchants, industrialists, and other investors in the economic development of Hong Kong. On the other hand, the government would not hesitate to involve itself in controlling the price of rice, public utilities, transport, medicine and healthcare, education and housing because these help provide cheap labour for Hong Kong's export-oriented industrialization (Schiffer, 1985). Only the political events of recent years have helped to raise the status and involvement of urban planners, particularly in relation to the Territorial Development Strategy (TDS), the Port and Airport Development Strategy (PADS) and Metroplan. Long-term plans for Hong Kong's development can be traced all the way back to Abercrombie's 1948 plan which recommended sites for coastal reclamation, cross-harbour tunnels, new communications and the new towns. The original intention of Abercrombie's plan was to relieve congestion in the main urban area. The development of eight new towns and the approved relocation of the airport to Chek Lap Kok have dispersed, and will continue to disperse, the population of Hong Kong, thus transforming Hong Kong from a uni-centre city state into a multi-centred one. However, the government will also focus on the redevelopment of the main metropolitan area around the harbour – the lifeblood of Hong Kong. Hong Kong urban planners are well trained and knowledgeable about planning development in Western countries. They are typical examples of the technocrats who are essential if Hong Kong is to attain its world city status. The new towns were on the whole quite well planned. They are success stories for Hong Kong's planners, although one must admit that there were failures in the course of implementing their plans. An obvious failure was the lack of co-ordination among individual departments involved in the project. The completion of the public housing in the new towns was not always accompanied by an equally complete provision of transportation facilities, education and other necessary services for the people who moved in. This lack of co-ordination in fact reflects the low status of the Town Planning Office at that time. Another major weakness of Hong Kong planning is the absence of participation by ordinary citizens in the planning process. Fortunately, the planners are aware of all these weaknesses and are trying to rectify them. The current policy of inviting public comment on Metroplan is a good example, although one would imagine the silent majority will remain mute while the influential merchants and industrialists will be more vocal.

Clearly, development in Hong Kong will become more and more complex in the future, and this explains why the government set up a Land Information System Unit in 1989 in the Buildings and Lands Department. Based on a number of Sun Workstations and ARC/INFO software, it will provide land information in digital form to planners and other officials in the government (*Arc News*, Spring 1989, vol. 11, no. 2). In the past planning in Hong Kong had focused on the territory comprised of Hong Kong Island, Kowloon Peninsula, New Kowloon and the New Territories. However, after 1997 when Hong Kong will have become a Special Administrative Area (SAR), Hong Kong's planners will have to consider the impact of the Shenzhen Special Economic Zone and the city of Guangzhou on Hong Kong's future development. More co-ordination with the Chinese planners will certainly be needed. On the other hand, the increased affluence of the population in Hong Kong has forced planners to be more conscious of their needs, particularly in raising the quality of the residential environment. Also, because limited democracy is permitted by the joint Sino–British agreement (the first ever direct election of 18 candidates to the Legislative Council by the people of Hong Kong was successfully carried out on September 15, 1991), the planners will have to be even more responsive to the people's needs, although one must admit that democracy in Hong Kong is still in its infancy. The implications of such political changes in the governing of Hong Kong over recent years and in the future will be discussed in Chapter 8.

References

Bristow, R. 1987. *Land-use planning in Hong Kong: history, policies and procedures.* Hong Kong: Oxford University Press.

Bristow, R. 1981. Planning by demand: a possible hypothesis about town planning in Hong Kong. *Hong Kong Journal of Public Administration*, 3 (2): 199–223.

Chiu, T.N. and So, C.L. (eds). 1986. *A geography of Hong Kong*, Second Edition, Hong Kong: Oxford University Press.

Choi, Y.L. 1985. The LUTO model and its applications in Hong Kong. *Planning and Development* (Journal of the Hong Kong Institute of Planners), 1 (1): 21–31.

Cuthbert, A.R. 1987. Hong Kong 1997: the transition to socialism – ideology, discourse, and urban spatial structure. *Environment and Planning D: Society and Space*, 5: 123–50.

Eason, A.G. 1985. Territorial development strategy studies: a view of the process. *Planning and Development* (Journal of the Hong Kong Institute of Planners), 1 (1): 4–7.

Hong Kong Government, 1985. *Planning for growth.* Hong Kong: Government Printer.

Hong Kong Government, 1990. *Metroplan initial options.* Hong Kong: Government Printer.

Leung, W.T. 1986. The new towns programme. In *A geography of Hong Kong*, T.N. Chiu and C.L. So (eds). Hong Kong: Oxford University Press, pp. 251–78.

Pun, K.S. 1984. Urban Planning in Hong Kong: its evolution since 1948. *Third World Planning*, 6 (1): 61–78.

Pun, K.S. 1986. Urban Planning. In *A geography of Hong Kong*, T.N. Chiu and C.L. So (eds). Hong Kong: Oxford University Press, pp. 305–27.

Schiffer, J.R. 1985. Anatomy of a *laissez-faire* government: the Hong Kong growth model reconsidered. In P. Hills (ed), *State policy, urbanization and the development process.* Hong Kong: Centre of Urban Studies and Urban Planning, University of Hong Kong, pp. 1–29.

Strategic Planning Unit, 1990. *Metroplan: the foundations and framework.* Hong Kong: Government Printer.

Tregear, T.R. and Berry, L. 1959. *The development of Hong Kong and Kowloon as told in maps.* Hong Kong: Hong Kong University Press.

Wigglesworth, J.M. 1971. The development of new towns. In D.J. Dwyer (ed), *Asian Urbanization: a Hong Kong Casebook.* Hong Kong: Hong Kong University Press, pp. 48–69.

6
Quality of life

The quality of urban life is less influenced by the factors of scale and density than by the values and organization of the society itself.

Schmandt, H.J. and Bloomberg, Jr.: 'Introduction', *The Quality of Urban Life*, Sage Publications, Beverly Hills, CA, 1969

Living in a high-density city like Hong Kong is extremely stressful, particularly because nearly every day many people have to commute to work in the Central Business District in the Central District of Hong Kong Island and Tsim Sha Tsui in Kowloon. Despite the careful siting of the new towns, many residents still have to travel long distances to work in offices located in the main metropolitan area around the harbour, because, as has been indicated in the previous chapter, these new towns do not have enough tertiary and quaternary jobs to offer their inhabitants. All this commuting depends on an efficient multi-modal public transport system and conflicts between drivers and passengers or between passengers themselves are common daily occurrences. Any casual traveller to Hong Kong will not fail to notice the way Hong Kong people walk in the street – everybody seems to be hurrying to meet a late appointment. They are also not the most polite people in the world when they are working. Most people work a five and half day week. Some probably have to work seven days a week. But even during the public holidays or Sundays, it is still difficult for anyone to relax because the parks are full of people, the tea houses have long queues of customers and most people's homes are too small to stay in all day. This explains why a popular pastime is a game of 'mah-jong' which can be played by four people at home or in a reserved room in a restaurant where friends can chat as they play. What they need is simply a table for four, and they can spend a whole day playing it. It is interesting to note that 'mah-

126

jong' is a game of numbers and strategy so that Hong Kong people continue to train their minds even in games. So, what kind of quality of life do people enjoy in Hong Kong?

Quality of life criteria

Most people have a strong personal interest in their own quality of life, which can be translated as how satisfied or happy people are with their lives. Quality of life is therefore highly subjective and is rather difficult to measure. Obviously, quality of life is also related to demographic and socio-economic variables such as age, income, education and marital status. Liu (1976) presented three approaches to measuring quality of life: (1) using precise definitions such as happiness, satisfaction, wealth etc., (2) using specific types of subjective or objective indicators such as GNP, health or welfare, educational and environmental, and (3) using an indirect definition by specifying a special group of variables or factors such as social, economic, political and environmental. The present discussion will utilize a mixture of the three approaches, and focus on income distribution, housing, urban services and environmental protection. Finally, the perceptions of some residents from different districts of Hong Kong will also be presented.

Income distribution

Since 1950 Hong Kong has become rapidly industrialized with an emphasis on the export of manufactured goods. Hong Kong's Gross Domestic Product (GDP) grew. It was calculated that over the three-decade period of 1952–81 the GDP averages grew 10.1 per cent per annum while in per capita terms the growth was 6.4 per cent per annum (Chau, 1984). Between 1981 and 1989, however, these declined to 7.1 per cent and 5.6 per cent respectively. But such growth rates are high by world standards. It should be noted that in 1964 Hong Kong's GDP in absolute amount was HK$8,827 million (US$1,765.4 million at the exchange rate at the time of US$1.00 = HK$5.00), but by 1989 it was estimated to be HK$490,550 million (US$62,891.0 million at the official exchange rate of US$1.00 = HK$7.80). The corresponding per capita GDP was HK$2,519 (US$503.8) in 1964 and HK$85,144 (US$10,915.9) in 1989. Certainly, there has been a great improvement in income for the people of Hong Kong. The study by Chau (1984) revealed three different periods of income distribution, based on the Gini coefficient computed: (1) 1953–61 when fledgling export-led industrialization resulted in great inequality in income distribution with a Gini coefficient of 0.48;

Quality of life

(2) 1961–73 when sustained high growth and full employment resulted in stable prices and falling inequality and poverty with a Gini coefficient of 0.43; and (3) 1974–83 when mixed development occurred with the Gini coefficient climbing up to 0.48, indicating an increased inequality in income distribution. It is noteworthy that the third period was a period of robust growth, but inflation rates fluctuated widely. Politics came into play in this period. It is doubtful if the fruit of economic progress trickled down as much as it did in the previous period. That was also the case after the signing of the joint Sino–British agreement on the future of Hong Kong in 1985. In September 1991, when this chapter was written, the inflation rate reached a high of 12.7 per cent, and the cost of purchasing a home skyrocketed. Nevertheless, the income per household of the poorest 20 per cent of the population did grow at about two-thirds of the growth rate of the per capita national income over 1971–6, and at 37 per cent of the overall growth rate during 1976–81. But, allowing for the decrease in household size between 1971 and 1981, the proportionate growth of their income was about 49 per cent of the per capita GDP. For the population as a whole the median monthly household income has increased from HK$3,259 in 1976 to HK$5,160 in 1986, or an increase of about 58 per cent. Therefore, despite some uneven distribution of income, people in Hong Kong did experience a genuine improvement in their standard of living even after inflation has been taken into account. The affluence of the Hong Kong population in recent years is shown by the fact that Hong Kong boasts having the greatest number of Rolls Royces per square kilometre in the world, which works out at over 1,000 Rolls Royces for the whole of Hong Kong – something for the Guinness Book of Records. Expensive cars such as Mercedes Benz, Volvos and BMWs are seen everywhere in Hong Kong. Only the top 10 per cent of the population can afford all these luxuries. The majority of the population are living in overcrowded public or private housing and travelling to work or play by means of public transport. One should note that Hong Kong's economic development has been shifting from secondary to tertiary and quaternary sectors where wages are much higher than those in the secondary sector. In fact, according to the projection for Metroplan, employment in manufacturing will decline by 2011 (Strategic Planning Unit, 1990). If this trend can be maintained, income distribution will be improved, and Hong Kong people will enjoy an even better quality of life.

Housing

A major measure of the quality of life in Hong Kong is housing because this represents the most important need of the Hong Kong people whether they are rich or poor. Indeed, the demand for housing in Hong Kong has never declined despite changes in the political climate, which only dampen speculative activities in the property market temporarily. The Hong Kong Housing Society, originally formed as a branch of the Council of Social Services in 1948, was the first body to provide housing for people on low incomes. Their first estate was built in 1952 with support from the Hong Kong Government Development Loan Fund. The government got itself more fully involved in the provision of public housing in December 1953 when a disastrous fire wiped out the squatters in Shek Kip Mei and rendered 50,000 people homeless. The squatters were the result of the post-1949 influx of Chinese refugees fleeing communist rule on the mainland. This kind of involvement is not typical of a *laissez-faire* government, particularly because of the high cost, but it was realised that the refugees would not voluntarily return to China, and that the land occupied by the squatters was inside the main urban area which could be used more profitably for other purposes. The cost of the emergency relief measures which the squatter fires required might have turned out to be even higher if the resettlement housing programme had not been adopted. Thus, the resettlement housing programme was undertaken strictly for economic rather than welfare reasons (Bristow, 1987). The government set up a new housing body called the Resettlement Department to plan, construct and manage the housing in co-operation with the Public Works Department. This provided the impetus for the establishment in April 1954 of a Housing Authority charged with the duty of advising the Governor on all housing policy matters as well as planning and building public housing estates.

Because of the need to charge a rental which bore a strict relationship to the ability of the squatters to pay, as well as paying towards the initial construction costs of the buildings, the quality of the housing provided was very low. Also, because of the need to erect the buildings as quickly as possible in order to resettle the squatters, a very simple and highly utilitarian design was adopted. This gave rise to the six-storey H-shaped blocks with the long arms of the H containing 64 rooms per floor and the cross piece a service core containing six communal flush latrines per sex, two water standpipes, and an open communal laundry space (Will, 1978) (Figure 6.1 – see Will's paper p. 98 Figure 5.1). This is known as the Mark I block with a space allocation of only 24 sq ft (2.2 sq m) per adult and a room size of 11.1 sq m. The cost of such a 120 sq ft (11.1 sq m) unit was HK$2,374 (US$475) including the purchase price of the land in 1954. Later in 1961–4, the H-shaped blocks were modified by filling in the ends of the H to become the Mark II blocks. These were later evolved into the L-shaped eight-storey Mark III blocks and E-shaped 16-storeyed Mark IV blocks, with increased improvements

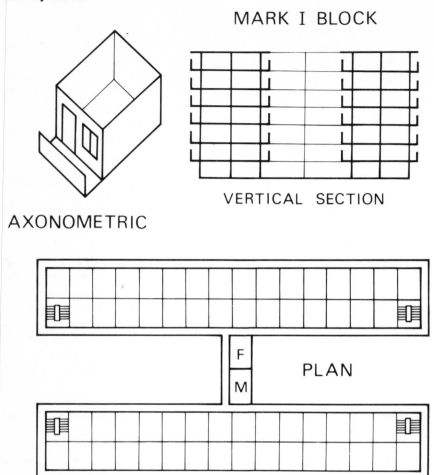

Figure 6.1 Plan of Mark I resettlement block
Source: Will, 1978

in privacy. Individual water supplies, a private balcony and lavatories shared by two families were provided in Mark III blocks while Marks IV and V blocks were fully equipped with private services for each housing unit. The latest type built in 1970, the Mark VI blocks, had the space allocation increased to 35 sq ft (3.3 sq m) per adult in units equipped with individual lavatories, a private balcony with a cooking bench and a water tap. These geometrically shaped resettlement blocks formed distinctive landmarks from the bird's eye view of an aerial photograph (Figure 6.2). Thus, even in the provision of housing for the lowest social class, quality had been gradually improved.

130

Figure 6.2 A portion of an aerial photograph of North Kowloon taken on January 10, 1985 showing the distinctive geometric forms of the public housing estates

Source: Survey Office, Building and Lands Department, Hong Kong Government

After beginning with squatter resettlement, the Hong Kong government expanded its involvement to the provision of housing for other income groups. In 1964 a new type of public housing – Government Low Cost Housing – was introduced to cater for the needs of low income families (less than HK$500 (US$100) a month) living in overcrowded and sub-standard accommodation. The standard of accommodation provided for this group was essentially the same as the Mark VI Resettlement Blocks mentioned above. Both the Housing Authority and the Housing Society attempted to meet the housing needs of middleincome families with higher quality government or government-aided housing. The Housing Authority aimed at families with monthly incomes

131

of between HK$400 (US$80) and HK$900 (US$180) and up to
HK$1,250 (US$250) for high rent units. The Housing Society aimed at
families with even higher incomes, up to HK$1,000 (US$200) or
HK$1,250 (US$250) for high rent units. They all built self-contained
units although the same standard of space allocation, 35 sq ft (3.3 sq m)
was maintained. It is worthy of note that, unlike Resettlement Housing
and Government Low Cost Housing, both the Housing Authority and
Housing Society houses were financed by the Government Development
Loan Fund plus being self-financing from rental returns. As a result, any
increase in capital or operational costs would result in rent increases. On
the other hand, the Resettlement Housing and Government Low Cost
Housing were financed directly from government revenue so that any
increase in construction, maintenance and management costs could be
absorbed by government revenue without the need for rent increases.
One common characteristic of these four categories of housing was that
they were all rental housing with the government or other statutory
bodies as the landlords.

In 1972 the governor announced a new public housing programme
that would rehouse some 1.5 million people in public housing within the
next 10 years. This represented a new approach to public housing. The
quality of the housing was emphasized, and it was to be related to the
development of new towns in the New Territories. Three new towns
were identified at the start of the programme: Kwai Chung, Tuen Mun,
and Shatin. Public housing was developed in conjunction with commercial and other uses to produce a balanced community (Fung, 1983).
Because of the availability of land, the emphasis was on self-contained
units in a sound living environment. The aim therefore was clearly to
improve the quality of life of the population. In 1973 the government
administrative structure was reorganized, a Housing Branch, headed by
the Secretary of Housing, was established and the Resettlement Department was replaced by a Housing Department. This indicated the government's determination to treat housing as a long-term policy matter rather
than as an *ad hoc* solution to a social problem. Public housing has now
become an integral part of new town development (Pryor, 1983). Also
in 1972, the government began to redevelop the Mark I and Mark II
estates in the city area which affected 84,000 families. The redevelopment programme was stepped up in 1983, so that by 1990–1 the
living conditions of all families living in Mark I–II estates could be
improved.

As the people living in the public rental housing become more affluent,
they increasingly want to own their own homes. In 1978, the Housing
Authority started the Home Ownership Scheme by constructing self-
contained flats of a design and quality better than those of public rental
housing for sale to the lower middle-income families at prices below

market value, with preference given to those living in public rental housing (Wong, 1986). More favourable mortgage terms were also arranged for these purchasers. It was hoped that these families would be encouraged to vacate their rented units to make room for the more needy lower-income households. By 1990 a total of 136,000 flats were sold to eligible families, of which about 45 per cent were public housing tenants. This scheme is quite popular, and is certainly providing a way for the public housing tenants to improve their living conditions.

By March 31, 1990, there were 2,759,100 people or 48 per cent of the total population of Hong Kong living in public housing of one form or another. On average, public housing tenants pay seven per cent of their income as rent. The government claimed that the rent levels represented about one-third to one-quarter of the current market rents. In other words, the government has subsidized public housing tenants quite heavily. All these developments clearly have a great impact on the quality of life of these lower middle- and lower-income groups. The government's public housing programme is considered to be quite successful and comparable to that of Singapore (Yeh, 1975). One should note however, that there are people still living in temporary structures. The most recent official figure available at the time of writing is 291,100 persons (end of March, 1990). In other words, the problem of squatters has not been totally eliminated even today.

People living in private housing constituted 45 per cent of the total population in 1990, which is slightly smaller than the number living in public housing. But living in private housing does not necessarily mean better living conditions. In the private housing sector, there is a great variety of design, and the costs or rents fluctuate according to the location, type and age of the building as well as supply and demand in the property market. In 1972 there were 296,000 permanent domestic accommodation units in private housing, of which 67.4 per cent were classified as tenement floors. About half of the tenement floors had an effective area of not more than 300 sq ft (27.9 sq m) (Wong, 1978). Most of the pre-war tenements had poor ventilation and lighting. Even for the post-war non-tenement dwelling units, the majority were small flats with an effective area of not more than 650 sq ft (60.4 sq m). In a survey of private housing undertaken by Maunder (1968) in 1963, it was found that of all the households paying not more than HK$500 (US$100) per month in rent, only 11 per cent were living in one whole flat or floor, while the rest were sharing accommodation in one form or another. From the mid-1950s onwards, redevelopment of the pre-war tenements took place rapidly, and all permanent domestic dwelling units built since then have been provided with piped water, flush toilets and kitchens.

Despite the massive public housing programme, the property market in

Quality of life

Table 6.1 Percentage of distribution of domestic households by tenure, 1971, 1981 and 1986

Tenure	1971 %	1981 %	1986 %
Owner–occupier	18.1	27.9	35.1
Sole tenant	45.5	44.0	45.5
Main tenant, sub-tenant, and co-tenant	30.2	21.2	12.7
Rent-free and accommodation provided or subsidized by employer	6.2	6.9	6.8
Total	100.0	100.0	100.1

Source: Census and Statistics Department, 1971, 1981, and 1986 census and By-Census reports

Hong Kong boomed. In 1973 private developers began to develop on large sites so that communities, including residential, commercial, educational, cultural and recreational activities, were developed all at the same time. The first of these projects was Mei Foo Sun Chuen built on an extensive former Mobil oil storage site on the coast in western Kowloon. It became very popular because of the high quality of housing and management. Its success led to other projects such as Chi Fu Fa Yuen on a former farm site in the western part of Hong Kong Island. Another successful project was Tai Koo Shing which occupied a former dockyard in the eastern part of Hong Kong Island. There have been many more of this type of real estate developments in different parts of urban Hong Kong in recent years. All these projects seemed to have met the needs of the more affluent upper middle-income groups desirous of owning their own home as protection from inflation. One thing that emerges clearly from this type of development is the conversion of cheap agricultural and industrial land into expensive residential/commercial land. Many of the warehouses, dockyards or even factories inside the main urban areas have been converted into private estates.

The development of the Mass Transit Railway in the late 1970s and early 1980s promoted further residential and commercial developments in the vicinity of the stations. Better financing terms (such as a small downpayment, longer repayment periods and low mortgage interest rates) have permitted more people in Hong Kong to own their own homes. From Table 6.1, one sees the great increase in the percentage of owner-occupier households from 18.1 per cent in 1971 to 35.1 per cent in 1986. Owner-occupiers tend to be more willing to improve their own living quarters than renting households. Indeed, the provision of private housing is just as important as the provision of public housing because the general increase in the level of household income renders many households ineligible for public housing. The supply of land in Hong Kong is always limited and, after the signing of the Sino–British agreement on the future of Hong Kong, the supply of land for sale from the government has been restricted to 50 hectares per year. At the time of writing, the property market is at an all time high, being stimulated by limited supply, low interest rates and rising inflation. The market price of a flat now ranges from HK$2,000 (US$256.4) to HK$3,000 (US$384.6) per sq ft. While on the whole all social classes have enjoyed much better housing quality in recent years, there is always the worry that the newer generation of Hong Kong citizens will find it increasingly difficult to purchase their homes.

Urban services

Rapid urbanization has increased the demand for urban services. The provision of minimum, basic levels of services is essential to raise living standards. This problem is now drawing much attention from urban planners in developing countries (Rondinelli and Cheema, 1988). Urban services include basic sanitation, water, housing, education, health, transportation and other municipal services such as garbage and solid waste disposal. It is important to ensure that even the poor will have access to such services. In Hong Kong, basic services in the urban areas on Hong Kong Island and Kowloon are provided by the Urban Council. This is a statutory council consisting of 40 members, 15 elected from district constituencies, 15 appointed by the Governor of Hong Kong and 10 representative members from the urban district boards. The Council therefore has a good representation of people from different parts of the city. The council makes decisions, and the council's chief executive, the Director of Urban Services who controls the operations of the Urban Services Department with a staff of 18,000, is charged with the duty of implementing the policies of the council. The council is financed by a share of the rates of properties and various licence fees and other charges. The services provided by the council are very varied and include street cleansing, refuse collection, control of environmental hygiene, the hygienic handling and preparation of food in restaurants, shops, abattoirs and other places, the control of hawkers and street-traders, the management of all public recreation and sporting facilities, museums, public libraries and several major cultural venues. The power of the Urban Council is not extended to the New Territories where the authority to provide the basic services lies with the Regional Council. Because the New Territories are leased territories with an essentially rural economy in the past, the native villagers' rights have to be respected, and their involvement in the Regional Council is ensured through the participation of the chairman and two vice-chairmen of the Heung Yee Kuk (literally the Village Affairs Council) who are *ex-officio* members.

The other members are made up of twelve by direct election, nine from the elected representatives of the nine district boards in the New Territories and twelve from appointment by the Governor. There are a total of 36 members in the Regional Council. Their financial sources are also from rates from properties in the council area and from fees and charges. Both the Urban Council and the Regional Council are financially autonomous.

Other basic services such as water supply, medical and health services, education and transportation are the responsibilities of other government departments. Drinking water is provided by the Water Supplies Department (formerly the Water Works Department). Water is a scarce resource in Hong Kong. Before the Second World War, Hong Kong prided itself on being able to supply its citizens with sanitary drinking water. With the rapid post-war industrialization and population increase, the water supply was no longer sufficient. Because of Hong Kong's monsoon climate, rainfall, the major source of Hong Kong's water supply, can fluctuate greatly in amount. Reservoirs had to be built to store up water (Tregear and Berry, 1959). Water rationing was a common occurrence during the 1950s and 1960s. Before the 1980s, the government spent a lot of money building increasingly larger reservoirs, the most recent being the High Island reservoir, completed in 1978, which was formed by joining islands together with dams in the Rocky Harbour area of eastern New Territories and then drawing out the sea water to artificially produce a massive fresh-water lake. A desalination plant was also built in Lok On Pai near Tuen Mun in 1977. However, the plant was never fully utilized because it was too expensive to operate. The government was striving for self-sufficiency in water out of fear of China's potential stranglehold. However, such a goal could not be achieved because the drought in 1963–4 forced the Hong Kong government to purchase water from Guangdong Province across the border in China. China used to pipe 22.7 million cubic metres of water a year from Dong Jiang to Hong Kong. As China opened up in 1978 and its relationship with Hong Kong became warmer, China supplied more and more water to Hong Kong. Today, China is the single major source of water supply for Hong Kong, and the annual amount has increased to over 500 million cubic metres. This will continue to increase to 660 cubic metres by 1994–5. Nevertheless, water remains a scarce resource, and could potentially limit not only the quality of life of the population but also Hong Kong's economic growth.

Hong Kong people enjoy good medical and health services. This is borne out by the fact that there has been a steady improvement in life expectancy. In 1990 the life expectancy for men was 74.6 years while women could look forward to 80.3 years. The infant mortality rate, which is very sensitive to the accessibility of health services, was only 5.9

per thousand live births in 1990. The crude death rate of the population as a whole was steady at 5 per thousand of population in recent years. All these figures compared well with those of economically advanced countries. Because of Hong Kong's status as a British colony, the provision of medical and health services has been influenced by the British way of thinking. The government, through its Department of Health and Hospital Services, provides subsidies to the public through the establishment of government and government-assisted hospitals as well as government maternity homes and clinics. All of these supply 22,464 hospital beds or 88.8 per cent of the total number of hospital beds in Hong Kong. The remaining beds are provided by private hospitals which are much more expensive. However, compared to the number of population (estimated at 5,800,600 in 1990), the number of hospital beds is still insufficient. There were 6,260 registered medical doctors in 1990, but only 1,864 of them (or 30 per cent) worked for the government. This worked out to be 926.6 persons per doctor, which is totally inadequate. Many people in fact rely heavily on the services of private doctors, who do excellent business but do not necessarily offer a good service. The concept of medical insurance, like that in the United States, is not found in Hong Kong, although in recent years there has been talk about the matter from the government. The general health of the population is good largely because of government efforts focusing on anti-epidemic and disease-surveillance measures, a comprehensive range of preventive, promotive and personal health services. The greater affluence of the population means that people eat better and enjoy an improved state of health. The leading causes of death today are cancer, heart disease and cerebrovascular diseases.

The success of Hong Kong as an international financial centre hinges heavily on the skill and technical know-how of its populace. Since 1971 free primary education has been provided to all children of suitable school age. In 1978, free education was also extended to junior secondary classes and subsidised senior secondary education was provided for about 85 per cent of the 15 year old population by 1991. There are three main types of secondary schools in Hong Kong: grammar, technical and prevocational. The majority of students are enrolled in grammar schools, which offer a five-year secondary course in a broad range of academic, cultural and practical subjects. The technical and prevocational schools are designed to prepare students with an interest and aptitude for technical and practical subjects. All these schools are under the supervision of the Department of Education. Hong Kong has a number of post-secondary colleges, polytechnics and universities. There is even an open learning institute (modelled after the Open University in Britain) to cater for the needs of more mature students who are in employment. The three major universities are the University of Hong Kong, the Chinese

University of Hong Kong and the Hong Kong University of Science and Technology. The latter is the most recently founded university, incorporated by statute in April 1988 and opened in October 1991. There are two polytechnics: Hong Kong Polytechnic and City Polytechnic of Hong Kong. The latter is a new institution founded in January 1984. The government also fully funds the Hong Kong Baptist College, founded in 1956, and partially supports two post-secondary colleges: Hong Kong Shue Yan College and Lingnan College. Strong government support for post-secondary school education is a reaction to the brain drain which began in 1984 when many Hong Kong professionals emigrated to Canada, Australia, the United States and other countries. By providing more opportunities for Hong Kong youngsters to have high quality university educations, it is hoped that they will make up for those who have left. This change in post-secondary education policy makes higher education more accessible to the general public, which is in significant contrast to the past when university education was considered to be only for the elitist few. In 1990 government expenditure on education constituted almost 15 per cent of the total public sector expenditure. The high level of education enjoyed by the population is indicated by the fact that the percentage with primary or above education increased from 81.5 in 1976 to 86.2 in 1986 while the percentage with technical or tertiary education increased from 5.4 in 1976 to 9.4 in 1986.

Only a very brief mention about transportation needs to be made here because a more detailed discussion of this essential service has already been carried out in Chapter 4. The Transport Department has provided an efficient multi-modal public transport system through the bus, MTR, mini-bus, tram and ferry services to supply people's needs in moving from place to place and attending to their daily business. However, traffic congestion on land is not uncommon because the high-density land use pattern of the urban areas tends to generate bottlenecks at road junctions. The cost of public transport which has always been kept low by the government is now on the rise due to an inflationary climate brought about by the government's recently announced massive programme to re-locate the airport to Chek Lap Kok on Lantau Island. Transport is an important item of household expenditure and has to be watched with care. One major characteristic of Hong Kong is the large number of pedestrians, particularly in the major office areas, and transport planners have made use of elevated bridges and walkways to keep them separate from road traffic (Plate 6.1). This is an ingenious solution to ensure the freer and quicker circulation of people and vehicles in a physically restricted environment.

Plate 6.1 An elevated walkway in the Central District of Hong Kong. This links up the whole Central District from east to west

Social welfare

Hong Kong is a modern city with a booming economy and everybody in Hong Kong has a lot of opportunities to make money. But because of differences in occupation, not everybody is doing equally well. Income inequality is always present and has already been discussed above. Another measure of the quality of life must be the availability of social welfare to the less fortunate section of the population.

Hong Kong's *laissez-faire* government did not accept social welfare as its responsibility until 1947 when the Social Welfare Office was set up. This became the Social Welfare Department in 1958. The slow development of social welfare was partly caused by the fact that before the Second World War, the bulk of the population was transient in nature. They were drawn into Hong Kong from China by the prospect of employment and as soon as they made enough money, they would return to China. They did not settle in Hong Kong. The Hong Kong government therefore saw no need to spend money on the welfare of temporary residents. The government was also worried that doing so would attract more people from China. There were also no pressure groups asking the government for change (Hodge, 1981). Any social welfare services delivered at that time took the form of charity carried out by private voluntary agencies. However, the government's attitude changed when the Director of Social Welfare stated in 1964 that 'the public provision of social services was not a gratuitous act of charity, but a concomitant privilege of citizenship'. In 1972 a government White Paper defined social welfare as 'any social services provided by the community as a whole for the benefit of particular members or sections of the community, or for the benefit of the community generally' (Social Welfare Department, 1972). As Hong Kong became financially more stable and its residents more and more permanent in nature the government's commitment to social welfare increased; a fact borne out by the increase in government expenditure in this area. In 1977 the White Paper on Rehabilitation announced a ten-year development programme to provide more and better services to the disabled. As Hong Kong has become more prosperous, the nature of social welfare has shifted from massive emergency relief to individual quality care (Kwan, 1989). Economic development always precedes social development. Despite the government's involvement, most of the welfare work in Hong Kong is done by voluntary agencies with both overseas and local financial supports. These agencies include religious organizations and the residential neighbourhood (known as kaifong in Cantonese) groups. The social services provided by the government and the voluntary agencies include social security, family welfare services, community services, rehabilitation services, services for offenders, services for young people and services for the elderly (Kwan, 1989). While there is no doubt that the government is determined to improve the general standard of living for everybody, there is still a big gap between the demand for services and their provision. In addition, the government's willingness to promote further social welfare services is still not strong enough. This goes back to the availability of resources. The massive airport relocation project will drain away financial resources which otherwise would have gone to social welfare. The need arises for the community and local leaders to negotiate with the government to secure better social services for the urban poor in the future.

Environmental protection

Intense industrial activities require abundant use of fossil fuel-based energy and generate a lot of smoke and waste which pollutes the air, land and water of Hong Kong. The high population concentration has also given rise to problems of solid waste disposal. Mixing small-scale industrial units with residential structures has also posed severe health hazards to the population. Hong Kong's *laissez-faire* government has its mind set on economic growth and so has been and still is reluctant to legislate for clean air or clean water or pass any measures to protect the environment because this will increase the cost of industrial production. It was only in the 1970s that the government began to realize the importance of environmental protection. The public's awareness of environmental issues has also increased. In 1974 the Environmental Protection Advisory Committee (EPCOM) was established to advise the government on various environmental matters. In 1977 the Environmental Protection Agency (EPA) was set up by the government under the Secretary for Health and Welfare to advise on measures to combat pollution and to set environmental quality standards. EPA was upgraded to become the Environmental Protection Department (EPD) in 1986 with the intention of centralizing the pollution control units into one administrative department (Keen and Lo, 1989). But it remains doubtful whether other government departments will co-operate fully with the EPD.

The government did make some laws to control environmental pollution. These were the 1980 Water Pollution Control and Waste Disposal Odinances, and the 1983 Air Pollution Control Ordinance. However, these ordinances have been criticised not only for the excessive length of time taken for them to be drafted and enacted, but also the confusion of their contents which makes enactment difficult (Lam, 1986; Keen and Lo, 1989). These ordinances reflected the seriousness of pollution problems in Hong Kong.

Basically, Hong Kong shows similar pollution problems to those faced by other cities in economically advanced countries. First and foremost is the disposal of about 8,100 tonnes of solid waste per day. This is expected to increase to 16,000 tonnes per day by 2001. This waste comes from both industry and residential usage. More than half of this sold waste is disposed of by landfill, about 25 per cent is incinerated and 4 per cent treated by composting. But landfill sites, which are located very close to the coast and to the urban areas, are expected to be full by the early 1990s, and new sites will have to be found very soon. Using incinerators produces toxic gases and so contributes to air pollution although some have now been equipped with electrostatic precipitators to remove air pollutants (Keen and Lo, 1989). According to a 1971 survey (Lam, 1986), sources of air pollution in Hong Kong also include power-stations and gasworks (44 per cent), automobiles (31 per cent) and manufacturing industries (9 per cent). The major pollutants are sulphur dioxide (44 per cent), carbon monoxide (30 per cent), and nitrogen dioxide (16 per cent). Although the annual average sulphur dioxide content in the air from most power-stations in Hong Kong ranged from 15–50 ug/cubic metres during 1984/6 (Table 6.2), which is within the acceptable range, a daily sulphur dioxide level of 350 ug/cubic

Quality of life

Table 6.2 Air quality data (annual average) from six monitoring sites around Hong Kong during 1984–86

Pollutant	Station	1984/85	1985/86
		ug/cubic metre	
SO$_2$	Kwun Tong	59	53
	Shum Shui Po	25	22
	Tsim Sha Tsui	29	43
	Central/Western	14	16
	Junk Bay	14	30
NO$_2$	Kwun Tong	65	152
	Central/Western	40	68
	Junk Bay	33	46
pH	Kwun Tong		4.92*
	Central/Western		5.16*
	Junk Bay		4.78*

* Values expressed in pH unit: the lower the value, the more acidic

Source: Yang and Wong, 1989

metres has been recorded on several occasions, suggesting that sulphur dioxide pollution is a potential threat to the environment. The low pH value of the rain also indicates the occurrence of acid rain which is of course related to the amount of sulphur dioxide and nitrogen dioxide in the atmosphere. With a traffic density ranging from 500 to 700 cars per km a day, automobile exhaust emission produces a large amount of lead. The use of low lead gasoline was only introduced in 1985, and in 1991 unleaded gasoline fuel began to be sold at the gas stations. But drivers are still reluctant to use this fuel. The Police Department is now enforcing checks on vehicles with excessive smoke emission.

The most serious pollution problem in Hong Kong is water pollution, which involves both the sea and the rivers. Because of the concentration of population around the harbour area, Victoria Harbour receives about 80 per cent of the total sewage effluent, which is responsible for most of the water pollution problems in Hong Kong (Yang and Wong, 1989). Although the current flow of Victoria Harbour is quite fast, about 0.5– 0.85 metres per second, the typhoon shelters built inside the harbour have made the water within them immobile. The inhabitants of these shelters live on boats and dispose of their waste directly into the water. In addition, there are sewage outlets inside these shelters. The resulting stink has pinpointed these shelters as the worst water pollution spots in the harbour. In the sea water near Shum Shui Po and Yau Mai Tei in West Kowloon coast, where the level of dissolved oxygen is less than 40 per cent saturation and the biochemical oxygen demand is the highest within the harbour, the water is practically lifeless. The water inside the harbour is also contaminated with toxic chemicals. At the bottom of the harbour near the same two sites, high levels of heavy metals such as lead, arsenic, copper, nickel, chromium, organic carbons and chlorinated hydrocarbons are found in the sediments. These are deposited from the industrial waste water pouring into the harbour. The coastal waters around Hong Kong also contain a lot of bacteria because Hong Kong has been using the strong tidal flushing effect of the harbour to get its sewage discharge out to the open sea. The continuing reclamation along the coast has decreased the size of the harbour, and hence the strength of its flushing effect. About 22 per cent of all the beaches around Hong Kong have high E-coli counts, which makes the water unsuitable for swimming. Again the Sham Shui Po site has the highest E-coli number, and is well over the standard set by the Environmental Protection Department. As Hong Kong constructed more new towns in the New Territories, coastal water pollution also increased in these areas. In fact, even the river water in the New Territories is badly polluted by agricultural waste including pig and poultry manure. About 2,000 tonnes of raw animal waste are discharged into the streams and inshore waters every day. Hong Kong's neighbours – Shenzhen and its adjoining territories over whom Hong Kong has no control whatsoever – have also contributed to the water pollution problem. Agricultural, domestic and industrial waste has also found its way into the coastal waters and the area near Deep Bay in North West New Territories is severely contaminated with infectious agents as a result. There used to be extensive oyster culture beds in the Deep Bay area around Lau Fau Shan, but the pollution contaminated the oysters with bacteria and viruses. The economic suffering of the oyster farmers has been very severe.

Hong Kong's economic achievement was marred by serious environmental pollution which the government chose to ignore until recently. This problem has already adversely affected the quality of life of the population. On the other hand, the people of Hong Kong have become more concerned about their environment. As a result, the future growth of Hong Kong, such as the relocation of the airport and coastal reclamation in conjunction with the Metroplan, will be constrained by the capacity of the public sewage treatment and disposal facilities. Currently, there are five primary and four secondary sewage treatment plants in operation in Hong Kong (Figure 6.3). The primary treatment removes 30–40 per cent of the total biochemical oxygen demand from the waste water, followed by a secondary treatment which removes a further up to 85–93 per cent before the waste water is discharged into the sea.

Fortunately for Hong Kong's residents, the New Territories have many scenic spots in the mountains and on the coasts. Since 1976, the government Forestry Department has conserved much of the land under the category of 'Country Parks' for recreational purposes. No development of any kind is allowed without government permission inside a 'Country

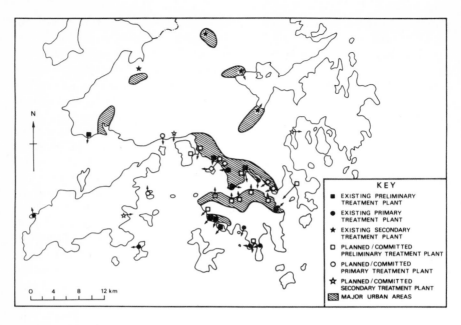

Figure 6.3 Public sewage treatment and disposal facilities in Hong Kong

Source: Yang and Wong, 1989

Park'. These parks should be valuable to the Hong Kong people for occasional relief from a life of stress in the concrete jungle (Lam, 1986).

Finally, Hong Kong is probably the noisiest place in the world because of ever-present construction work, traffic (particularly the double-decker buses) and the fact that the airport is located inside the main urban area. The government did try to control noise pollution with a number of ordinances enacted on December 31 1986. All these ordinances were subsequently consolidated into one noise control ordinance in 1988. The ordinance restricts the hours when excessive noise is allowed from the general neighbourhood, construction sites and industrial and commercial premises. Traffic and airport noise is governed by another set of ordinances or regulations. The noise threshold for workers is usually agreed to be 90 dBA (decibels) based on an 8-hour daily exposure with a 16-hour recovery period. Areas with extensive commercial and industrial activities are the most noisy so that Central District, Tsim Sha Tsui, and Kwun Tong have spots which exceed 70 dBA, caused mainly by large buses and trucks. Similarly, the area around Kai Tak Airport, particularly the Kowloon City area, is seriously affected by aircraft noise. Research by Ko *et al* (1976) indicated that Hong Kong residents suffered from a higher noise burden factor than those in New York, Tokyo and London.

Citizens' perceptions of their quality of life

How good or bad is the quality of life in Hong Kong? This is a totally subjective question and is best answered by the residents of Hong Kong. Some limited research was carried out on this aspect in the Chinese University of Hong Kong. The well-being of a sample of 539 Hong Kong residents living in Kwun Tong was measured in 1986 (Lau and Wan, 1987). The majority of residents interviewed had a household income of less than HK$7,000 (US$897.4) per month, all exhibited positive feelings about their lives and were optimistic about their future. They were found to be even more satisfied with their families and friends than they were with their material well-being. However, it was found that some of the interviewees felt some degree of helplessness towards political changes in Hong Kong and lacked confidence in themselves. On the whole, younger, better educated and higher paid interviewees were more satisfied with their lives than those who were older, less well educated, and lower paid in their jobs. It was also interesting to note their mixture of Chinese and Western cultural values towards marriage, sex, birth, divorce and abortion, and their attitude towards Chinese and Western medicines. Chinese traditional values prevailed in such matters as raising children, the role of women and filial duties.

A second research project was conducted by Chow (1988) through the University of Hong Kong on the quality of life of Tuen Mun new town residents to evaluating how well the new town has met their needs. In 1987, 932 households consisting of 3,831 persons were interviewed. It was noted that, when compared with the entire population of Hong Kong (as estimated by the 1986 By-Census), these households had a much higher percentage of children under 15 years old and a lower percentage of elderly aged 60 and over. Because of the high percentage of public housing units in the new towns, there were more nuclear-type families in the sample. By asking questions on the relationship between husband and wife, the relationship with neighbours, the sense of belonging to the community, the ability to adjust to the new environment, the sense of security in living in the new town and the degree of satisfaction with present living conditions, the author has been able to construct a quality of life scale based on the responses of the interviewees which seemed to show a positive improvement in their quality of life. However, this study also revealed some inadequacies in the new town particularly in the provision of medical, educational, transport, community and social welfare services. The new town environment, its remoteness from the main urban area, seemed to have adversely affected the relationships between members of households. They also felt that the new town was far from self-contained and balanced.

The two pieces of research cited above, although limited in spatial extent, did focus on the perception of the lower-middle class and lower-class population on their quality of life in Hong Kong. They bore out the fact that, despite some deficiencies in the environment, people still thought that Hong Kong was a good place for them to live. The high degree of adaptability of the people and the more positive outlook on life of the younger and better educated population have given Hong Kong a stable foundation for economic development.

Conclusions

The quality of life of the Hong Kong population can generally be described as good. A number of government programmes have helped to achieve that goal, including housing and urban services. The government's public housing programme in conjunction with the new towns programme has helped to ameliorate the living environment of the lower income and lower-middle income groups, despite the substandard provision of facilities in the early resettlement estates. In the urban area, the provision of basic urban services in terms of transportation, education, sanitary, water and health services are excellent. Hong Kong has always maintained a very efficient infrastructure to support commerce and industry. Residents have benefited from the excellent outside contacts made possible through all kinds of telecommunications necessitated by Hong Kong's role as an international financial centre. People in Hong Kong have also enjoyed better freedom of speech and the right to know than many people in East Asia, particularly in comparison with China. On the other hand, the Hong Kong government has been negligent over environmental protection. Although laws controlling land, air, water and noise pollution have been passed in recent years, they are not as thorough as one would like. The government took action only when pressured by environmental advocates. Obviously, environmental protection is costly in the short run, particularly to industrialists, but, in the long run this makes economic sense. This issue must be addressed seriously if the quality of life of the population of Hong Kong is to be sustained or even improved.

Although Hong Kong residents are enjoying a higher GNP per capita, the income distribution has still been unequal over recent years. Speculative activities in the property market are rampant. This, together with the fact that Hong Kong has to rely on foreign imports for most of its needs, has fuelled high inflation. Importing contract manual labour from foreign countries is now being advocated by the government as a means to combat labour shortage and inflation, but the local labour force sees this as government action to depress the wages of the labour for the protection of the industrialists. Common citizens in Hong Kong do have a lot of complaints, and life in this bustling city is stressful with a noisy environment and restricted living space. Surprisingly, many people have accepted all these as necessary evils. They value the freedom, albeit limited, given to them by the British administration, which makes it possible for them to excel or get rich if they work hard. Hong Kong people are amazingly adaptable and show a high degree of flexibility. Hong Kong is an excellent example to justify the statement quoted at the beginning of this chapter that, 'The quality of urban life is less influenced by the factors of scale and density than by the values and organization of the society itself.' This will form the subject of discussion in the next chapter.

References

Bristow, R. 1987. *Land-use planning in Hong Kong: history, policies and procedures.* Hong Kong: Oxford University Press.

Chau, L.C. 1984. Economic growth and income distribution of Hong Kong since early 1950's. Hong Kong: Department of Economics, University of Hong Kong.

Chow, N.W.S. 1988. The quality of life of Tuen Mun inhabitants. Hong Kong: Centre of Urban Studies and Urban Planning, University of Hong Kong.

Director of Social Welfare, 1964. *Annual Departmental Report, 1963-4.* Hong Kong: Government Printer.

Fung, T. 1983. Public housing management in Hong Kong's new towns. In *A place to live: more effective low-cost housing in Asia*, Y.M. Yeung (ed). Ottawa: IDRC, Canada, pp. 199-213.

Hodge, P. 1981. The politics of welfare. In *The common welfare: Hong Kong's social services*, J.F. Jones (ed). Hong Kong: The Chinese University Press, pp. 17-20.

Kwan, A.Y.H. 1989. Social welfare and services in Hong Kong. In *Hong Kong Society*, A.Y.H. Kwan (ed). Hong Kong: Writers' and Publishers' Cooperative, pp. 131-83.

Liu, B.C. 1976. *Quality of life indicators in US metropolitan areas: a statistical analysis.* New York: Praeger, p. 12.

Keen, R.C. and Lo, C.K. 1989. Pollution control in Hong Kong: progress so far. In *Hong Kong society*, A.Y.H. Kwan (ed). Hong Kong: Writer's and Publishers' Cooperative, pp. 235-74.

Ko, N.W.M., Kwan, A.S.H., and Chan, W.T. 1976. Noise pollution in Hong Kong. *Hong Kong Engineer.* 4 (5): 27-34.

Lam, K.C. 1986. Environmental problems and management. In *A geography of Hong Kong*, T.N. Chiu and C.L. So (eds). Hong Kong: Oxford University Press, pp. 350-93.

Maunder, W.F. 1968. *Hong Kong urban rents and housing.* Hong Kong: Hong Kong University Press, p. 76.

Lau, S.K. and Wan, P.S. 1987. *Preliminary report on the social indicators research in Hong Kong* (in Chinese). Hong Kong: Hong Kong Research Centre, Chinese University of Hong Kong.

Pryor, E.G. 1983. Housing needs and related urban-development programs and process in Hong Kong. In *A place to live: more effective low-cost housing in Asia*, Y.M. Yeung (ed). Ottawa: IDRC, Canada, pp. 185-98.

Rondinelli, D.A. and Cheema, G.S. 1988. *Urban services in developing countries: public and private roles in urban development.* London: Macmillan Press.

Schmandt, H.J. and Bloomberg, Jr., W. 1969. *The quality of urban life.* Beverly Hills, California: Sage Publications, Inc.

Social Welfare Department 1972. *Social welfare in Hong Kong: the way ahead.* Hong Kong: Government Printer.

Strategic Planning Unit 1990. *Metroplan: the foundations and framework.* Hong Kong: Government Printer.

Tregear, T.R. and Berry, L. 1959. *The development of Hong Kong as told in maps.* Hong Kong: Hong Kong University Press.

Will, B.F. 1978. Housing design and construction methods. In *Housing in Hong Kong,* L.S.K. Wong (ed). Hong Kong: Heinemann Educational Books (Asia) Ltd., pp. 91–127.

Wong, L.S.K. 1978. An overview of housing provision and housing needs in Hong Kong. In *Housing in Hong Kong,* L.S.K. Wong (ed). Hong Kong: Heinemann Educational Books (Asia) Ltd., pp. 23–54.

Wong, L.S.K. 1986. Urban housing and the residential environment. In *A geography of Hong Kong,* T.N. Chiu and C.L. So (eds). Hong Kong: Oxford University Press, pp. 279–304.

Yang, M.S. and Wong, M.H. 1989. Air, water and land pollution in Hong Kong. In *Hong Kong society,* A.Y.H. Kwan (ed). Hong Kong: Writers' and Publishers' Cooperative, pp. 275–311.

Yeh, S. 1975. Housing conditions and housing needs in Singapore. In *Public housing in Singapore,* S. Yeh (ed). Singapore: Housing and Development Board.

7
Ecological structure and urban form

Like it or not, Hong Kong is one of the most interesting cities mankind has ever created, and it deserves some stateliness at the heart: for as the *feng shui* geomancers have always said,nothing is more auspicious for the well-being of a people than the shape of the city they inhabit.

Mo.ris, Jan: *Building Hong Kong*, FormAsia, Hong Kong, 1989

Hong Kong exhibits typical characteristics of a Third World colonial city, as described by McGee (1967) in his book on South-east Asian cities. The more salient characteristics include the highly mixed land use and multi-functional use of buildings. There is a modern 'firm-type' economy coexisting with a traditional 'bazaar-type' economy. In other words, the dualism of formal and informal sectors identified by Milton Santos as the upper and lower circuits of the urban economy (1979). There is a port zone which forms the urban centre and where population density tends to be high. The spatial growth of the city is largely centrifugal, with the outer areas of the city growing at faster rates than the inner core. At the urban periphery there are illegal squatter settlements founded by the impoverished rural in-migrants. All these characteristics remain true of Hong Kong even now. However, today more than ever before, Hong Kong is at the threshold of change as the government embarks on the development of a new airport and the subsequent implementation of the Metroplan in the old urban area. The city form of Hong Kong is a product of its people, and its evolution reflects changes in the social process over time.

Changes in Ecological Structure, 1966–81

The author has traced the evolution of the ecological structure of Hong Kong since 1966 using population census statistics and the methods of factor analysis and cluster analysis (Lo, 1972, 1975, 1986). The variables employed in the analyses have included population densities, age–sex structure, employment, housing and internal population movements. In 1966, the author was able to identify seven socio-economic types at the census district level. These were:

1. Mixed high-class commercial and residential type covering the Central District, Tsim Sha Tsui, and the Mid-levels-Tai Hang district on Hong Kong Island.
2. The overcrowded old middle-class commercial area with residential uses comprising the coastal area districts of Sheung Wan, West District, and Wan Chai on Hong Kong Island in close proximity to the first type.
3. A high-class residential area mixed with squatters which covered the unique Kowloon Tong area in Kowloon.
4. A new industrial and residential area with rural characteristics consisting of six New Territories districts and three peripheral urban districts including the new town of Tsuen Wan.
5. A new middle-class residential area with commercial activities, comprising all those districts with predominantly private housing in the eastern coastal belt of Hong Kong Island and the central part of the Kowloon peninsula.
6. The overcrowded old industrial area with residential and intense commercial activities found only along the eastern and western coastal belts of Kowloon Peninsula.
7. The old rural agricultural area in north-western New Territories.

The generalized spatial model of the ecological areas derived is shown in Figure 7.1. It reveals a very interesting mixture of sectoral and concentric zonal patterns. Kowloon was typically sectoral while Hong Kong was predominantly concentric zonal. While part of the cause may be the nature of the landscape (Kowloon peninsula having a less rugged terrain), the major shaping force for this pattern is the orientation of the road network. The sectoral pattern is generally regarded as representing variations in economic status while the concentric zonal pattern is related to family structure or life-cycle stages (Berry, 1965). It is worthy of note that no multiple nuclei pattern had yet emerged at that time. The Central Business District (CBD) was very prominent and straddled both sides of the harbour: the southern tip of Tsim Sha Tsui and the northern coast of Hong Kong Island. This CBD was really the port zone where warehouses and storages were found. However, in 1966, the CBD on Hong Kong Island was not spatially contiguous but interrupted at Wan

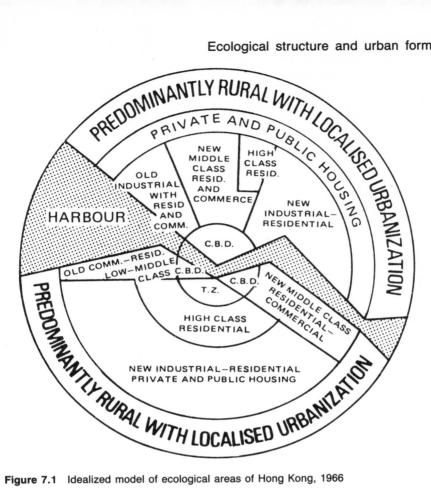

Figure 7.1 Idealized model of ecological areas of Hong Kong, 1966

Source: Lo, 1972

Chai because of the British army barracks there. In the rural area of the New Territories, some degree of urbanization had already occurred but was confined to the market towns and public housing sprang up in the suburbs surrounding the main urban area. This model reveals characteristics typical of a Third World city.

In 1971, the ecological model of Hong Kong underwent some modifications (Lo, 1975). The most important of which was the emergence of the public housing belt occupying the rural–urban fringe. The high-class residential area on Hong Kong Island expanded southwards, and public housing estates were also established in the southern and eastern parts (Figure 7.2). The city had expanded in size. The CBD showed little change except that its Tsim Sha Tsui component expanded eastwards. The sector pattern was still predominant and was also mixed with the concentric pattern. Because of the development of new towns, new

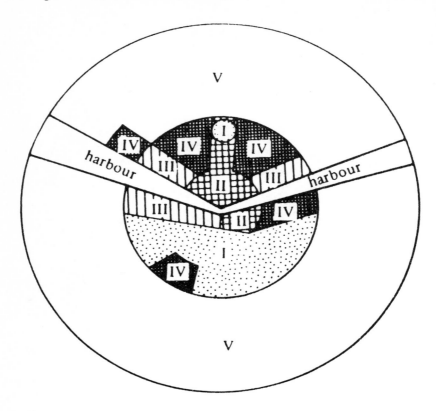

Figure 7.2 Idealized model of ecological areas of Hong Kong, 1971. Key: I = exclusive high-class residential area; II = middle-class commercial-residential mixed area; III = old established blue/white-collar workers belt; IV = government public housing belt in 1971; V = rural area

Source: Lo, 1975

centres were established in the New Territories, and the multiple nuclei pattern also emerged.

By 1981, the analysis revealed some drastic changes in the ecological model of the whole of Hong Kong and a much more complex pattern emerged (Lo, 1986). Eight factors were identified in the factor analysis, which were, in descending order; high socio-economic status, low socio-economic status, the elderly, public housing households, young female factory workers, farmers and fishermen, young children and large households with extended or combined nuclear families. These factors revealed bi-polar contrasts among the population in Hong Kong. Because of the difference in spatial scale between the main urban area and the New Territories, they were treated separately in the analysis. For Hong

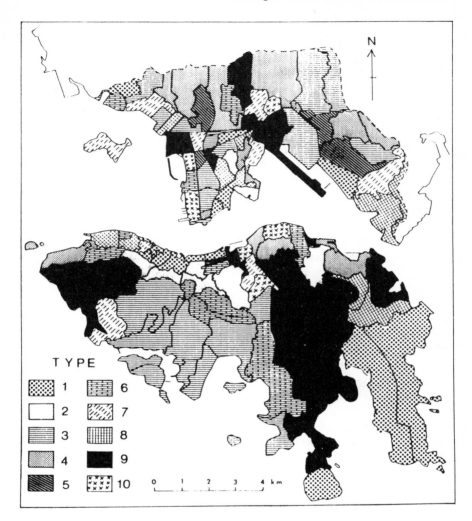

Figure 7.3 Ecological types of Hong Kong and Kowloon, 1986

Source: Lo, 1986

Kong and Kowloon, the factor analysis revealed eight factors which were also bi-polar contrast. These were; blue-collar workers versus high-income professionals, recent Chinese immigrants versus local residents, the elderly versus the young, self-employed farmers or fishermen, private housing tenants and subtenants, white-collar and service workers, South-east Asians and young children. Two ethnicity factors, namely recent Chinese immigrants and South-east Asians, appeared for the first time. Based on these factors, ten ecological types were identified for the main urban area of Hong Kong and Kowloon. (Figure 7.3). Type one was the Central Business District (CBD) similar to that identified in previous models. The main difference was the spread of the CBD to the eastern part of the Kowloon peninsula (on reclaimed land) and the coastal strip at Wan Chai on Hong Kong Island. The gap along the northern coast of Hong Kong Island between Central District and Wan Chai was closed, and became a part of the Central Business District after the removal of the army barracks. Today, this new business district, which is located in the current Admiralty underground station, is the site of three fancy hotels (Merriot, Conrad, and Shangri-la Island), a huge shopping mall, a multi-storey central government office complex and a new park (Hong Kong Park). Type two was the high class and upper-middle class residential district, consisting of the Mid-levels and Tai Hang, which was the same as the one identified in the 1966 model. Type three was a mixed area of high- and low-density housing for the upper-middle and middle-class population. Type four was high-density housing for the lower-middle and lower-class population mostly associated with public housing. Type five was mostly high-density private housing for the lower middle-class population while type 6 exhibited low-density high class residential characteristics in such famous spots as Repulse Bay and Kowloon. Type seven indicated middle-class high-density housing whereas type eight was high-density housing in an industrial setting. Type nine indicated high-density housing on hilly lands or reclaimed coastal areas for a wide range of social classes. Finally, type ten was extremely mixed in land use and socio-economic characteristics. The lack of uniformity in the overall spatial pattern suggests the high degree of juxtaposition of different socio-economic groups and the multifunctional nature of the buildings, especially in the lower- to middle-class residential districts.

By 1981 the New Territories had been considerably transformed by the spread of new towns. These attracted a large number of the urban population from the Kowloon area, particularly New Kowloon. This is a good illustration of the distance decay principle. New Kowloon, being geographically much closer in location to the New Territories than Kowloon and Hong Kong Island, felt more pull from the new towns. Also New Kowloon was characterised by a high percentage of industrial use and hence a concentration of blue-collar workers who would be attracted by the relocation or establishment of industries in the new towns. A separate factor analysis revealed that for the New Territories alone, ten significant factors, in descending order of importance, could be identified: elderly population, blue-collar workers, low-rent public housing residents, private housing main and sub-tenants, nuclear families, large household size, high-income professionals, highly educated group, farmers and fishermen and the armed forces. These ten factors

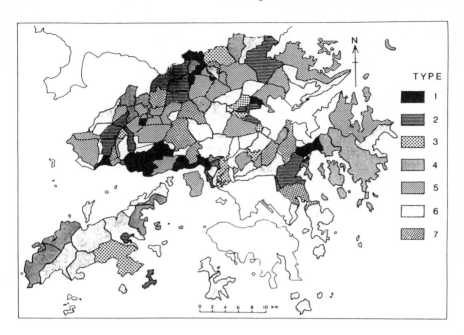

Figure 7.4 Ecological types of the New Territories, 1986
Source: Lo, 1986

describe the diverse characteristics of the New Territories which were the result of urban in-migration. The location of the Chinese University of Hong Kong in Sha Tin, New Territories, was responsible for the highly educated group and high-income professional factors. The elderly population factor suggested emigration of young people from the villages in the remote corners of the New Territories to the urban area in Hong Kong or overseas. Because of the new towns, many people worked in the factories which accounts for the blue-collar workers factor. On the other hand, farmers, fishermen and military personnel were also found. People living in the New Territories tended to have larger household sizes, and because of the public housing programme they were basically nuclear families. For the private housing sector, the housing conditions were not good because of the need for flat-sharing, hence the tenants and subtenants factor. These factors were very different from those identified for Kowloon and Hong Kong. These ten factors combined to produce seven ecological types for the New Territories. For each new town, a core (type one) was developed in the market town proper adjoining an industrial area (type two), a residential area (type three) or traditional villages (types four and five). These towns were separated from each other by mountains interspersed with depopulated villages and mining

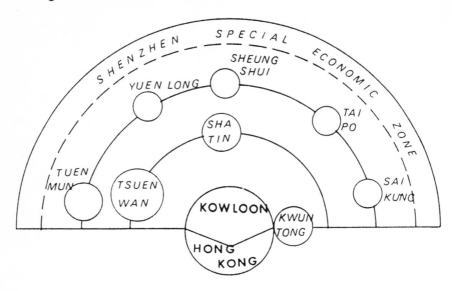

Figure 7.5 Multi-centred relationship between the main urban area of Hong Kong and the new towns

Source: Lo, 1986

settlements (types six and seven). The overall spatial pattern which resulted can be described as 'multi-centred' (Figure 7.4). The ecological structure which emerged in the New Territories was much more regular than that of the urban area of Hong Kong and Kowloon. When viewed as a whole at the correct spatial scale, Hong Kong and Kowloon constituted the largest and the most important centre which can be labelled as the 'core' (Figure 7.5). The observed pattern seemed to correspond to Stage three of Friedmann's core-periphery model when secondary cores were formed during the period of industrial maturity, thereby reducing the periphery to smaller intermetropolitan peripheries (Friedmann, 1966). The model in Figure 7.5 also reveals that two tiers of secondary cores probably developed in the New Territories. The first tier was comprised of the older and larger inner cores, namely Kwun Tong, Tsuen Wan and Sha Tin, while the second tier was made up of the newer but smaller outer cores, namely Tuen Mun, Yuen Long, Sheung Shui, Tai Po, and Sai Kung. The outermost belt is the Shenzhen Special Economic Zone located immediately across the border in China. The intense urban development of Shenzhen Special Economic Zone have prepared it to become a potential main core located in the opposite direction to the main Hong Kong-Kowloon core and capable of attracting population from the New Territories (according to the distance decay principle).

156

Although no similar factor analysis has been carried out using data from the 1986 By-Census, the Social Atlas produced by the government revealed the continuation of the decentralization and multi-centred development trends (Census and Statistics Department, 1987). The population loss from New Kowloon and Kowloon as well as the northern coastal area of Hong Kong Island continued. The New Territories gained population, most spectacularly in the market towns, namely Tuen Mun, Sha Tin, Tai Po, Sheung Shui, Fanling and Tin Shui Wai (right at the border of Shun Chun River in north-western New Territories), where the new towns are located. It is interesting to note that the areas immediately adjoining the new towns lost population, presumably to the new towns. The Atlas also revealed that there were more children aged 0–5 living in the north-western and north-eastern parts of the New Territories than in the urban areas of Hong Kong and Kowloon. Similarly, elderly population (aged 65 and over) was found predominantly in the remote and more rural parts of the New Territories where new towns had not been founded. This seems to imply that as one moves away from the main urban area, one finds larger families. On the other hand, there was a sharp contrast in the level of education attainment and income between the urban areas of Hong Kong, Kowloon and the New Territories. In both cases, the New Territories lagged far behind. This illustrates that even though the traditionally rural New Territories have been undergoing urbanization, the regional disparities between the main urban area and the New Territories persist. It is interesting to note from the point of view of ecological structure that the *really* high-class residential areas are still found in the main urban area: the Peak, the Mid-levels, Repulse Bay area, Kowloon Tong and other old established areas not far away from this main economic core.

Urban form and architecture

The city-state of Hong Kong is built on reclaimed land on the coast or terraced sites on mountains. On Hong Kong Island, the major urban area is confined to the northern coastal strip stretching from east to west, and buildings crawl up the hillsides. In Kowloon there is more flat land, and the built-up area covers the whole peninsula from the southern tip to the foothills of Kowloon Hills. In the New Territories, where new towns are located in isolated spots, a dispersed form of urbanization has emerged. In all cases, building density is extremely high in order to maximize the use of a piece of land and to recover the high cost of site formation. Multi-storey buildings for both commercial and residential uses are the norm. Despite the recent decentralization trend, the urban form of Hong Kong still shows the dominance of the port zone around the harbour.

Plate 7.1 Hong Kong Island waterfront on a misty day as viewed from the Star Ferry

The port zone, which is the area immediately located along the water-front, forms an important part of the Central Business District (CBD). This is the area first seen by a tourist when he or she crosses the harbour, particularly from Kowloon to Hong Kong, on the Star Ferry (Plate 7.1). In the past, the port zone was marked by wharves and storages and the southern tip of Kowloon peninsula, as well as the neighbouring east and west coasts, formed a typical wharf and warehouse zone. Today, these areas are occupied by large commercial buildings and modern hotels. Only the Ocean Terminal (now called the Ocean Centre) in Tsim Sha Tsui, which is also a shopping mall, retains some of the characteristics of the old port zone (Plate 7.2). The port zone has now been totally transformed into a commercial and cultural centre and forms the core of the Central Business District (CBD). On Tsim Sha Tsui waterfront, the peach-coloured spherical dome-shaped Space Museum is an imposing landmark amidst the hotels. The eastern coast of Tsim Sha Tsui has been reclaimed to form a special office, shop-ping, restaurant and entertainment complex, including the educational Science Centre (with an exhibition hall for commercial use) and Hong Kong Polytechnic. This is the famous Tsim Sha Tsui East which attracts a lot of tourists and local residents. On the western side of the Kowloon peninsula coast, immediately adjacent to Tsim Sha Tsui, the former

Plate 7.2   The ocean terminal in Tsim Sha Tsui, Kowloon

wharf zone of Kowloon Docks has been transformed into an office and hotel complex.

On Hong Kong Island, the Central Business District (CBD) spreads inland right from the waterfront. The CBD now consists of two parts: the old part, known as the Central District, extending from the Central Market and the new Heng Seng Bank Building in the west to the Hong Kong and Shanghai Bank Building in the east; and a new part focused around the Admiralty MTR station just before reaching Wan Chai District to the east. There are some excellently designed and constructed buildings in the eastern part of the CBD. The Jardine House (formerly the Connaught Centre) built by Palmer and Turner in 1973 for Jardine Matheson and Company for HK$258 million, a colossal sum at the time, is a 52-storey building with a lot of 'holes' (Plate 7.3). The Hong Kong and Shanghai Bank Building at One Queen's Road on Statue Square, designed by the Englishman Norman Foster, is a high-rise building conceptualized as a series of towers supporting bridges, from which floors of diminishing sizes are reached by external lifts and criss-crossing escalators (Plate 7.4). The orientation of the building and the angle of inclination of the escalators have been determined with reference to Chinese 'feng shui' or geomancy. Literally meaning 'wind and water', 'feng shui' can be regarded as a pseudo-science practised by the Chinese

159

Plate 7.3 Jardine House (formerly Connaught Centre) on Hong Kong Island waterfront showing its characteristic 'holes'

Plate 7.4 The new Hong Kong and Shanghai Bank headquarters building designed by Norman Foster

Plate 7.5 The 70-storey new Bank of China headquarters building designed by I.M. Pei

in locating a house or a whole settlement. In essence, the prosperity of a structure can be affected if the balance between its orientation direction and the nature of the terrain is disturbed. The geomancer uses a Chinese compass to determine the proper orientation of the structure for such a cosmic balance to be achieved. Even the arrangement of furniture items inside the house could affect the lives of the occupants. The belief in 'feng shui' is deeply embedded in the culture of Hong Kong.

The Bank of China to counterbalance the dominance of the Hong Kong and Shanghai Bank building and following the spirit of 'feng shui', engaged the famous Chinese–American architect, I.M. Pei, to build a 70-storey headquarters building in a new site near its old headquarters in the eastern part of the CBD. The Bank of China building is believed to be the tallest in Hong Kong and consists of four triangular glass shafts rising to varying heights. These symbolize bamboo nodes which, according to a Chinese saying: 'rising higher and higher like a bamboo one node at a time', signify continuous growth and prosperity (Plate 7.5). Bamboo is one of the fastest growing typical Chinese plants. It was widely believed by the people of Hong Kong that the result of erecting this building which rises above Government House where the Governor of Hong Kong lives, is that the good 'feng shui' of Government House will have been affected. To deflect this bad force, 'weeping willows' were planted on the lawns of Government House.

In the new CBD located around the Admiralty MTR station in the east, a number of new buildings have sprung up. These include Pacific Place which houses the Merriot Hotel and a large shopping mall. There are also the Conrad Hotel, the Island Shangri-la Hotel, the massive Central Government Office Buildings and the new Supreme Court building which overlooks a man-made Hong Kong garden built on the ground of the former army barracks. A famous building in the same area is the Bond Centre, designed by American architect Paul Rudolph, which consists of two hexagonal multi-faceted glass towers (Plate 7.6). In the western part of the CBD, a building of interest is the 52-storey tower on Exchange Square which houses the Unified Hong Kong Stock Exchange and is located right on the waterfront. It has distinctive alternating bands of pink Spanish granite and silver reflective glass, and was designed by Remo Riva with a team from Palmer and Turner (Plate 7.7). It attempts to integrate art and architecture in the building. There is a sculpture by Henry Moore at the entrance, bronzes by Dame Elizabeth Frick and the Taiwanese artist Ju Ming in the outdoor plazas, and the four-storey Rotunda houses exhibits from around the world.

All in all, the CBD is typically western in appearance. It is interesting to note that the CBD extends eastwards rather than westwards. This is partly because land for expansion happened to be available in the west only after the military structures which formerly occupied the area were

Plate 7.6   The Bond Centre designed by Paul Rudolph

Plate 7.7 Exchange Square designed by Remo Riva

Plate 7.8 Chinese stores specializing in selling dried sea products in the Sai Ying Pun area of Hong Kong

removed and partly because the west is occupied by the Chinese business centre where the port warehouses and wharves are concentrated. This part of the CBD extends all the way to Sheung Wan and the building structures are much older, not as high and less imposing. The further west one goes, one encounters more and more shophouses run by traditional Chinese merchants. These represent the informal business sector, in contrast to the 'firm-based' formal sector in the east. From the extreme western edge of Sheung Wan extending westwards to Sai Ying Pun, there is a concentration of shops selling dried sea products, such as salted fish, shark fins, dried shrimps, dried mushrooms, dried abalones, dried sea urchin etc., which are Chinese delicacies (Plate 7.8). There are also Chinese herbal medicine stores, selling ginseng, birds' nests and other expensive health foods. In the same district there are small firms handling the import and re-export of these special foods and medicines. The origin of most of these products is from China in the north and South-east Asia in the south. Hence, these small firms are called 'nan bei hong' in Chinese (literally 'South and North Firms').

Going back to the eastern end of the northern coastal strip on Hong Kong Island, just beyond Admiralty MTR Station is Wan Chai which is famous for its Suzie Wong bars. It is the location of the American fleet

166

Plate 7.9 New style Repulse Bay Hotel, Hong Kong

club and is in close proximity to the British naval base. The building structures have been designed to allow commercial activities of all types to be carried out on the ground floor and residential use on upper storeys. Its land use is extremely mixed. Although residents in the district are trying hard to change the image of Wan Chai, it remains an entertainment district with night clubs, bars and restaurants. Beyond Wan Chai one comes upon Causeway Bay, a Japanese shopping centre where four major Japanese department stores Dai Maru, Sogo, Matsuzakaya and Mitsukoshi are located. This area has a very different architectural style from that of Wan Chai. Massive modern buildings designed for department stores on the lower floors and offices on the upper floors are characteristic. This area replaces the CBD as the heart of Hong Kong Island at night.

From the above description, it is clear that the urban morphology of Hong Kong is highly mixed. Although many old shophouses have been demolished during the government's slum clearance activities of the past years, some still survive. They are just Chinese buildings and old tenements with poor conditions and monotonous design. Unlike the CBD where architecturally distinctive buildings abound, the other parts of Hong Kong are drab. Particularly notorious are the old H- and L-shaped public housing estates which have the minimal amount of basic services

Plate 7.10   University of Hong Kong main building built in 1910

provided. Many of these old public housing estates have been demolished. However, more modern public housing estates are mere high-rises with no aesthetic appeal. The other private high-rise buildings for commercial and residential uses are of a standard modernist mediocrity. One exception perhaps is the newly reconstructed Repulse Bay Hotel which features a modern wavy-form multi-storey building with a big square hole open on one side (Plate 7.9). This peculiar style permits an open-air podium to be built at each level of the building.

A common style of large-scale high-density private residential development aimed at the upper middle-income group is to erect high-rise multi-storey buildings for residential use and low-rise buildings for shops, restaurants, cinemas, markets, schools and doctors' offices to serve the residents' needs. Mei Foo Sun Chuen in Western Kowloon and Tai Koo Shing in Eastern Hong Kong Island are forerunners of this type of development. Many other developers have followed suit but, in order to keep costs down, the architectural styles of these high-rise buildings are not outstanding.

As Jan Morris (1988) observed, Hong Kong is an architectural hotchpotch. There are still many old buildings in Hong Kong which remind one of the British influence. These buildings include the Government House on Upper Albert Road (1855), St. John's Cathedral on

Plate 7.11 The old Supreme Court building designed by Sir Aston Webb in 1905, now dwarfed by the modern high-rise commercial buildings

Garden Road (1849), the former residence of commanders of British military forces Flagstaff House (1846), now a tea-ware museum located inside Hong Kong Garden, the University of Hong Kong Main Building (1910) and the old Supreme Court building (designed by Sir Aston Webb, the architect of the Victoria and Albert Museum in London, in 1905) (Plates 7.10 and 7.11). The only Chinese building that has some architectural distinctiveness is the Taoist Man Mo Temple located on Hollywood Road in the heart of the CBD (Plate 7.12). All these buildings are found on Hong Kong Island where the original settlement started.

In the New Territories, there are Chinese village houses built by the Hakka or Punti villagers. The ridges of the rooves of some village houses are characteristically decorated with brightly coloured porcelain figurines, and the eaves are painted with pictures of people or flowers. Unfortunately, many of the village houses have fallen into disrepair or been totally demolished and replaced by Spanish-style villas or Western townhouses – the inevitable result of Western influences and a rising standard of living. In the new towns of the New Territories, standard modern high-rise buildings surrounding a civic centre or a shopping mall is the most common design, as seen in the recently developed Sha Tin New Town. There is a characteristic intermixture of public and private

Plate 7.12 The Man Mo Temple located on Hollywood Road in Hong Kong Island

housing with the obvious purpose of achieving a more balanced community through a mixture of different social classes. In the older new towns, such as Tsuen Wan New Town, industrial structures, commercial structures and high-density private and public housing are located on separate sites rather than mixed together.

Conclusions

Hong Kong has inherited its ecological structure and urban form from its colonial past. The focus of the city of Hong Kong has always been the port zone or the waterfront surrounding Victoria Harbour. The core of the port zone is the Central Business District (CBD) which has now expanded eastward on Hong Kong Island. Much attention has been paid to the modernization of the CBD with the result that many buildings of distinctive architectural styles have been erected. This is the western style CBD where the financial and commercial business is carried out every day. This is the heart of Hong Kong. Coexisting with the western CBD is a more traditional Chinese CBD which deals mostly with China and South-east Asian countries to satisfy the needs of the domestic population. The two CBDs complement each other very well. The result is an extremely mixed land use and a hotchpotch of architectural styles. There are still many old structures in Hong Kong, and slum clearance has not yet been fully accomplished. Despite the government's decentralization emphasis since 1970, the focus of Hong Kong's development has always been the main urban area. The new Metroplan bears witness to this.

The drive to new town developments in the New Territories has created a number of mini-centres of commerce and industry which take up excess population from the main urban areas. Hong Kong has gradually transformed from a uni-centred city to a multi-centred one although the mini-centres can never seriously challenge the dominance of the main centre. Such a development conforms to Friedmann's (1966) spatial development model of core and periphery, and the idea of the spread effects from the core. With the construction of a new airport in Lantau Island in the far western part of Hong Kong, another new growth centre is emerging. One finds the presence of two opposite forces of development in Hong Kong, centrifugal and centripetal, taking place at the same time.

The ecological structure of Hong Kong tends to display a sectoral pattern which is the result of the importance of socio-economic status as a discriminatory component. This also has an historical root. As a colony, there was distinct segregation of different ethnic groups in the past. For instance, the Peak and the Mid-levels on Hong Kong Island were preferred as residential sites by the Europeans. But, after the Second World War, ethnic segregation was replaced by socio-economic segregation. People with high incomes and high social status tend to live together. Not surprisingly, because of the excellent service facilities, these people prefer to live in the main urban area. The siting of public housing estates, usually on the peripheries of the main urban area and in the New Territories, tends to emphasize the residential location contrast between high income and low income groups. The sectoral pattern is therefore a common occurrence being dictated by the topography. There is also a zonal variation of family status from the main urban area. More old and young people are found in the periphery and the contrast in income between the core and the periphery remains great.

Finally, one should note that the spatial structure of Hong Kong is the result of the combination of highly pragmatic economic policies and the minimum of environmental regulation. Its form also shares characteristics of both Chinese and British cultures. While this form may be mixed and aesthetically unappealing, it is nevertheless extremely efficient in meeting the needs of the people at work and play. With the impending return of Hong Kong to China in 1997, the spatial structure will be subjected to change and its external relationship with the neighbouring Shenzhen Special Economic Zone will be altered. There is a possibility of a Greater Hong Kong through integration with the Shenzhen Special Economic

Ecological structure and urban form

Zone. This and other aspects of Hong Kong after 1997 will be discussed in Chapter 9.

References

Berry, B.J.L. 1965. Internal structure of the city. *Law and Contemporary Problems*. 31: 111–19.
Census and Statistics Department, 1987. *Hong Kong 1986 By-Census Social atlas*. Hong Kong: Government Printer.
Friedmann, J. 1966. *Regional development policy: a case study of Venezuela*. Cambridge, MA: MIT Press.
Lo, C.P. 1972. A typology of Hong Kong census districts: a study in urban structure. *Journal of Tropical Geography*. 34: 34–43.
Lo, C.P. 1975. Changes in the ecological structure of Hong Kong 1961–71: a comparative analysis. *Environment and Planning A*. 7: 941–63.
Lo, C.P. 1986. The evolution of the ecological structure of Hong Kong: implications for planning and future development. *Urban Geography* 7: 311–35.
McGee, T.G. 1967. *The Southeast Asian city: a social geography of the primate cities of Southeast Asia*. London: G. Bell.
Morris, J. 1988. *Hong Kong: the end of an empire*. Harmondsworth: Penguin Books.
Morris, J. 1989. *Building Hong Kong*. Hong Kong: FormAsia.
Santos, M. 1979. *The shared space: the two circuits of the urban economy in underdeveloped countries*. London: Methuen.

8
Government and politics

The decision process in Hong Kong is frequently made up by an amalgam of three elements, interest groups, influential and determined elites, and the bureaucracy.

Harris, P.: *Hong Kong: A Study in Bureaucracy and Politics*, Macmillan, Hong Kong, 1988, p. 50

Hong Kong is ruled by the Jockey Club, Jardine Matheson, the Hong Kong and Shanghai Bank and the Governor in that order.

Hughes, R.: *Hong Kong Borrowed Places, Borrowed Time*, Deutsch, London, 1975, p. 17

These two quotations are really addressing the same thing although Harris's is more general and Hughes's is more specific. As is clear from earlier chapters, Hong Kong is a British colony which exists primarily to serve the interests of merchants and industrialists. Colonialism, according to Leninists, is expected to promote underdevelopment. But surprisingly, the Colony of Hong Kong prospered after 1949, and has emerged as one of the world's foremost financial centres as well as an important world city. The success of Hong Kong can be explained by many factors, of which the hard-working and highly adaptable nature of the Chinese people must count as one, but the British government must be given credit for creating a favourable environment in which the Chinese could prosper, despite whatever shortcomings a *laissez-faire* style of government might have.

While the Chinese government never recognised the unequal treaties on the basis of which Hong Kong was ceded as a British colony, it implicitly condoned the British rule, provided that Britain would not jeopardize China's future control of Hong Kong. One of the Chinese government's major fears was, and still is, that an independent, democratically elected government could emerge in Hong Kong. The form of government established by the British in Hong Kong has always been slow to encourage local democracy, and has met with silent approval from China.

Harris (1988) has used the term 'administrative no-party state' to describe Hong Kong. As a no-party state, Hong Kong is not governed by representatives of the people through elections. Instead, the Hong Kong government is made up of officials appointed by the British government. Therefore, these officials cannot be removed by the people. Government decisions are made 'administratively' according to a bureaucratic type of compromise. The government officials are administrators and bureaucrats, who are therefore above the kind of political influences that one would find in other countries in Asia although an authoritarian form of government is quite common in East Asia. The absence of politicians in Hong Kong means that the Hong Kong government can devote all its energies to the economy and society. As a pure administrative state, the high-ranking government officials are generalists with professionals as their subordinates. Finally, Hong Kong has no ideology, and as a borrowed place in a span of borrowed time, people are just interested in making as much money as possible before they scram at the last moment. The government of Hong Kong seems to have facilitated that, because this 'non-ideology' also pleases China which has no desire whatsoever to see political parties or universal suffrage being promoted in Hong Kong. In the following sections, the salient characteristics of such an administrative government are explained, and the recent changes brought about by the signing of the Sino–British Agreement of 1984 are examined.

The government structure

The way how Hong Kong should be governed is specified in two separate legal documents issued by the British government to the colonial government. These are Letters Patent and Royal Instructions (Miners, 1986; Ngan, 1989). These may be regarded, in a very broad sense, as the constitution of Hong Kong. The Letters Patent contain 21 clauses creating the office of the Governor of Hong Kong and defining the Governor's powers. The Governor's power is only restricted by Her Majesty's Government in London. They also authorize the creation of the Executive and Legislative Councils as the central political organs of the government of Hong Kong. The Royal Instructions contain 37 clauses, which fill in some of the gaps left by the Letters Patent, laying down the details of the composition, powers and procedures of the Executive and Legislative Councils as well as the methods of appointment and dismissal of government members. In addition to these two documents, the

Governor has to adhere to the Colonial Regulations which give general guidance from the Crown through the Secretary of State for Foreign and Commonwealth Affairs on the appointment and disciplining of officials as well as financial matters. Until 1985 Hong Kong's basic government structure was basically unchanged from that established when the colony was first founded in the nineteenth century. However, the bureaucratic structure in the Hong Kong government has greatly expanded in recent years as compared to the past. In 1949 there were only 17,500 people working for the government. By 1988 this had increased to 180,000 and, as Harris (1988) has pointed out, the government is now the biggest employer in Hong Kong. The administrative structure of the Hong Kong government as it has evolved to the present day is shown in Figure 8.1. At this point, it should be noted that there is no separation of powers between the executive, legislative, and judicial branches as this figure seems to suggest. For one thing, the membership of the Executive and Legislative Councils usually overlaps. In other words, a member can serve in both councils simultaneously. On the other hand, the Governor's role is very similar to that of the President of the United States except that the Governor is not elected.

The Governor

The Governor is a super-bureaucrat acting both as head of state and head of government. As head of state, the Governor is the Queen's representative in Hong Kong. He is also the titular Commander-in-Chief of the British Forces stationed in Hong Kong. As head of government, the Governor presides at meetings of the Executive and Legislative Councils. The Governor posesses all powers except that of the Judiciary but he does have to consult the Executive Council when deciding important government policy matters. He is assisted in his administration by the Chief Secretary who heads the Government Secretariat. The Governor is appointed by the Queen at the recommendation of the Secretary of State for Foreign and Commonwealth Affairs in Britain normally for a five-year term, which can be extended by the British government. The Governor is therefore directly responsible to the British Crown and not to the people of Hong Kong. As the visible symbol of the British Chief Executive the Governor cannot be a local Chinese. While the Governor has the powers of a despot, he has to use them with care and espouses the beliefs of Western liberal constitutionalism rather than those of the rulers of the other Asian little dragons like South Korea, Taiwan and Singapore. As a symbol peculiar to Hong Kong the existence of the Governor may explain Hong Kong's success in attracting foreign investments from the West despite its rather shaky political future. The

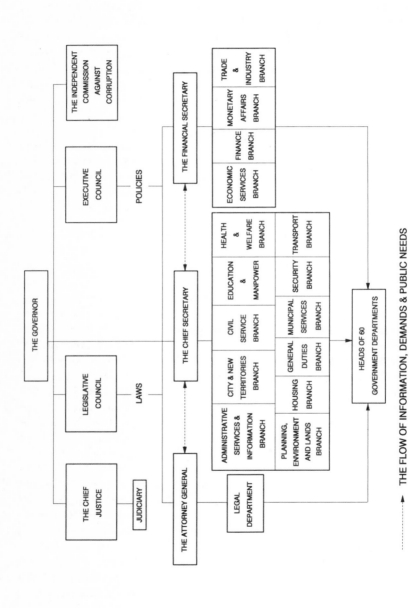

THE GOVERNOR

THE CHIEF JUSTICE — LEGISLATIVE COUNCIL — EXECUTIVE COUNCIL — THE INDEPENDENT COMMISSION AGAINST CORRUPTION

JUDICIARY

LAWS

POLICIES

THE ATTORNEY GENERAL — THE CHIEF SECRETARY — THE FINANCIAL SECRETARY

LEGAL DEPARTMENT

ADMINISTRATIVE SERVICES & INFORMATION BRANCH | CITY & NEW TERRITORIES BRANCH | CIVIL SERVICE BRANCH | EDUCATION & MANPOWER | HEALTH & WELFARE BRANCH

PLANNING, ENVIRONMENT AND LANDS BRANCH | HOUSING BRANCH | GENERAL DUTIES BRANCH | MUNICIPAL SERVICES BRANCH | SECURITY BRANCH | TRANSPORT BRANCH

ECONOMIC SERVICES BRANCH | FINANCE BRANCH | MONETARY AFFAIRS BRANCH | TRADE & INDUSTRY BRANCH

HEADS OF 60 GOVERNMENT DEPARTMENTS

- - - → THE FLOW OF INFORMATION, DEMANDS & PUBLIC NEEDS

———→ THE FLOW OF LEGISLATION, INSTRUCTIONS AND POLICIES

Figure 8.1 The structure of Hong Kong government, 1990

Governor, however, has no say in foreign matters concerning Hong Kong. Those are the responsibilities of the British government. Despite the enormous power bestowed to the Governor, he has a difficult role to play. He has to be sensitive to the pressures both from within Hong Kong and from China, and must show sympathy to Chinese sentiments. The present Governor, Sir David Wilson, who assumed office on April 9 1987, had been in the British diplomatic service and had experience in negotiating with China on matters related to the 1984 Sino–British Agreement on the future of Hong Kong. It was announced by the British government on December 31 1991 that his term of office will expire before the end of 1992.

The Executive Council

The Executive Council is the policy-making body in Hong Kong with which the Governor is required to consult as stipulated by the Royal Instructions. The Royal Instructions also specify the composition of the Executive Council. As of October 1, 1990, there are four ex-officio members (namely, the Chief Secretary, the Commander of British Forces, the Financial Secretary and the Attorney General), one appointed official member (Secretary for the Civil Service) and ten appointed unofficial members. The number of appointed official members has dropped from two to one in recent years and the positions were held by the Secretary for Trade and Industry and the Secretary for District Administration. The appointed unofficial members are all high ranking managers, company chief executives, lawyers and rich merchants. These are the people who belong to the Jockey Club, Jardine Matheson and the Hong Kong and Shanghai Banking Corporation, as stated in Hughes's famous quotation at the beginning of this chapter.

The role of the Executive Council is to advise the Governor on all important matters and policies. The Governor does not have to follow the advice of the Councillors, and can act against it if he so chooses although he has to report his reasons to the Secretary of State. But there is no instance in recent times of the Governor having done this. In practice, decisions are arrived at by consensus. In other words, the Governor attempts to maintain harmony and some form of balance among the various kinds of interests represented. The proceedings at the meetings of the Executive Council are confidential but in recent years many of the decisions arrived at in these meetings were made public. This represents a gesture to improve the transparency of the government. The Executive Council considers all principal legislation before it is introduced into the Legislative Council, and makes subsidiary legislation when acting as the Governor-in-Council. Therefore, the executive and legislative arms of the

177

government are blurred. The Executive Council also advises the Governor on matters of policy involving the use of public funds, but this is subject to the approval of the necessary funds by the Finance Committee of the Legislative Council. The Governor-in-Council also considers appeals, petitions and objections.

Legislative Council

The Legislative Council has the specific duty of assisting the Governor in making laws for peace, order and good government by virtue of the Letters Patent, and is the most important law-making body in Hong Kong. This body also controls finance, and the unofficial members are supposed to question government policies and decisions from Executive Council. But in practice there is no debate in the parliamentary sense. As Harris (1988) observed, the Legislative Council is a bureaucratic rather than a legislative arm of the machinery of government. Before 1985 the Legislative Council was entirely composed of government officials and unofficial members selected by the Governor. After the signing of the Sino–British agreement in 1984, the Governor was under some pressure from local people to open up the Legislative Council membership for election. In 1985, the government adopted a form of election by functional constituencies and indirect election by District Boards on the recommendation of a White Paper on Representative Government published in November 1984. Professionals in Hong Kong were divided into nine functional constituencies, namely, commercial, industrial, financial, labour, social services, education, legal, medical, engineers and associated professions. Members in these functional constituencies elected 12 members to the Legislative Council. Geographically, Hong Kong was also divided into 10 districts, each representing about 500,000 people, from which 10 members were elected. It should be noted that this was still only indirect election because they were elected among the District Board members. In addition, one member each from two special constituencies, the Urban Council and Regional Council, was also elected. In total, 24 unofficial members were elected to serve in the Legislative Council. In 1988, two additional functional constituency members were added. In 1990 the Legislative Council consisted of 57 members: the Governor, who is the President; three ex-officio members, namely, the Chief Secretary, the Financial Secretary and the Attorney General; seven official members selected by the Governor; 20 appointed members selected by the Governor and 26 elected members. The elected members are in a minority, and can be easily outvoted. In reality, the government quite often makes concessions and accepts amendments to legislation in response to the members' views although it is never in danger of being defeated in a vote (Miners, 1990). In addition, the Governor also appoints Legislative Council members to be members of the Executive Council concurrently. Obviously, those who show strong support for government policies will be appointed.

The Legislative Council controls the expenditure of public funds through the Finance Committee and the Public Accounts Committee. The Finance Committee consists of the Chief Secretary, the Finance Secretary, one official member of the Council and all members other than official members. Its function is to consider requests for public expenditure and the supplementary provision of funds. The approval of this committee is required for all government proposals involving public expenditure. The Public Accounts Committee consists of a chairman and six members, none of whom is an official member of the Council. Its main role is to consider reports from the Director of Audit on the government's annual statements of account, and to see that public expenditure has not been incurred for purposes other than those originally intended. The Legislative Council can examine, discuss and approve the annual budget submitted by the Finance Secretary. Its unofficial members can neither change the decisions of the Financial Secretary, nor recommend the increase in expenditure of a certain item, nor move to increase government revenue. They can however reduce expenditure.

As compared with the past, the composition of the Legislative Council has changed quite considerably. In 1950 there were only 15 members in the Council, consisting of five ex-officio, three official and seven unofficial members. In 1984 the size of the Council increased to 46, the number of ex-officio members decreased to three and the number of official and unofficial members increased to 13 and 30 respectively. With the introduction of some form of election in 1985, the size of the Legislative Council continued to increase. On September 15 1991 the first ever direct election took place, replacing the indirect election among the District Board members. 18 members altogether were elected by registered voters from nine districts (two from each district). The voter turn-out was about 39 per cent which was regarded to be disappointingly low. Candidates from the United Democrat Party, a local party led by a British-trained Hong Kong barrister, Martin Lee, regarded as the 'father of democracy in Hong Kong', won 12 out of the 18 seats. This party emphasizes a greater degree of democracy in Hong Kong and is very critical of China's hardline policies and its brutal handling of the June 4, 1989, incident in Tiananmen Square, Beijing. The anti-China attitudes of Mr Lee and his party have worried some of the elite groups who are keen to preserve the *status quo* of Hong Kong and keep a friendly relationship with China. While Martin Lee maintained that the election gave the party a clear mandate from the people of Hong Kong that democracy was important, the Chinese authorities, who were obviously displeased with the outcome of the election, pointed out that there was a silent majority who had not voted. All this direct election in the Legislative Council requires the consent of the Chinese government in accordance with the Sino–British agreement. Hong Kong is now in the so-called transitional period towards the return of sovereignty to China. China has to be consulted on many important matters, particularly those which have an impact on Hong Kong after 1997. It is quite clear that significant political changes, necessitated by the change in sovereignty, have begun to take place in Hong Kong. The rules of the game of governing Hong Kong have to be changed, and such changes are most obviously seen in the Legislative Council. The Governor is facing increasing difficulty in maintaining the interest of business people and the elites.

The Urban Council and the Regional Council

Both the Urban Council and the Regional Council are subordinate local government bodies, much lower in status than the Legislative Council and Executive Council. The Urban Council is composed of elected and appointed members. In 1990, there were 40 members, 15 elected from district constituencies, 15 appointed by the Governor and 10 representative members from the urban district boards. In fact, election of Urban Council members can be dated back to 1883 when the body was known as the Sanitary Board and there were two elected seats. In 1936, the name was changed and the election of Urban Council members provided the model for the Legislative Council elections. However, voter apathy is typical in Urban Council elections because the Council lacks political power. However, elected members may find it a stepping stone to the Legislative Council. From the city management point of view, the Urban Council is an important body. As has been observed in Chapter 6, the Urban Council is responsible for the provision of municipal services to about 3.6 million people who live within the urban ares. Waste disposal, the maintenance of environmental hygiene, the control of hawkers, the provision of recreational and cultural activities and the sale of liquor are all carried out by the Urban Council. Since 1973, the Council has been financially autonomous thanks to rates on properties and licensing fees and, unlike other government departments, can retain any surplus of its revenue. It makes out its own budget and is not subject to the approval of the Legislative Council. In 1989–90 it spent over HK$3,000 million (or US$384.6 million). The Governor can intervene if the Council fails to carry out its statutory duties.

The Regional Council was only established in 1985 as a counterpart of the Urban Council for the New Territories. This was despite objections from the Urban Council which saw it as logical to extend its own area of jurisdiction to include the New Territories. The whole of the New Territories was traditionally a rural area, and the political power of the rural committees of village representatives was very strong because of the special lease conditions of the New Territories. There are 28 rural committees and an executive council. The rural committees formed themselves into an advisory body known as the Heung Yee Kuk (literally, the Village Council). In 1990 the Regional Council consisted of 36 members. 12 were directly elected, 12 appointed by the Governor, nine indirectly elected by the nine District Boards in the New Territories and three ex-officio members who were the chairman and two vice-chairmen of the Heung Yee Kuk. The Regional Council provides the same types of services as the Urban Council to about 2 million people living in the New Territories. Its revenue comes mainly from rates levied on properties and from an annual government grant. Because of the creation of new towns in the New Territories, more and more people will live in both private and public housing in these new towns. The Regional Council has therefore assumed an increasingly important role although it suffers from the same voter apathy which can be seen in the Urban Council elections.

District boards

The lowest level of administration in Hong Kong is the district board which was established in 1982. In 1990, the whole of Hong Kong and the New Territories were divided into 19 district boards according to the physical development as well as the growth, movement and geographical spread of the population. Each district board consists of appointed unofficial members, elected members from the respective constituencies and, in the case of the New Territories, rural committee chairmen. From 1988 to 1991, there were 264 elected and 141 appointed members for all 19 district boards. The major function of the district boards is to advise the government on the quality of life of the people living in each district. For each district there is also a district management committee chaired by a district officer, a senior member of the government administrative service. The committee identifies the needs of the district and can bring together senior government officials from relevant departments to help meet the needs. The District Board advises the district management committee, monitors the work of the government departments in the district and sounds out complaints to the committee when the services provided are inadequate or unsatisfactory. The residents in the districts are encouraged to meet the board members and express their views on any district problems or suggest ways for improvement. On the other hand, the district office provides information to residents and educates them on matters of environmental hygiene and protection. This level of administration therefore provides an outlet for the common people to express their frustrations, if any, with top government officials or policies.

The Government Secretariat

As an administrative state, the Hong Kong government places great emphasis on its civil service. The head of the civil service is the Chief Secretary who is the Governor's deputy. Within the Government Secretariat, he directs and supervises the various administrative departments and is the Governor's principal adviser on local policy. In 1990, the Secretariat was organized into sixteen branches, each of which was headed by one Secretary. The five branches concerned with economic and financial departments come under the overall control of the Financial Secretary, and the remaining eleven branches come under the control of the Chief Secretary. There is also the Legal Department which is separately organized under the Attorney General with 60 departments responsible for all day-to-day operations, each of which has a department head. With this type of administrative structure, all government operations can be tightly controlled from the centre. As a result, the Governor and his immediate staff are fully informed of everything that happens in Hong Kong. Unfortunately, this structure necessitated an increase in the size of the Secretariat and the result was an increase in the size of the civil service. Between 1979 and 1989 the size of the civil service increased by 46 per cent. The side-effect of all this was excessive government expenditure on staffing (about 65 per cent of recurrent government expenditure in 1990) and an increased fragmentation of responsibilities. As the hierarchy branches out further, the degree of bureaucracy correspondingly increases and delays are caused. The government was aware of this problem and, in fact, the size of the civil service was trimmed in 1990. As of April 1989 there were 186,054 civil servants, which was 10,802 below the authorized establishment of 196,856. About 98.6 per cent were local Hong Kong Chinese officers while only 1.4 per cent were expatriates, mostly from Britain and other British Commonwealth countries (Miners, 1990). Since 1984, a policy for the localization of the civil service has been established, and more local Chinese are to be employed in higher ranking positions in the government. In the past the top Secretaries were expatriates, and only in recent years have some senior local Chinese administrative officers been appointed to these positions.

The Hong Kong civil service attests to the classical management or Weberian theories of bureaucracy which emphasize a hierarchical structure of government and a division of labour; the task to be performed rather than the individual performing it; recruitment and selection based on technical qualifications and examinations; remuneration by salary and the formal prohibition of the use of public office for private gain (Weber, 1947). It is clear that the power of the government is almost entirely in the hands of a small, expatriate, bureaucratic elite with an emphasis on law and order and value for money (Scott, 1984). This system has the support of the business community, of course, and has not resulted in any great social conflict because of the Chinese tradition of deference to authority. Indeed to the Chinese people in Hong Kong, this style of British administration is much less autocratic than the system in pre- and post-Communist China. Scott (1984) observed that both the British and the Chinese have a high regard for bureaucratic formality which helps to dampen potential causes of friction. However, with increased Western influences and better education, the younger generation in Hong Kong began to realize that their social needs were not being adequately met by the government. The 1967 riot, triggered off by the Cultural Revolution in China, revealed the social discontent among some groups of people in Hong Kong and led the government to change its emphasis slightly. Government involvement in the public housing programme could be seen in that light although it could also be seen as the government subsidizing industry by providing their workers with low-cost housing. The present structure of the government as outlined above is an outcome of the recommendations by McKinsey and Company, management consultants commissioned by the government to review government operations in 1972. The structural reforms were intended to meet the needs of a more socially responsive government. It has been observed that the Hong Kong civil service represents a hybrid of British colonial tradition and Chinese cultural values (Scott, 1984). This mixture provided stability in Hong Kong over long periods of its isolation from changes in values which have affected Britain, the United States and other places. British laws are not automatically applicable to Hong Kong. Until recently, the classical management theories of Weber mentioned above have strongly influenced management behaviour at senior levels in civil service. Part of the values of bureaucracy are efficiency and merit, which are criteria to recruitment and promotion. This belief in efficiency distinguishes Hong Kong from other countries in South-east Asia, thus adding to its suitability as an international financial centre and a world city. Therefore, the contributions of the civil service to Hong Kong's economic growth must not be underestimated.

The Independent Commission Against Corruption (ICAC)

Since 1974 the acronym ICAC has become a household word in Hong

Kong, and is very much feared by the civil servants and employees of private companies. The ICAC was set up in 1974 to investigate corruption in the Police Force. Previous to that, an anti-corruption unit had been set up inside the Police Department itself. However, that became a joke because corruption was most rampant among the police at that time. The ICAC is directly responsible to the Governor who charged it with investigating all instances of bribery and corruption which came to its knowledge, both those involving civil servants and the private sector, and to prepare cases for prosecution or disciplinary action. The staff of the ICAC is recruited without reference to the Public Service Commission, some on secondment from the civil service, some directly on contract. It is totally separate from the rest of the civil service and is not even subjected to the supervision of any of the branch secretaries in the Secretariat except on financial matters. The ICAC is therefore free to investigate the affairs of civil servants or business people at any level of seniority. While the ICAC has not completely stamped out corruption in Hong Kong it makes Hong Kong a better place to do business, at least from the foreign investors' point of view. In this part of the world where 'relationships' are important for business success or for getting things done quickly, Hong Kong is the exception rather than the rule.

The Judiciary

In Hong Kong, the Judiciary is an arm of the administrative state, but it is theoretically independent of the executive and legislative branches of government, which is fundamental to the English common law system. The head of the Judiciary is the Chief Justice, who is assisted in his administrative duties by the Registrar, seven Deputy Registrars and one Assistant Registrar of the Supreme Court. The court system of Hong Kong consists of ten magistrates' courts to deal with minor criminal offences, a Small Claims Tribunal to hear civil claims not exceeding HK$15,000, a Labour Tribunal for labour disputes, the Lands Tribunal to deal with landlord and tenant matters, three District Courts with civil jurisdiction over monetary disputes involving amounts between HK$15,000 and HK$120,000, the High Court to try civil disputes and serious criminal offences and the Court of Appeal to hear appeals from both civil and criminal cases. The High Court and the Court of Appeal form the Supreme Court of Hong Kong. The final court of appeal for Hong Kong cases is the Judicial Committee of the Privy Council in London. The judges are trained in Britain, Hong Kong or other British Commonwealth jurisdictions. In 1990 there were 49 Permanent Magistrates, 12 Special Magistrates, 31 District Judges, 19 High Court Judges and 9 Justices of Appeal. All the judges have security of tenure, to safeguard them from executive interference, in accordance with the principle of judicial independence (Chen, 1990). The legal system as practised in Hong Kong was imported from Britain in the mid-nineteenth century and has left its mark on Hong Kong even today. This English-style legal system has provided Hong Kong with a more attractive business environment for foreigners who are familiar with the system, and has contributed to Hong Kong's stability and prosperity.

There is a Legal Department which provides legal advice to the executive branch and undertakes the prosecutions of suspected criminal offenders on behalf of Hong Kong. This is headed by the Attorney General who is the Governor's top legal adviser. The Legal Department also drafts regulations. As of May 1990 there were about 230 lawyers on the staff of the Legal Department. The Department is organized into six divisions, each of which has a division head. They are Legal Policy, Administrative, Civil, Prosecutions, Law Drafting and International Law.

On the whole, the Hong Kong legal system, although foreign to the Chinese majority, has provided adequate protection for the social and political freedoms of its citizens. In order to ease the anxiety of the Hong Kong people over any violation of their human rights beyond 1997, the Legislative Council passed the 'Hong Kong Bill of Rights' Bill of 1990, which gives effect in local law to the relevant provisions of the International Covenant on Civil and Political Rights, as applied to Hong Kong.

The Sino–British Agreement and the Basic Law

The Sino–British Agreement, which was signed between Britain and China on December 20 1984, must rank as one of the most important documents affecting the destiny of Hong Kong since the signing of the Treaty of Nanking between the same two countries in 1842. This agreement has triggered changes towards a higher degree of accountability of the Hong Kong government in recent years although this was clearly not its original intention. The Agreement contained some basic principles aimed at maintaining the economic prosperity of Hong Kong when the sovereignty of Hong Kong passes back to China on June 30 1997. Hong Kong will become a Special Administrative Area (SAR) in accordance with Article 31 of the Constitution of the People's Republic of China, and will be known in full as Hong Kong – China. It was stressed that it will enjoy a 'high degree of autonomy' after 1997 while China will take on the responsibility for defence and foreign policy. Capitalism as practised in Hong Kong will continue unchanged. Basic rights and freedoms will also continue. The legislature as constituted by election will make laws, and the executive will be responsible to the legislature. The Chief Executive (equivalent in status to the Governor) will be appointed by the

Chinese government after elections or local consultations. The legal system of Hong Kong, including English common laws, will be retained, but the Final Court of Appeal will be in Hong Kong. The Special Administrative Region of Hong Kong may, as required, invite judges from other common law jurisdictions to sit on the Court of Final Appeal. The judiciary will be free from political interference from China. The civil service will be retained and staffed by local Chinese, particularly at the highest level. The free enterprise economy will remain and the Hong Kong dollar will be freely convertible into other foreign currencies. Individuals can own and dispose of their properties as they wish, and investors can freely deposit or withdraw funds in and from Hong Kong. Hong Kong can continue to hold memberships of international bodies and associations in tariffs and trade. People can move in and out of Hong Kong with no restrictions. The International Covenants on Civil and Political Rights and on Economic, Social and Cultural rights which have been extended to Hong Kong since 1976 will be continued beyond 1997, and are guaranteed in the Joint Declaration. All these specific conditions will be stipulated in a Basic Law of the Hong Kong SAR, and will remain unchanged for 50 years until 2047 when Hong Kong will hopefully be unified with China. The Basic Law will be drafted under the control of the Chinese government in consultation with representatives of Hong Kong residents.

It is quite clear from this summary of the Agreement that China accepts the *status quo* of Hong Kong as it existed in 1984 when the Agreement was signed. This means that China likes the efficient, non-democratic and highly centralized style of government in Hong Kong, and hopes that it can be continued unchanged up to June 30, 1997. In fact, when the Chinese government appointed members to the Basic Law Drafting Committee in July 1985, the twenty-three Hong Kong representatives were prominent businessmen and leading professionals, similar in nature to the membership of the Executive and Legislative Councils. In so doing, the Chinese government showed that it was keen to uphold establishment interests in Hong Kong. Therefore, any changes in the government after the signing of the Agreement, particularly in the area of a more representative government, will be viewed as antagonistic to the Chinese government. The drafting of 'the Basic Law of the Hong Kong Special Administrative Region of the People's Republic of China' was completed on April 28 1988. After a period of consultation during which Hong Kong people showed extreme apathy towards the document, the Basic Law was formally enacted and promulgated by the National People's Congress of the People's Republic of China. Despite the enactment of the Basic Law, the general feeling of pessimism prevailed among the people of Hong Kong, particularly after the Tiananmen Square incident, who believed that if freedom, human rights and democracy cannot be guaranteed in China then they cannot be protected in Hong Kong after 1997 (Cheng, 1990). More discussions on the future of Hong Kong as a world city can be found in Chapter 9.

Conclusions

It has been shown in this chapter that the success of Hong Kong as a world city was heavily dependent on its highly structured and centralized government, being constituted by the Letters Patent and the Royal Instructions, with the Governor at the helm. There were no party politics in Hong Kong, at least not until 1991 when the first ever direct election for Legislative Council members took place. The Governor had all the power he needed to carry out policies to protect the interests of the business and professional elites. The Governor relies heavily on an efficient civil service, headed by the Chief Secretary, to do the job for him. The civil service represents a hybrid of British colonial traditions and Chinese cultural values. This system promotes efficiency and merit. Efficiency in Hong Kong means 'value for money' (Scott, 1984). The Chinese tradition of accepting authoritarian rule matches this style of administration well. The government's style is administrative. It aims at providing an attractive environment in which business can thrive. The legal system, based on common English laws, has protected local citizens and foreigners alike. The strong anti-corruption stance of the government presents a clean image to the civil service and Hong Kong's business sector. All these 'good' qualities are possible at the expense of democracy. Hong Kong cannot be viewed as a democratic city-state.

After the signing of the Sino–British Agreement in 1984, the Hong Kong government was under some pressure to change more quickly in order to become more 'democratic' or, in other words, more representative of the wishes of the people of Hong Kong. This change will certainly affect the power of the Governor and the administrative nature of the government. There is also another force at work which people in Hong Kong cannot ignore: Chinese influences. The Basic Law enacted by the Chinese government, which amplifies all the promises made in the Sino–British Agreement, will supplant the Letters Patent and the Royal Instructions and become the new constitution of Hong Kong on June 30 1997. Some people in Hong Kong are actively engaged in party politics. They hope to get as much democracy as possible from the government now before it becomes too late. They are trying to appeal to the lower income groups for their support. Obviously, this type of activity does not meet with the approval of the established elites who are keen to maintain a friendly relationship with an anti-democratic China. The elites fear that antagonising China will spell the end of economic prosperity for Hong

Kong. How this will evolve remains to be seen. Meanwhile, the Governor is trying hard to control the new political forces and to uphold the existing structure of the government.

References

Chen, A.H.Y. 1990. The legal system. In *The other Hong Kong report 1990*, R.Y.C. Wong and J.Y.S. Cheng (eds). Hong Kong: The Chinese University Press, pp. 65–86.

Cheng, J.Y.S. 1990. The basic law: messages for Hong Kong people. In *The other Hong Kong report 1990*, R.Y.C. Wong and J.Y.S. Cheng (eds). Hong Kong: The Chinese University Press, pp. 29–63.

Harris, P. 1988. *Hong Kong: a study in bureaucracy and politics*. Hong Kong: Macmillan.

Miners, N.J. 1986. *The government and politics of Hong Kong (4th edn)*. Hong Kong: Oxford University Press.

Miners, N.J. 1990. Constitution and administration. In *The other Hong Kong report 1990*, R.Y.C. Wong and J.Y.S. Cheng (eds). Hong Kong: The Chinese University Press, pp. 1–28.

Ngan, R.M.H. 1989. The overall governmental structui · in Hong Kong. In *Hong Kong society*, A.Y.H. Kwan (ed). Hong Kong: Writers' and Publishers' Cooperative, pp. 91–112.

Scott, I. 1984. Organization and personnel. In *The Hong Kong Civil Service, personnel policies and practices*, I. Scott and J.P. Burns (eds). Hong Kong: Oxford University Press, pp. 1–16.

Weber, M. 1947. *The theory of social and economic organization*. New York: Oxford University Press, pp. 333–34.

9
The future of Hong Kong as a world city: 1997 and beyond

After the lease expires – Hong Kong's new horoscope 1st July, 1997. We find the same wild energy which has always marked Hong Kong and dominated its life and we also find the same concentration on money-making. . . . Even with a new form of government, the making of money is still going to be the focal point of the new Hong Kong.
Gormick, T. and Bloomfield, F. (1983): *Hong Kong 1997: a new lease on life? An astrological analysis of Hong Kong and its future*

Such was the prediction of Astrologist Gormick for the day Hong Kong will be turned over to China. The above statement illustrates a simple and yet correct insight that Hong Kong exists solely to make money, and that its future survival will depend on how successfully it can continue to do so in order that China will tolerate the existence of a capitalist enclave on its socialist soil. Indeed, the question, 'What will happen to Hong Kong after 1997?', has stimulated so much interest from politicians, economists, social scientists, journalists, university professors, researchers and intellectuals, both local and foreign, that it forms a special Hong Kong study of its own. The views expressed are also diverse, and can be categorized as pessimistic or optimistic, depending on which scenario one wishes to believe. In fact, both scenarios share some common elements, and both have an equal chance of occurrence according to a recent analysis by Mushkat (1990). From the analysis presented in the previous eight chapters, it will become clear to the reader that there are certain important ingredients which have made Hong Kong succeed and survive as an international financial centre and a world city. A crucial question is therefore: will these ingredients be diminished or enhanced after 1997?

189

Ingredients for Hong Kong's prosperity

Geographic location and natural factors

Foremost among these ingredients is Hong Kong's geographic location. Situated on the Pacific rim right at the door of China which, with a population of 1,133.7 million in 1990, is generally regarded as a large market with great economic potential. One of the reasons for Hong Kong's selection as a world financial centre in the 1970s was its time-zone location which allowed a 24-hour banking service in relation to the United States. Hong Kong also occupies a central position in relation to other countries in South-east Asia and East Asia. Hong Kong is also famous for its deep natural harbour and port facilities. These geographic and natural advantages of Hong Kong will not be diminished after 1997. With the construction of the new airport (which should be partially completed by 1997) and new container terminals, Hong Kong will be in a strong position to enhance its port facilities. However, by being integrated into China in 1997, Hong Kong will have to compete with other Chinese ports and potential financial centres where major technical, manufacturing, and educational institutions already exist (Wu, 1987). A serious competitor will be Shanghai with its equally good geographic location and potential to become another world city. Most important of all, Shanghai will have the strong support of the Chinese government in Beijing. After all, the General Secretary of the Chinese Communist Party, Mr. Jiang Zemin, was the former mayor of Shanghai.

The administrative no-party government

The government of Hong Kong is very efficient because, as has been pointed out by Harris (1988), it is essentially an administrative structure with the office of the Governor as the centrepiece. Because the Governor is appointed by the British Queen he cannot be removed from office by Hong Kong citizens. There are therefore no party politics in Hong Kong. At least, this was true until 1991. The Governor, in consultation with the expatriate elites and local bureaucrats, rules Hong Kong with his full energy devoted to economic growth. The government upholds a modified form of a *laissez-faire* economic philosophy, known locally as 'positive non-interventionism'. Apparently, this policy works very well. A distinctive advantage of this policy is that it gives Hong Kong a high degree of adaptability to adverse economic conditions in the world. The Hong Kong government calls the Hong Kong economy a self-regulating one and the classical economists' dream. The wage/price flexibility is very high in Hong Kong so that Hong Kong can quickly respond to any fall in employment and output by lowering real wages followed by a decrease in prices, as predicted in the classical macroeconomic model (Chen, 1984). Rabushka (1979) also identified such factors as the absence of external barriers to the flow of goods and services, the 'non-stickiness' of wages and the high mobility of capital and labour as conducive to the working of the automatic corrective mechanism.

Under the shadow of the impending sovereignty change in 1997, the people of Hong Kong are becoming more and more politically vocal. The joint Sino–British declaration in 1984 stipulated that Hong Kong will enjoy a 'high degree of autonomy', under the 'one country, two systems' arrangement, advocated by Deng Xiaoping. It is not clear whether under such an arrangement the people in Hong Kong will enjoy freedom and democracy. People are now interested in forming themselves into political parties in an attempt to ensure that a more democratic form of government can be established before the take-over by China in 1997. The Hong Kong people have obviously lost confidence in China and in the usefulness of the Basic Law, drafted by the Chinese government with minimal input from Hong Kong, after the Tiananmen Square incident. The people of Hong Kong wanted a more representative government but, because of the objections of the Chinese government, direct elections to the Legislative Council were postponed in 1988 until 1991. The United Democrat Party emerged from that election as a strong party advocating a greater degree of democracy. Some of the leaders of the Party are vocal critics of China's Tiananmen Square crack-down which has not endeared them to the Chinese government. Scott (1989) has observed that the Hong Kong government has been increasingly facing difficulties in making and implementing authoritative decisions over recent years which he called a crisis of legitimacy. The government's support base is being eroded. The government also seems to have lost some degree of autonomy because it has to be sensitive to reactions from China. A good example is the construction of the new airport to which the Chinese government objected. The matter was only settled after lengthy negotiations involving high-level British government officials and their Chinese counterparts, with the result that the Chinese government must be consulted over all matters regarding Hong Kong which extend beyond 1997. This interference from China is a major concern to Hong Kong because it presages things to come after 1997. China will certainly tamper with the automatic corrective mechanism of Hong Kong, which will in turn adversely affect Hong Kong's adaptive capacity. Certainly, after 1997 there will be more party politics, and Hong Kong will no longer be able to maintain the type of efficient administrative government from its colonial past.

The future of Hong Kong

Human resources

A major advantage of Hong Kong as an industrial and financial centre is the quality of its labour force. Hong Kong has a highly disciplined and enterprising labour force which is a reliable source of growing output and sustained innovation (Mushkat, 1989). The Hong Kong Chinese have been educated to uphold the Confucian philosophy of hard work and frugality. Labour unions are not strong in Hong Kong because there are many illegal Chinese immigrants who are always willing to work and, up until the 1980s, labour supply was still abundant. With the provision of free primary education in 1971 and free secondary education in 1978, Hong Kong has a well educated labour force. Tertiary education in Hong Kong has been able to provide the necessary professionals for work in both the public and private sectors, despite its limited annual enrolment. But many Hong Kong students study overseas and, after they have completed their study, normally opt to return to Hong Kong where the working environment is quite favourable from both the cultural and financial points of view. Hong Kong being a British colony also attracts a lot of British expatriates. As a place open to foreign investment, Hong Kong also attracts other foreign nationals. The rise in the importance of Hong Kong as a financial centre owes much to its cosmopolitan nature and the availability of a highly skilled work force in the upper echelon of the economy.

It has been noted that the Hong Kong economy changed from an entrepôt port function to industries, and then to finance and services. When China adopted a more open policy in 1978, its relationship with Hong Kong became more and more intimate. China created the Shenzhen Special Economic Zone right at the border of Hong Kong and also carried out rural reforms with the introduction of the agricultural responsibility system. The result was a surplus rural labour force in China. To accommodate this change, China has encouraged the development of rural enterprises and the Zhujiang Delta, at the mouth of which Hong Kong is located, was opened up as an 'Open Economic Zone'. Foreign investment, including that from Hong Kong and Macau, is encouraged by the Chinese government in order to develop industries in the delta for the export market. At the same time, China also actively participated in investing in Hong Kong and, between 1984 and 1988, Chinese investment has risen at least seven-fold from an estimated US$5.8 to US$7.7 billion. After the United States and Japan, China is the third biggest investor in manufacturing in Hong Kong. Measured by deposits, China-owned banks are the second largest group in Hong Kong. Hong Kong's entrepôt trade has also been revived, with a lot of foreign goods being shipped to China through Hong Kong. Hong Kong industrialists have also invested heavily in China, taking advantage of the much cheaper labour there. Much of Hong Kong's manufacturing industry has been re-located to the Shenzhen Special Economic Zone and the Zhujiang Delta area. The opening up of China helps to propel Hong Kong's economy upward with a consequent decline in the manufacturing sector and a rise in importance of finance and service sectors. Hong Kong's industry has to move towards high-technology. Thus, the Chinese and the Hong Kong economies complement each other very well.

In this process of economic transformation, the social structure of Hong Kong has also been changed. There is now an increasingly large group of middle-class people who are engaged in the service and finance sectors and doing very well financially. They are obviously nervous about the impending sovereignty change. The Chinese government did not want any Hong Kong citizens to be represented in the negotiations with Britain, because, to the Chinese there is never any question that the territory of Hong Kong belongs to China and that the Hong Kong people are Chinese. The middle-class group felt that their existence was largely ignored in the drafting of both the joint agreement and the Basic Law. Their options are to protest or to emigrate. Those who are protesting are pressuring the Hong Kong government for direct election so that their views can be better represented. Those who emigrate have initiated the so-called brain drain. The 1997 issue has become the most important macrostructural issue to Hong Kong's people (Emmons, 1988). Between 1980 and 1989 over 260,000 people emigrated. In the early 1990s emigration became a major concern. The Hong Kong government estimated that about 62,000 people were leaving Hong Kong every year and that this figure had increased from around 20,000 a year in the years before 1987 (Skeldon, 1991). Popular destinations are Canada, Australia and the United States. Over one-quarter of the emigrants were in the entrepreneur and investor categories. Large numbers of the emigrants in other categories were highly educated and skilled managers, administrators and professionals. These are the people who have contributed to the economic success of Hong Kong. Although a small percentage of these emigrants will return to Hong Kong after they have established residency in foreign countries, the brain drain problem is serious. The Hong Kong government reacted by establishing a new university (Hong Kong University of Science and Technology) and increasing the number of places in tertiary education institutes with the hope that the lost talents can be replenished in the future.

The China factor

It should be remembered that the existence of Hong Kong depends heavily on the goodwill of the Chinese government. Had the Communists adopted a hardline policy towards Britain after their take-over of China in 1949, Hong Kong could not have remained as a colony under British rule. Although at the early stages, the Hong Kong government tried not to be overly dependent on China for important resources such as water and food supplies, it became obvious that the economic growth of Hong Kong could not be sustained without the support of China. It was therefore very important for the Hong Kong government to maintain a good relationship with China. The 1967 riot in Hong Kong, inspired by the Cultural Revolution in China, was a major crisis which threatened the British rule. It was only with the Hong Kong people's strong support of the British government that the riot was quelled. The relationship between Hong Kong and China became more and more intimate after China began to open up to the West in 1978. After the declaration of the Sino–British Joint Agreement in 1984, China's investment in Hong Kong intensified and Hong Kong benefited economically from trading with China. Indeed, by now, China is Hong Kong's number one trade partner. Hong Kong serves as China's window to the West through which it acquires new information and technology. With the relocation of Hong Kong's manufacturing industries to China, Hong Kong benefited from a supply of cheap labour. Hong Kong's economy is now very intertwined with China's. A case in point is that the granting of the 'most favoured nation' status to Chinese imports by the United States can affect Hong Kong as much as China.

This was all very well until June 4, 1989 when China's image as a liberalizing country was shattered by its bloody crack-down on the students' pro-democracy demonstration in Tiananmen Square, Beijing. Deng Xiaoping stressed that the modernization of China should proceed in accordance with the 'Four Cardinal Principles' of adherence to the socialist road, the people's democratic dictatorship, leadership of the Communist Party, Marxist-Leninism and Maoist thought. The more liberally-minded premier, Zhao Ziyang, was replaced by the Soviet trained Li Peng. Zhao Ziyang was the one who told the Hong Kong people not to worry about its return to China. Now he has been purged from the Party. After June 4 1989, the confidence of the Hong Kong people was at an all time low. The stock market in Hong Kong also fluctuated. However, Hong Kong's economy recovered very quickly from this setback, displaying once again the resilient nature of Hong Kong's economy. Fortunately, investor confidence in Hong Kong has not subsided, and China has also tried to prop up Hong Kong's economy. Any political incidents in China will send ripples to Hong Kong, and one can expect to see more of these coming from China in the future.

The future of Hong Kong as a world city

Changes in Hong Kong are inevitable now and in the years to come. Despite the possible adverse changes in the ingredients of Hong Kong's prosperity, the outlook for Hong Kong is not necessarily very grim. Hong Kong has become prosperous because its government has been responsive in providing a favourable environment for everyone to make money, and because the people of Hong Kong have devoted their full energies to the task. Hong Kong exists because it can make money for China. Hong Kong's survival also depends on foreign investment. As long as such an environment exists, Hong Kong will do well in the future. According to a 1984 survey of foreign investors, the five factors which were found to be important in making Hong Kong an attractive investment location were: 1. Freedom to move capital and assets, 2. Freedom to repatriate earnings and interest, 3. Low tax ceiling, 4. Availability of efficient labour, and 5. The stability of the Hong Kong government (Tung Ho, 1984). After 1997, the only worrisome item in this list is the stability of the Hong Kong government. The Hong Kong government can only maintain its stability and authority without undue interference from China. Only when there is a strong Hong Kong government can the other items in the list be maintained. If Hong Kong can prove that it will do well after 1997, many emigrants will return, because Hong Kong is one of the best places in this world to make money – if making money is your prime objective. If the Chinese government can keep its promise of letting Hong Kong have a 'high degree of autonomy' in dealing with internal matters, Hong Kong's world city status can be further developed on the basis of its new airport and container port facilities. Whether or not China will keep its promise depends on who is in control of China at the time of the change over. This, of course, is an unknown factor. On the other hand, the collapse of communism in the world during the late 1980s and early 1990s makes it hopeful that China will become more democratic in its ruling policy.

Inevitably, the return of Hong Kong to Chinese rule in 1997 can affect its spatial structure. Hong Kong will have to be governed according to the 'Basic Law'. Cuthbert (1987) suggested that this will provide a new set of rules which, over time, will affect the use of space and urban planning in Hong Kong. For one thing, the zoning and density policies which affect the spatial distribution of different socio-economic classes will be changed, and the controls over the privatization of space both between and within buildings will be eliminated. Any capitalist and imperialist symbolism on the identity of buildings, streets, and places will be demolished. All these will be valid only under the assumption of the existence of a socialist city. My research into Chinese cities, such as Guangzhou, in recent years seems to indicate some degree of convergence between socialist and capitalist cities in design as a consequence of the western influences on Chinese city planning. Therefore, it is very likely that the future change towards a socialist urban form for Hong Kong will be more in name than in substance.

References

Chen, E.K.Y. 1984. The economic setting. In *The business environment in Hong Kong*, D.G. Lethbridge (ed.). Hong Kong: Oxford University Press, pp. 1–51.

Cuthbert, A.R. 1987. Hong Kong 1997: the transition to socialism – ideology, discourse, and urban spatial structure. *Environment and Planning D*. 5: 123–50.

Emmons, C.F. 1988. *Hong Kong prepares for 1997: politics and emigration in 1987*. Hong Kong: Centre of Asian Studies, University of Hong Kong.

Gormick, T. and Bloomfield, F. 1983. *Hong Kong 1997. A new lease on life? An astrological analysis of Hong Kong and its future*. Hong Kong: Gulliver Books.

Harris, P. 1988. *Hong Kong: a study in bureaucracy and politics*. Hong Kong: Macmillan.

Mushkat, M. 1989. Environmental turbulence and the economic prospects of Hong Kong. In *Hong Kong: the challenge of transformation*, K. Cheek-Milby and M. Mushkat (eds). Hong Kong: Centre of Asian Studies, University of Hong Kong.

Mushkat, M. 1990. *The economic future of Hong Kong*. Boulder, Colorado: Lynn Rienner.

Rabushka, A. 1979. *Hong Kong: a study in economic freedom*. Chicago: University of Chicago Press.

Scott, I. 1989. *Political change and the crisis of legitimacy in Hong Kong*. Hong Kong: Oxford University Press.

Skeldon, R. 1991. Emigration, immigration and fertility decline: demographic integration or disintegration. *The Other Hong Kong Report 1991*. Hong Kong: Chinese University of Hong Kong Press, pp. 233–58.

Wu, Y.L. 1987. Comments on two papers. In *Hong Kong and 1997: strategies for the future*. Y.C. Jao, C.K. Leung, P. Wesley-Smith, and S.L. Wong (eds). Hong Kong: Centre of Asian Studies, University of Hong Kong, pp. 289–92.

Index

Index

Index